D0948189

BUGS

OF THE

WORLD

BUGS
OF THE
WORLD

George C.
McGavin

Photography by
Ken Preston-Mafham

Facts On File

For Amy

Yet let me flap this bug with gilded wings –
This painted child of dirt that stinks and sings.[1]

With apologies to Alexander Pope.
An Epistle from Mr Pope to Dr Arbuthnot, 1735

[1]At the risk of offending those familiar with the works of Pope, I have intentionally changed the final word of the quotation from '*stings*' to '*sings*'. Had Pope been an hemipterist, I feel sure that he would have forsaken alliteration for scientific accuracy. While it is true that many bugs produce noxious and repellent odours from special glands within their bodies, no species has a stinging organ comparable to that of wasps or bees. Many, however, use acoustic signals for sexual attraction and in mating rituals.

BUGS OF THE WORLD

Copyright © 1993 Blandford, an imprint of Cassell plc, London
Text copyright © 1993 George C. McGavin
Photographs copyright © 1993 K. G. Preston-Mafham/Premaphotos Wildlife

Facts On File, Inc.
11 Penn Plaza
New York NY 10001

Library of Congress Cataloging-in-Publication Data

McGavin. George.
    Bugs of the world/George C. McGavin; photographs by Ken Preston
-Mafham.
        p.   cm.
    Includes bibliographical references (p.   ) and index.
    ISBN 0-8160-2737-4 (acid-free paper)
    1. Insects.   I. Preston-Mafham, Ken.   II. Title.
QL 463.M34   1993   92-38040
595.7'54 — dc20

Printed and bound in Hong Kong

10 9 8 7 6 5 4 3 2

This book is printed on acid-free paper.

Contents

Acknowledgements   6

Preface   7

Introduction.   9

1   Collecting Bugs   15

2   The Structure of Bugs   21

3   Bug Classification   34

4   Diseases and Enemies   96

5   Bug Defences   121

6   Food and Feeding   139

7   Mating and Egg Laying   159

8   Bugs and People   177

Further Reading   188

Index   189

Acknowledgements

I would like to thank many friends and entomological colleagues in the University Museum and the Department of Zoology in Oxford and at the British Museum (Natural History) in London for discussions, advice, facts and figures. In this book I have attempted to give the general reader an outline of the major features of bugs, their classification and biology, in a form that is neither indigestible nor simplistic. While books in this series can never hope to be comprehensive in their coverage, I have tried to strike a balance between essential facts and interesting stories. To achieve this I have consulted nearly a hundred reference and academic textbooks and nearly one thousand papers and articles in scientific journals. I would like to thank Graham Floater for his assistance in searching the literature. To the very many entomologists and authors, past and present, some of whom are colleagues and friends and on whose work I have depended, I extend my appreciation and thanks. I would particularly like to mention some of these eminent hemipterists and researchers, with whom I have had a long association and share a love of bugs; they are Professor Sir Richard Southwood, Dr Bill Knight, Bill Dolling and Ivor Lansbury.

I am most grateful to Rosemary Wise (Figs 1, 2 and 4–6), Alan Rollason (Fig. 17) and especially Richard Lewington (Figs 3, 7–16 and 18–19), who made a splendid job of the black-and-white line illustrations.

Although I have dedicated this book to my five-year-old daughter, I do not suppose for one minute that she takes much consolation from the honour at the moment. By the time she is grown up with children of her own it is likely that the Earth will have, at the hand of humans, lost up to half of all its plant and animal species. Many of the species, extinguished forever, will undoubtedly be bugs; although a few may be preserved for posterity in celluloid, the superb photographic skills of Ken Preston-Mafham will serve only as a mute testament to their beauty and our lack of understanding.

Preface

The opening few words of this book do not necessarily refer to bugs but rather seek to highlight wider problems soon to become all too urgent and which will affect us, them and all other species. Most, if not all, of our current difficulties are environmental. They stem from an ignorance of the fundamental processes that govern the continued survival of every living organism on this grain of inter-stellar debris in orbit around a minor star, itself one of billions in our galaxy, the Milky Way.

The major, global problem, and one to which an answer will have to be found in the very near future, is man's explosive population growth. The current world human population stands at 5.4 billion. By the year 2000 it is expected to be around 6.3 billion, and conservative projections for the year 2025 put the human population at well over 8 billion.

Around this time, without immediate and cooperative effort, most of the tropical forests with their natural treasury of species and resources will be gone. By this time it will be difficult to find sufficient fresh water that does not contain damaging levels of heavy metal ions and other types of pollution. By this time the cumulative and virtually undiminished effects of greenhouse gases will have changed the global climate to such an extent that increasing areas of the Earth's surface will be subject to frequent and unremitting drought.

It does not take too much imagination, based on our present knowledge, to foresee the scale of the problems and shortages which will be experienced by the majority of the world's human inhabitants a mere 35 years from now. Setting aside the problems of pollution, acid rain, ozone depletion, global warming, desertification, urbanization and relentless, worldwide habitat destruction – a direct result of our unchecked growth and development – the primary tasks of providing adequate supplies of food and clean drinking water for every human being will ultimately defeat us.

Nearly one billion humans are undernourished or starving today. The massive increase in food production seen 20 or 30 years ago was brought about by culti-vating more and more land, and by the increasing use of biocides, fertilizers and high-yielding crop plant varieties. It has not been, and cannot be, sustained. Water quality and availability is now a crisis issue in many parts of the world. The prospects for the next two generations are bleak indeed.

As a species, our acquisition of knowledge has been staggering; but it is not yet clear if we have learnt anything to help us in our present plight. We wrestle with the complexities of sub-atomic particles and the origins of the cosmos; from quarks to quasars and from bosons to the big bang. Our large brains have unravelled the secrets of DNA, the molecule of life, and we are currently putting vast resources into working out the exact sequence of the human genome (a scientifically questionable exercise). All these and other things are not in them-

7

selves bad or undesirable, but we have forgotten or ignored some very simple facts. You may have heard all this before, but it bears repetition.

We are just another species of animal and, as such, totally dependent on every other living organism for what we eat, drink and breathe. The planet sustains us but, given the demands being made on its finite resources, it cannot do so for ever. Animal and plant populations are all subject to natural regulatory processes and physical laws. We have, by virtue of our intelligence and cunning, avoided and modified some of these processes; but it will not be too long before they take effect again. When this happens in earnest, many Earth Conferences will have come and gone. We will have most of the facts and none of the answers.

In the gloom of a dark forest at Kakamega the glare of the flash gun makes terminal wax filaments on the bodies of these flatid nymphs shine like skeins of fibreglass. Kenya.
Flatidae

Introduction

Insects have been present on Earth for several hundreds of millions of years longer than humans, and many aspects of their beneficial, destructive or disease-causing nature are documented in our earliest known records, writings and paintings. Insects are by far the most ubiquitous and successful organisms that evolution has produced in the 2000 or so million years since organic life first developed on Earth. No other single animal group has as much impact on the planet's ecosystems, or is as important to their continued maintenance and survival. Insects represent a major component in every single terrestrial and aquatic food chain, and pollinate the vast majority of the Earth's flowering plants. Of the estimated $1\frac{1}{4}$ million species of all animals that have been described to date, a staggering 932,000 – that is, 75 per cent – are insects. Our knowledge of the world's fauna is still far from complete, and notwithstanding mass habitat destruction (particularly of tropical forests where the diversity of plant and animal life has been shown to be higher than anywhere else on Earth), there may be somewhere between 2 and 6 million more insect species alone awaiting discovery. Despite the negative effects of disease and crop destruction that insects may directly have on mankind, we are, ultimately, totally dependent on them.

Virtually any statistic concerning insects is likely to generate disbelief. It has been calculated that every square kilometre (0.4 sq miles) of land may contain some 10 billion individual insects. An average locust swarm may weigh some 80,000 tonnes, comprise some 50 billion individuals and eat four times as much food in a day as the human populations of New York or London. The reproductive potential of some insect species is so great that, given suitable breeding conditions and freedom from predation, the numbers generated in one year from a single pair of small flies could theoretically reach 10^{40} (write the figure 1 with 40 zeros after it).

Those readers with a calculator and a mathematical bent can spend some time, armed with this information and the fact that you could probably pack about 60 adults into a cubic centimetre (1000 per cubic inch), estimating the space that this number of flies would fill. When you work out the incredible volume that 10^{40} flies represents, you will certainly want to check your sums several times. Even when only very small insects are involved, the effect of this awesome breeding output is likely to be serious. Insects have had a major impact on the short course of human history, decimating populations, cities and armies and laying waste to crops. Despite our inexorable progress, knowledge and success in many fields, even today humans lose up to 20 per cent of all their crops to the insect multitudes, and one in six of us are suffering from some insect-borne illness.

Classification and taxonomy may at first seem a dull procedure, but it is a primary and characteristic function of the human brain and the cornerstone of all the sciences. Without classification it would be impossible to make sense of the highly complex and diverse world around us. We group related objects together on the basis of shared features or characteristics and, as a result of this, can make logical inferences about newly encountered objects. For example, before even picking this book from the shelf the reader could infer a great deal about it: that it was a book, that it might have drawings and/or colour photographs, that it would have printed text of a dark colour on white pages, and so on. In short, we are all taxonomists.

When dealing with large numbers of related insects, the process might become more complex but remains essentially the same. Large groups are divided into smaller groups on the basis of shared attributes, and then subdivided again and again until we reach the indivisible taxonomic level of the species.

To illustrate the hierarchical nature of classification and to outline the major taxonomic groupings the Common Bed Bug, *Cimex lectularius*, will serve as an example. A taxon is the proper name for any sort of taxonomic group; thus a phylum, order, suborder, family, subfamily, tribe, genus or species are all examples of taxa.

KINGDOM	ANIMALIA (all animals).
SUPERPHYLUM	ARTHROPODA (all animals with jointed legs). Includes the next taxon down plus spiders, ticks, scorpions, crabs, lobsters, tongue worms, velvet worms and water bears.
PHYLUM	UNIRAMIA (All arthropods with unbranched appendages and a single pair of antennae). Includes the next taxon down plus the millipedes, centipedes, symphylans and pauropods.
SUPERCLASS	HEXAPODA (all six-legged animals). Includes the next taxon down plus springtails, proturans and diplurans.
CLASS	INSECTA (all insects). Includes the next taxon down plus all the other insect orders.
ORDER	HEMIPTERA (bugs). Four suborders: the Heteroptera, Coleorrhyncha, Auchenorrhyncha and Sternorrhyncha.
SUBORDER	HETEROPTERA (true bugs).
INFRAORDER	CIMICOMORPHA The next taxon down plus another five superfamilies, which include palm bugs, lace bugs, plant bugs, assassin bugs and related groups.
SUPERFAMILY	CIMICOIDEA The next taxon down plus another six families including the bat bugs, flower bugs and damsel bugs.
FAMILY	CIMICIDAE (bed bugs and their allies). Approximately 80 species worldwide.
SUBFAMILY	CIMICINAE The next taxon down plus another four genera.
GENUS	*Cimex* A total of some sixteen species feeding on the blood

of bats, pigeons, man and occasionally other birds and mammals.

SPECIES   *lectularius* A cosmopolitan species feeding on the blood of man, chickens and a few bats.

The names of infraorders invariably end with -morpha, superfamilies with -oidea, families with -idae and subfamilies with -inae and tribes, when used, with -ini. (In this book, the names of the bug families are set in **bold type** to distinguish them from other insect families.) Generic and specific names are always italicized. Generic names begin with an upper case letter, specific names with a lower case letter. Although intentionally omitted in this book and more appropriate in taxonomic tomes, the author of a species, that is the surname(s) of the person(s) who first described it, follows the specific name thus, *Cimex lectularius* Linnaeus. Author names are sometimes shortened, the abbreviation for Linnaeus being L. When an author's name appears in brackets this indicates that the species was originally assigned to a different genus to that in which it is currently placed.

The origins of the word 'bug' are obscured by the passage of time, but may date back as far as the fourteenth century when the word 'bugge' was used to mean bogle or some such object of terror. 'Bugge' may have come from the earlier Welsh word *bwg*, meaning scarecrow, ghost or hobgoblin. It is possible that the current meaning of the word 'bug' may have been derived by transference from this earlier usage. One of the first recorded uses of the English word 'bug' in relation to an insect is in Massinger and Dekker's play *The Virgin Martyr*. In Act III, Scene iii a character refuses an embrace on entomological grounds:

> *Harpax*: Come, let my bosom touch you.
> *Spungius*: We have bugs, Sir.

It is unclear to what species of insect Spungius refers, but bed bugs are certainly prime candidates.

In modern usage the word 'bug' has acquired a wide range of meanings. As a noun, 'bug' is used to refer to such things as bacteria, general illnesses with cold or flu-like symptoms, a fault or problem in a machine or computer program and any small electronic listening device; while as a verb, it means to irritate or annoy. In keeping with this pattern, 'bug' has a variety of entomological meanings. Non-specialists may use the word to refer, in the broadest sense, to any insect and the use of common names such as ladybug (a ladybird beetle) further confuses the picture. The common name of bug should strictly be used only to refer to members of the insect order Hemiptera. But before describing the particular features and classification of this important insect order, I want to place the Hemiptera in a wider entomological context.

The class Insecta is divided into two subclasses of very unequal size. The first, the Apterygota or primitively wingless insects (0.07 per cent of all insect species), is made up of just two small orders, the Archaeognatha and Thysanura. The second subclass, the Pterygota or winged insects (99.93 per cent of all insect species), has 26 separate orders. Many of these, such as the dragonflies

(Odonata), beetles (Coleoptera) and butterflies and moths (Lepidoptera) will be familiar to the reader.

Below the level of subclass, the Pterygota are further divided into two infra-classes, the Palaeoptera and Neoptera. The Palaeoptera (having primitive wings), comprising the mayflies (Ephemeroptera) and the dragonflies and dam-selflies (Odonata), represent only 0.8 per cent of all insect species. The Palaeop-tera are characterized, among other features, by the way their wings are held out at right-angles to the body. Insects of all the other orders are contained in the very much larger infraclass Neoptera (or new wings); as adults, they have the ability to fold their wings back along the body when resting. Within the Neop-tera there are two very clear and distinct divisions: the Exopterygota (14 orders comprising 14.5 per cent of all insect species) and the Endopterygota (10 orders comprising 85 per cent of all insect species). These two are differentiated from each other mainly by the way in which development occurs.

The exopterygote orders are represented by the cockroaches (Blattodea), ter-mites (Isoptera), mantids (Mantodea), zorapterans (Zoraptera), grylloblattids (Grylloblattodea), earwigs (Dermaptera), stoneflies (Plecoptera), grasshoppers and allies (Orthoptera), stick insects (Phasmatodea), embiopterans (Embiop-tera), barklice (Psocoptera), parasitic lice (Phthiraptera), thrips (Thysanop-tera) and, finally, the dominant order in the division, the bugs (Hemiptera). In these orders, development from egg to adult is termed hemimetabolous – that is, occurring gradually through a number of immature stages or nymphal instars. In habits and morphology the nymphs are very similar to the adults, lacking only fully developed wings and genitalia. Another characteristic feature is that the wings develop gradually on the outside of the body, contained within nym-phal wing pads.

The Endopterygota are represented by the megalopterans (Megaloptera), lacewings and allies (Neuroptera), beetles (Coleoptera), strepsipterans (Strep-siptera), scorpionflies (Mecoptera), fleas (Siphonaptera), flies (Diptera), caddis-flies (Trichoptera), butterflies and moths (Lepidoptera) and bees, wasps and ants (Hymenoptera). In these, more advanced orders, the larval and adult stages are totally different in habit and morphology and their development is known as holometabolous. The immature stages are called larvae, and the adult stage is preceded by a resting or pupal stage inside which the incredible processes of metamorphosis occur.

Setting aside disagreements concerning the evolutionary history of bugs, such fossil evidence that exists suggests that the Hemiptera arose from an ancestral group around 280 million years ago (in geological terms, the Carboniferous–Permian boundary). Many Hemiptera-like fossil insects, already with special-ized sucking mouthparts (a characteristic of bugs), are known from this time. But it is likely that, as more and more palaeontological material is collected, the origins of the group will be pushed back further in time, into the Carboniferous Period. Morphological and other evidence shows that the Hemiptera are most closely related to the Psocoptera (booklice and barklice) and the Thysanoptera (thrips).

Global figures are notoriously difficult to obtain and are subject to a certain margin of error, but the best current estimate for world bug species is just under

Normally found on nettles and sometimes a predator of aphids and similar soft-bodied insects, this plant bug, *Calocoris stysi*, is feeding at a foxglove flower (*Digitalis* sp.). Great Britain. **Miridae**

82,000. The bugs, therefore, comprise 8–10 per cent of all known insect species and are the biggest and most successful of all the exopterygote orders.

As with virtually any other insect group, very many more species than are known remain undiscovered. Recent estimates, based on work in the tropical rain forests of Indonesia and obtained using a whole gamut of collecting techniques, suggest that just over 105,000 species of bug may remain undescribed worldwide, bringing the total species count to somewhere in the region of 187,000. We may never know for sure, as the rainforests, particularly those of the Old World tropics, are now in peril at the hand of man.

Beetles are renowned for their incredible diversity and ubiquity, butterflies for their spectacular grace and beauty, and flies for their aerial agility and medical importance. The bugs, however, although of less popular appeal, can be all of these things and more: for they can be jacks of all trades and masters of many. The species contained within the large order Hemiptera range from minute, wingless scale insects hardly resembling insects at all to ferocious-looking, giant water bugs with enlarged, fish-catching front legs.

Hemipteran species are very widespread across the world and can be found in a huge range of habitats from mountain and moorland to forest and fen. Virtually every conceivable type of terrestrial and fresh water habitat has a particular and characteristic bug fauna. Among the water dwellers there are surface and subaquatic specialists. Even hundreds of miles from land, floating out on the open ocean, and in the skies above us, drifting as aerial plankton, there are bugs of many species. During a survey of insects drifting or flying over the North Sea, biologists found species belonging to the families **Cicadellidae**, **Delphacidae**, **Psyllidae**, **Miridae** and **Nabidae**. In addition to these bugs, aphids were found to be very common with more that 20 species represented, some in very large numbers. The majority of bug species are plant-feeders (phytophagous), but many are predacious and some feed on the blood of vertebrate animals.

The division and arrangement of the order Hemiptera into its various subgroupings or taxa has been the subject of much debate among bug taxonomists for many years, and no one single system of classification should be regarded as written on tablets of stone. It is not even universally accepted that the order should remain as one – some authorities would split it into two or even four separate but closely related orders.

The word 'Hemiptera' is derived from two Greek words, *hemi* meaning half and *pteron* meaning wing. This is not to imply that bugs are partially winged (although some species do have long- and short-winged forms) but rather refers to the construction of the front pair of wings. In many bugs the front wings have two obvious portions, the basal area (nearest the body) being thickened and tough, while the apical area (furthest from the body) is thin and membranous. However this does not properly apply to all species in the order, as there are many whose front wings are either uniformly toughened or uniformly membranous.

The name Hemiptera was given to the order by Linnaeus in 1758 and it could be argued that the later proposal, Rhynchota – referring to all bugs' possession of sucking mouthparts – is a better one. The name Hemiptera, however, has stuck. The order has traditionally been divided into two large suborders, the Heteroptera (true bugs) and the Homoptera (treehoppers, planthoppers, leafhoppers, cicadas, aphids, plantlice, scale insects and related groups).

The name Heteroptera is derived from the Greek words *heteros* (different or other) and *pteron* (wing), referring to the non-uniformity of front wing texture. Homoptera is derived from *homos* (the same or uniform) and *pteron*, referring to evenly textured, membranous or tougher front wings. Up-to-date classifications recognize four suborders, the Heteroptera, the Coleorrhyncha (a small group more closely related to the Heteroptera than to the Homoptera), and two homopteran groups, the Auchenorrhyncha and the Sternorrhyncha.

In 200 years, the number of families recognized within the order has risen from a mere handful to somewhere between 140 and 150, depending on whether or not certain subfamilies are elevated to family rank. The number of species in a single family is very variable indeed: some have but a single species, while others encompass tens of thousands.

Species of bug in many families will never or only very rarely be encountered by the general collector or hobbyist. Common English names exist for some, but by no means all, bug families. Unlike scientific names, common names are not regulated by the scientific community and international agreement. Confusion can therefore arise from the use of a single common name for more than one family or from the use of more than one common name for the same family.

Chapter 1
Collecting Bugs

Before any kind of study can begin, insect material needs to be collected and preserved. Collecting should, of course, never be undertaken for frivolous or commercial reasons, and collectors should find out what legal restrictions apply in particular localities or to particular species. Several countries, at long last, have now imposed strict regulations covering the collecting and export of plants, insects and other animal species. In addition, many places of high wildlife and habitat value are designated as reserves, parks and sites of special scientific interest where only bona fide and controlled research work is allowed.

Many people's mental image of an insect collector is an eccentric, safari-suited, bearded gentleman, net in hand, dashing madly in pursuit of the elusive butterfly. These scenes are not completely fictional but the majority of collecting, particularly of bugs, relies on other techniques. Some are simple, others more involved. Methods of collection vary according to the habitat and the type of insects likely to be present.

Methods of Collection

Bugs occupy a wide range of habitats and require similarly varied collecting methods. Pond nets and trawls are used in aquatic habitats. Many pieces of collecting equipment can be made simply and need not be expensive. A small kitchen sieve or strainer taped to a cane makes an ideal water bug catcher. Stout, large-rimmed nets of heavy, close-woven, white cloth are used for sweeping bugs from vegetation. Folding beating trays or sheets can be held or placed under trees and bushes to catch dislodged bugs as the branches are jarred or shaken. One of the simplest and sometimes very productive techniques is just to look carefully at host plants, on the ground, under bark and other microhabitats, armed only with a collecting tube, forceps or perhaps a pooter. A pooter or aspirator is an elegant and cheap device used to suck up small insects into a tube. One of the best designs, illustrated in Fig. 1, uses a screw-topped, plastic, hospital specimen vial. The use of glass tubes in the field is inadvisable, but remember that mosquito repellents and killing agents such as ethyl acetate will dissolve many plastics on contact, and specimens should be transferred to a glass container for killing.

Ecologists often use what is, in effect, an enormous mechanical aspirator called a D-Vac. Working like a giant hoover, powerful suction is produced by fan blades driven by a small petrol engine. Insects are sucked from the ground or vegetation through a wide, flexible tube to be collected in a muslin net. The advantage of this system is that sampling from different areas can be standardized and made less subjective. Disadvantages of the D-Vac are that it is heavy and cannot effectively sample bugs from very tall or wet vegetation.

15

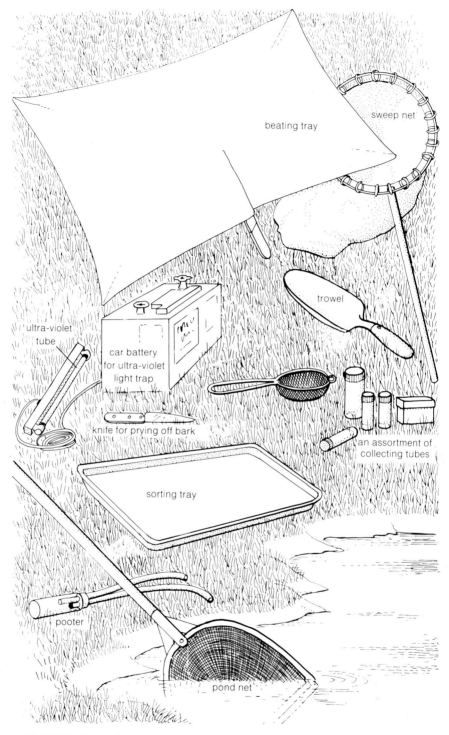

Fig. 1. Collecting equipment.

Relying on superb cryptic coloration rather than on warning coloration for protection, a pair of shield bugs (*Bromocoris foetida*) mate exposed on the bark of a tree. New Guinea.
Pentatomidae

One of the techniques that has recently revolutionized ecological entomology, particularly in tropical forest habitats, is the use of insecticidal knockdown by fogging or misting. Collecting sheets or bags are placed on the ground under the forest canopy while petrol-driven fogging or mist-blowing machines, charged with fast-acting pyrethroid insecticides, are directed at the foliage from ground level or hoisted into the treetops by means of ropes and pulleys. The insecticides used have very low persistence in the environment and do not harm higher organisms. Vast amounts of material can be collected in a very short time and the results from several tropical studies are providing incredible new species and very impressive data. Many people will have seen these techniques in use on television natural history programmes or in the film *Arachnophobia*.

In contrast to these active techniques, there is also a range of passive techniques in the form of pitfall traps, baited traps, water traps, sticky traps, aerial suction traps, light traps (tungsten, ultra-violet and mercury vapour), malaise traps and flight interception traps. With these methods, the operator sets up the trap for a specified period of time and returns to remove the catch. Not all trapping methods are particularly appropriate for bugs; for instance, pitfall traps tend to catch ground-running beetles and other invertebrates. Tent-like, malaise traps and other types of flight interception device are not very good at catching bugs, but are very good for flies and wasps. Some traps, however, are very effective for catching some types of bug. Yellow trays or pans filled with water and a surface tension-reducing substance such as washing-up liquid will attract aphids in large numbers. Aphids are also routinely sampled from large volumes of air by large, chimney-like suction traps. The results from this type of work are relayed to farmers and growers by various government agencies to provide early warning of potential outbreaks of pest species.

Many mass collection techniques such as light trapping or insecticidal knockdown will only provide presence or absence data, and cannot be used to infer anything much about the habits or host plants of the species caught. Careful observation and detailed field note-taking remain the mainstay of any investigation.

Labelling, storage and preservation

Once caught, the bugs should be preserved and/or mounted as soon as possible. Dead, dried bugs can be relaxed in humid, airtight boxes, but the process of mounting then becomes much more difficult and time-consuming. Here is an outline of the many techniques employed.

Killing the catch is done using fumes of ethyl acetate, cyanide or other poisonous substances inside a specially prepared jar. Nymphs and soft-bodied adult bugs such as scale insects and aphids can be killed and preserved directly in 70 per cent alcohol (one hundred per cent alcohol diluted to 70 per cent with distilled water). A short spell in a freezer will kill most species without the need for dangerous chemicals. For permanent storage, the majority of bugs (Heteroptera and Auchenorrhyncha) can be pinned directly, staged on micro-pins supported on small bits of foam or stuck with water-soluble adhesive to small cards or card points as shown in Fig. 2. When pinning directly or with micro-pins, the

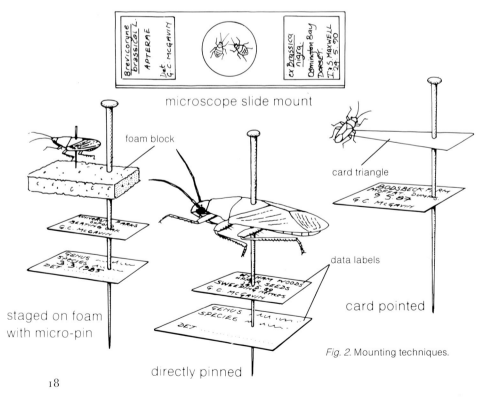

microscope slide mount

foam block

card triangle

staged on foam with micro-pin

data labels

card pointed

directly pinned

Fig. 2. Mounting techniques.

Not only good mimics of wasps and bees, many assassin bugs can resemble dead leaves or other objects. This brown and spiny species, *Sphagiastes ramantaceus*, lives in the savannas of South Africa. **Reduviidae**

pin should be made of stainless steel and must penetrate the body just right of the midline, through the scutellum.

In general, identifying species of the suborder Sternorrhyncha (aphids, scale insects, mealy bugs and so on) requires the examination of very minute morphological characteristics. For this reason, these bugs are best removed from alcohol storage and mounted on glass slides for examination (Fig. 2). Preparing a good slide mount can be quite complicated and involves the use of a number of chemicals and reagents. Various recipes can be found in entomological textbooks.

Whatever method is used to collect or store bugs, the associated data is of the utmost importance. A specimen with no details attached to the pin or slide is completely useless for scientific purposes – a waste of the bug and a waste of the time and effort expended to catch it.

The absolute minimum information that should accompany any specimen must include the precise locality, date, habitat and the collector's name. Additional information such as method of collection (fogging/at light/beaten from/ etc.), host plant identification in the case of a herbivore, and any other field observations can prove invaluable and must be recorded wherever possible. The more information that can be recorded, the better.

In many cases, the microscopic examination of male genitalia or other structures is required for an accurate species identification. The genitalia are dissected from the end of the abdomen and subjected to various cleaning and softening procedures before examination. Dissected structures should always be glued to the card mount alongside the specimen or stored in glycerol in a micro-vial attached to the main pin.

Pinned collections should be kept in special airtight entomological boxes or drawers – not in polystyrene (styrofoam)-lined shoe-boxes. The voracious larvae of several museum and household pest insects, such as carpet and museum beetles of the genus *Anthrenus*, will otherwise reduce a valuable collection to dust in a matter of months.

Faunal zones of the world

The world is divided into six major faunal zones: Nearctic, Palaearctic, Neotropical, Ethiopian, Oriental and Australian. The Nearctic is essentially the whole of North America from Mexico northwards, Canada, Baffin Island and Greenland. The Palaearctic region covers Europe, Asia north of the Himalayas and the Tibetan mountains, North Africa and a large part of Arabia. The Oriental region covers India, Asia south of the Himalayas and the Tibetan mountains, and Indonesia excluding Celebes and Papua New Guinea. The Ethiopian region is all of sub-Saharan Africa, Madagascar and the southern portion of Arabia. The Australian region includes Australia, New Zealand, Celebes and all islands east to New Guinea and the vast majority of the Pacific islands.

In broad terms, the northern hemisphere is made up of the Nearctic and Palaearctic regions (sometimes collectively known as the Holarctic region). The Neotropical, Ethiopian, Oriental and Australian regions make up the southern hemisphere. Fig. 3 shows the world's major faunal regions and the present extent of forested areas.

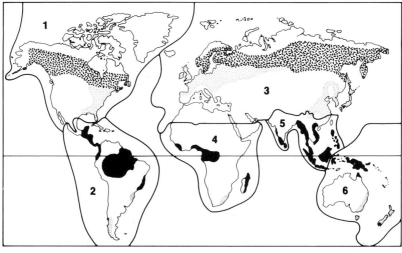

Boreal forests

Temperate forests

Tropical rain forests

1 Nearctic region
2 Neotropical region
3 Palaearctic region
4 Ethiopian region
5 Oriental region
6 Australian region

Fig. 3. World forests and faunal regions.

Chapter 2

The Structure of Bugs

Although varying in body length from just under 1mm (0.04 in) to over 100 mm (4 ins), and with a bewildering range of shapes and colours, the majority of the world's bug species nevertheless share many similarities in external and internal design. With certain exceptions bugs, like other insects, have a basic three-part body plan of head, thorax and abdomen. Setting aside the superb adaptations of many bugs which help to disguise them or make them resemble bark, lichen, thorns and other natural objects, many species are very good mimics of other insects. Some look like and sometimes behave like wasps, ants, flies, beetles and insects of other orders. Fig. 4 shows the major features of a typical heteropteran bug's body.

Especially vulnerable when soft, many bugs moult under cover of darkness. Anchored to a plant in the rain forest, this coreid bug (*Phythia pulchella*) emerges from its last nymphal skin as an adult. Brazil. **Coreidae**

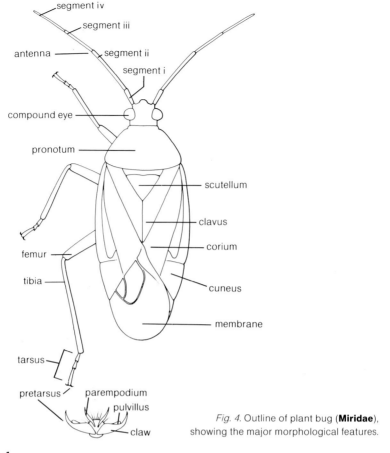

segment iv
segment iii
antenna
segment ii
segment i
compound eye
pronotum
scutellum
clavus
corium
femur
tibia
cuneus
membrane
tarsus
pretarsus
parempodium
pulvillus
claw

Fig. 4. Outline of plant bug (**Miridae**), showing the major morphological features.

Head

Rostrum

General appearance is not going to be of much use to novice bug hunters. They want a singular, distinguishing feature to separate hemipterans from all other, commonly encountered insect orders – in bugs, this is the head. It carries the mouthparts or rostrum, which alone provide the best recognition characteristics for the order and its constituent suborders.

The external head structure, showing the position of the rostrum in typical heteropteran, auchenorrhynchan and sternorrhynchan bugs, is shown in Fig. 5. In heteropteran bugs the rostrum, which arises from the front of the head and lies directed backwards under the body when not in use, can be hinged or swung forward to point downwards or even forwards in front of the head. This feat, allowing much greater flexibility and thus a more comprehensive choice of food (animal and plant juices), is made possible by the presence of a special region of cuticle called the gula which forms the underside of the head behind the base of the rostrum. In members of the Auchenorrhyncha and Sternorrhyncha, the rostrum, which arises from the posterior part of the head, sometimes apparently from between the front legs, lies permanently directed backwards along the underside of the body.

With stylets thrust deep into a hibiscus fruit, this Harlequin Bug (*Tectocoris diophthalmus*) sucks up its diet of sap. Australia. **Scutelleridae**

Antennae

Besides the mouthparts, the head carries the antennae, compound eyes and, when present, accessory light-receptive organs known as ocelli. The antennae are typically composed of a small number of segments. The first segment may join the head in a variety of positions. The jointing between the first segment and the head, and between the first two segments, allows the antennae great flexibility of movement. The remainder of the antennal segments bear the majority of the sense receptor organs.

Heteropteran bugs have elongate antennae of four or five segments which may be relatively short or long and variously thickened, ornamented or modified. Coreids in many parts of the world show some strange leaf-like antennal expansions. It is sometimes thought that weird and wonderful species are confined to the tropics, but within the **Miridae** males of a small, Holarctic, oak-living species by the name of *Harpocera thoracica* possess bizarre swellings at the end of the second antennal segments. These swellings are clumps of specialized, adhesive hairs whose function is to grip the smooth pronotum of the female bug as the male copulates.

Auchenorrhynchan bugs have short antennae with a bristle-like terminal portion. Sternorrhynchan bugs usually have fairly long, thread-like antennae, which in some species may have ten, twelve or even more segments. A few species of scale insect lack antennae altogether. In some bug groups such as the Aphidoidea, the position and nature of the sense organs or sensilla along the antennae are important distinguishing features.

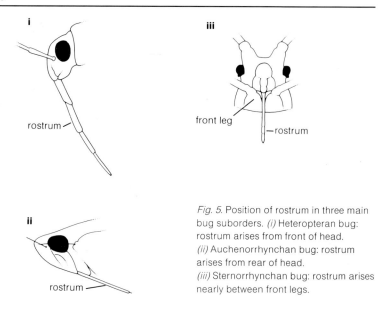

Fig. 5. Position of rostrum in three main bug suborders. *(i)* Heteropteran bug: rostrum arises from front of head. *(ii)* Auchenorrhynchan bug: rostrum arises from rear of head. *(iii)* Sternorrhynchan bug: rostrum arises nearly between front legs.

Eyes

The compound eyes, which are normally very noticeable, are placed laterally on the head. There is considerable variation in eye shape, size and orientation in bugs.

As in all insects, compound eyes are made up of a number of individual light-gathering units or facets known as ommatidia, whose number varies from hundreds per eye to fewer than five. The species in a number of families with underground or gall-forming habits have very reduced eyes, and some have none at all. Eye reduction or loss is particularly evident in sternorrhynchan groups such as the Aphidoidea and Coccoidea.

The presence and position of secondary light-receptive ocelli or simple eyes, usually on top of the head, can be of some use in differentiating bugs. Although several bug families lack ocelli, two ocelli are typical of heteropteran and many auchenorrhynchan families, while cicadas and many sternorrhynchan families possess three ocelli.

Thorax

The thorax, which is concerned mainly with enabling the bug to move about, is composed of three portions: from front to back, the prothorax, mesothorax and metathorax. In simple terms each part can be likened to a box – the dorsal and ventral surfaces are known as the notum and sternum respectively, while the walls or sides are called the pleura. The prothorax bears the front pair of legs, the mesothorax the middle legs and front wings, and the metathorax the hind legs and hind wings. The front wings are usually larger than the hind wings;

A denizen of the Peruvian rain forest, this shield bug (*Edessa* sp.) may gain some protection from the predatory attentions of small lizards and other animals by the possession of very stout, laterally directed pronotal spines. **Pentatomidae**

consequently, the mesothorax is the largest of the three thoracic segments.

The pronotum may be small and collar-like, but in many families it is structurally modified with spinous and other extensions and in some it is prolonged backwards. In the **Membracidae** the degree of pronotal development can be very marked. Large, posteriorly or laterally directed spines or bizarre and complex ant-mimicking structures, seemingly larger than the whole bug, are common in many species.

In heteropterans and auchenorrhynchans, the only part of the mesonotum that can generally be seen from above is a large, usually triangular area known as the scutellum (Fig. 4). It is effectively that part of the back behind the pronotum and bounded by the folded wings. In some species, especially those in the superfamily Pentatomoidea, the scutellum can be extremely large and may cover most of the abdomen and sometimes the wings as well.

In virtually all species in the suborder Heteroptera the metathorax contains a stink gland, whose mainly defensive secretions are passed to the outside through either an opening on the underside or, more typically, two lateral openings. The area of cuticle surrounding these lateral openings is often sculptured into microridges, pits, furrows and strange, mushroom-shaped bodies. The function of these evaporative areas, as they are known, may not be the apparently obvious one of enhancing or prolonging the effects of the secretions; it may instead prevent the secretions from spreading over the bug's body surface, where they might enter the thoracic breathing holes or spiracles.

Heteropteran nymphs do not have thoracic stink glands; instead, they have a number of abdominal glands whose secretions are vented through single or

This denizen of inner space is stranger than any science fiction. The processes of evolution have moulded the pronotum of this Costa Rican rain forest treehopper (*Heteronotus reticulatus*) into a grotesque and incredible shape resembling an open-jawed ant.
Membracidae

paired gland openings on the dorsal surface. The function and chemical nature of the many types of stink gland secretion produced by heteropteran bugs are discussed in Chapter 5.

Wings

The wings of Hemiptera are very varied and, although typically there are two pairs, many species have shortened wings (brachypterous), very reduced wings (micropterous) or none at all (apterous). An additional complication in some species is the occurrence of fully winged, short winged and wingless forms.

The hind wings, when present, are always membranous. At rest, they are folded beneath the front wings; while in flight, they are simply coupled to the hind edge of the front pair. The front pair of wings, known as the hemelytra, show structural differences characteristic of the suborders (Fig. 6).

In members of the Heteroptera there are several distinct regions which can be helpful in distinguishing certain superfamilies and families. These regions are separated by lines of folding or bending called furrows or fractures. The design of the wings, with these inbuilt flexions, is important for stable and efficient flight – the whole wing acts effectively as an aerofoil. In general, the heteropteran wing has a toughened basal area (subdivided, depending on the family, into the corium, clavus and cuneus) and a softer apical area called the membrane (hence *heteros* – different + *pteron* – wing). At rest, heteropterans hold their wings folded flat over the back with the membrane of one wing overlapping the membrane of the other.

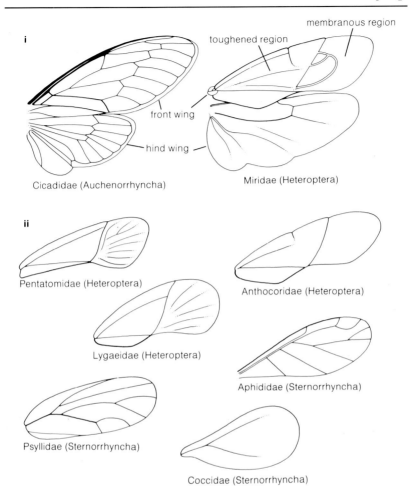

Fig. 6:i. Front and hind wings of an auchenorrhynchan and a heteropteran bug.
Fig. 6:ii. Typical front wing venation in some hemipteran families.

In members of the suborders Auchenorrhyncha and Sternorrhyncha the front wings tend to be of a uniform, membranous or slightly toughened texture (hence the name Homoptera, from *homos* – same + *pteron* – wing). At rest the front wings are generally held sloped like the sides of a tent over the body with little or no overlap, although some aphids and male scale insects may hold them flat.

Hemipteran nymphs grow their wings inside wing pads on the outside of the body. In early instars wing pads are not present, but by the third instar small outgrowths from the hind margins of the mesothoracic and metathoracic nota are just discernible. In the fourth instar they are clearly visible, and in the fifth – and usually final – instar the wing pads can be quite large, with the mesothoracic pads completely overlapping the metathoracic pads (Fig. 7).

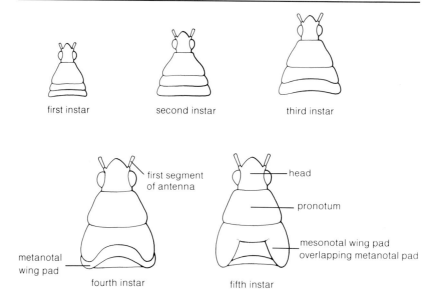

first instar   second instar   third instar

first segment
of antenna

head

pronotum

metanotal
wing pad

mesonotal wing pad
overlapping metanotal pad

fourth instar   fifth instar

Fig. 7. Wing pad development in a typical heteropteran nymph.

Legs

Hemipteran legs are mainly used for moving around, grooming, capturing food and mating. Keeping external body surfaces clean is very important and many species spend long periods systematically grooming their body parts. In many bug families special cleaning spines or bristles on the legs are used; in some, these bristles may be arranged like the teeth of a comb on the end of the front tibiae. The antennae can be drawn, one at a time, through the combs while the ends of the front legs are held together. The front legs are also used extensively to clean debris and the remains of previous victims from the rostrum. The rear part of the body is groomed by the middle or hind legs.

It is not surprising that evolution, driven by the unstoppable process of natural selection, has produced some extraordinary adaptations for jumping, digging, prey capture, filter-feeding, sexual signalling, mating, swimming, water-walking and many other functions. In many cases any special function may be restricted to one pair of legs. Members of the **Corixidae** are notable in that all three pairs of legs are modified for a particular purpose. The front pair are used for catching food, the middle pair for clinging to vegetation and the hind pair for swimming.

Many families contain prey-capturing species whose expanded or raptorial front legs may be armed with spines or teeth for gripping prey. One of the most fascinating ways in which bugs use their legs to catch food can be seen among some of the **Reduviidae** living in the Oriental region. Incredibly these bugs, which do not use their front legs much for walking, smear them with naturally occurring tree resins. Once covered with the slow-drying resin, the legs are held out in front of the body to act as living fly-paper. While some insects may simply blunder into the assassin bug's trap by accident, the bugs which use this trick carefully choose the tree species from which they collect their resin – it may be that some insects are actively attracted to the resin.

The body-cleaning rituals of these reduviids must be modified to minimize the risk of transferring resins from the front legs to sensitive areas. Similar care must be taken by aphids which wander across the surface of glandular-haired leaves such as those of the potato plant family (Solanaceae). These hairs release a very sticky substance if a careless insect ruptures the tip. Small bugs may be held fast and in any case attempts at grooming would soon transfer the adhesive mess to the antennae and mouthparts, resulting in death.

Plant bugs belonging to the mirid subfamily Dicyphinae, such as *Dicyphus* and *Cyrtopeltis*, are associated with host plants which have very hairy leaves or leaves covered with insect-trapping glandular hairs. These bugs have modified claws to grip the hair shafts and, when walking, move carefully and place their legs vertically almost as if walking on tiptoes. Interestingly, some dicyphine species living on the leaves of insectivorous plants are partly predacious and will feed on the juices of their host plant's victims.

Many male leaf-footed bugs (**Coreidae**), as the name implies, have leaf-like tibial expansions; while others have hugely swollen and spined hind femora. The fact that, in some species, it is only males which exhibit these distortions immediately suggests the possibility that they are concerned with mate selection, rival combat or courtship.

The first part of the leg, where it attaches to the appropriate thoracic segment, is known as the coxa. Next comes a small segment called the trochanter, which articulates with the femur. The tibia follows the femur, and its distal end articulates with the tarsus. The presence of a variety of tibial hairs, bristles, spines and spurs can be characteristic for many families.

The tarsus is made up of a number of segments but in some specialized bug groups may be lacking or fused with the tibia. Although three segments is typical in heteropteran bugs, in some families the tarsus of one or more pairs of legs may have fewer. The tarsi of the vast majority of auchenorrhynchan bugs have three tarsal segments, while those of sternorrhynchans have only one or two.

At the very end of the leg is the two-clawed pretarsus (Fig. 4). Exceptions to the two-claw rule can be seen in all the families of scale insects and mealy bugs comprising the superfamily Coccoidea and in some groups of water-dwelling heteropterans, where a single claw is present. Besides the claws, a variety of other minute but very important structures such as the parempodia and pulvilli are of great importance in maintaining grip and providing traction on surfaces of varying texture. Although as yet little studied, the micro-mechanics of pretarsal structures enable bugs to conquer anything from waxy-smooth, densely hairy or sticky leaf surfaces and spiders' webs to the surface of water in their quest for survival.

Abdomen

The abdomen, which in most species is concealed at rest by the folded wings, houses the digestive system (see Chapter 6) and the reproductive organs (see

A pair of leaf-footed bug nymphs, *Anisoscelis flavolineata*, feed on a passion flower (*Passiflora*) in Trinidad. The strange expansions on their hind tibiae may serve to divert a predator's attention away from vulnerable body parts. **Coreidae**

Chapter 7). Specialized functions, like the acoustic role played by the mainly air-sac-filled abdomen of male cicadas, are unusual. Typically, all bugs have 10 visible abdominal segments, although the last two may only be very small annuli or rings around the anus. In some groups, the outside of the abdomen may carry distinctive features. Aphids have defensive cornicles, some heteropteran families have long sensory hairs called trichobothria, and in members of the **Nepidae** the end of the abdomen carries an elongate breathing siphon. As already mentioned, the nymphs of heteropterans have abdominal stink glands, whose dorsal openings provide distinguishing features for many families.

The sides of a number of the abdominal segments carry the spiracles or external openings of the tracheal breathing system (see the section on gaseous exchange on p. 31). Normally, there are ten pairs of spiracles: two pairs on the thorax and eight pairs on the abdomen. In many bug families, especially those of the Sternorrhyncha, some species show a reduced number of spiracles.

Genitalia

At the posterior end of the abdomen are the external genitalia. The underside of most heteropteran and auchenorrhynchan females reveals a small cleft or slit in which the ovipositor is concealed when not in use. The ovipositor itself can be variously developed and enlarged depending on the egg-laying site. Those species laying eggs deep inside tough plant tissue, for instance, will need to be better equipped than those laying eggs shallowly or on surfaces, and have saw-like ovipositor blades. Females of the superfamilies Aphidoidea and Coccoidea, on the other hand, do not have an ovipositor at all; and in some other groups the structure may be reduced.

Male heteropteran and auchenorrhynchan bugs have complex genitalia, typically comprising an aedeagus or penis and a pair of small, laterally placed claspers or parameres. The size, shape, ornamentation and orientation of these and other associated reproductive structures are very useful when attempting to identify closely related and otherwise indistinguishable species.

The mechanics of male–female coupling are complex and varied. Depending on species, copulation may be end to end, side by side, beneath or above. In some species it may even not require the engagement of lock-and-key type genitalia to effect sperm transfer (see Chapter 7). Little is known about the details of reproductive behaviour in many bug species; amateur researches in this area are likely to be of great interest and to provide valuable results.

Gaseous exchange

Obtaining oxygen and getting rid of carbon dioxide is a necessity for all living organisms; but unlike the situation in higher animals, in insects the gases are not carried by special cells in the bloodstream and exchanged through lungs. Instead there is an open system terminating on the outside of the body in a number of small holes or openings called spiracles – in general, two pairs on the thorax and a further eight pairs on the sides of the abdominal segments.

The spiracles, which are internally linked to each other by large ducts called tracheal trunks, can be closed off to reduce water loss by means of special muscles. The spiracles are connected to an incredibly highly branched system of air passages or tubes which invade all parts of the insect's body. The larger air tubes or tracheae leading from the spiracles are spirally thickened, in the manner of a flexible vacuum cleaner hose, to resist collapse. The tracheae divide and branch repeatedly until ultra-fine, blind-ended tubes or tracheoles lie inside the tissues of the body and in close contact with individual cells. Gases are exchanged by straightforward diffusion across the thin walls of the tracheoles and the cells. When the bug is very active, and requires a high rate of oxygen supply, a flow of air can be generated through the body by the sequential opening of particular spiracles.

Although the tracheal system of hemipterans is essentially the same as in other insects, there are a number of modifications associated with underwater life (semi-aquatic and fully aquatic species are only found within the suborder Heteroptera). Many species employ air stores of various kinds which can be periodically renewed by making contact with the surface, head- or tail-first. The concave dorsal body surface beneath the tightly folded wings is a common site for the storage of air, but a bubble of air may also be trapped on the ventral body surface. Air can move front to back or vice versa by means of furrows and fields of closely-packed hairs.

Air stores are found in the **Corixidae**, **Notonectidae**, **Naucoridae** and

Belostomatidae. Nymphs, of course, do not possess wings under which to trap bubbles of air. Instead, many are able to absorb gases directly through the cuticle, and many use the trick of special air-trapping hair layers.

The trouble with air stores is that they need to be renewed. A major advance over a simple air store is seen in members of the **Aphelocheiridae**. Here a plastron, formed by a microscopically thin layer (approximately 6 microns thick) of silvery-looking air, trapped to the body surface by tiny hook-tipped, water-repellent hairs, acts as a physical gill. These hairs form a very dense pile of some 2 million per square millimetre which covers a large area of the body, especially the ventral surface, and is continuous with the tracheal system. The layer is very robust and virtually incompressible. As oxygen is used up by the bug's cells via its spiracles and tracheal system, more oxygen diffuses into the plastron. The reverse process happens in relation to carbon dioxide. To a certain extent, gases will diffuse from the surrounding water in and out of simple air stores and bubbles, allowing them to be renewed less often, but with a plastron the bug may never have to break the water's surface.

Nervous system

The central nervous system is very uniform throughout the order Hemiptera. As in most insects, there is a ventral nerve cord lying under the digestive system and running the whole length of the body. At intervals large numbers of nerve cells are lumped together into special centres known as ganglia. In the generalized

Defending them from parasitoids and predators, a female Australian Harlequin Bug (*Tectocoris diophthalmus*) stands guard over the clutch of eggs she has glued to a plant stem. A keen eye will spot the spiracles or breathing holes located along the lateral margin of her abdomen. **Scutelleridae**

insect there is a very large ganglion in the head known as the brain. Leading from it are two large connective trunks which join it with the first ventral ganglion, known as the suboesophageal ganglion and lying under the digestive tract. From here backwards there may be a variable number of thoracic and abdominal ganglia.

In Hemiptera, the ventral ganglia are frequently fused. The majority of bugs have three ganglia: the suboesophageal, the first thoracic, and a final one made up of the fusion of the second thoracic ganglion with all the abdominal ones. Aphids only have two, the suboesophageal ganglion and one other made up from the fusion of the thoracic and abdominal ganglia. In keeping with their small size and lack of body segmentation, scale insects retain only one ventral ganglion.

While the functioning of the nervous system in regulating and controlling the various activities of a bug's life and its response to outside stimuli is outside the scope of this book, I do not want readers to get the idea that bugs are simple creatures. On the antennae of a reduviid, blood-sucking bug there may be as many as twelve thousand individual sensory receptors. Not all will be of the same type, and the axons (the long parts of nerve cells responsible for conducting the nervous impulse) from each of these may join others to form 350–400 compound axons running from the base of each antenna towards the brain. We are still quite a long way from understanding anything but the simplest of matters concerning the insect's nervous system.

Haemolymph and circulation

As in all insects, the internal organs of a bug are bathed in a blood-like fluid called haemolymph which is moved around the body cavity by means of a combined heart and aorta (dorsal pumping organ) lying just under the dorsal body surface. In some bug families the heart lies well to the rear of the abdomen, while in others it extends along much of the dorsal surface of the abdomen. The main function of the haemolymph is concerned with the transport of nutrients and waste products. The heart-and-aorta structure is, in effect, an open-ended tube divided into a number of sections, and its job is to propel the haemolymph from the posterior end of the body to the anterior end in a cyclical fashion.

In addition to the main heart, all bugs have accessory hearts associated with each of their legs. These pulsatile organs are designed to avoid stagnation and to ensure a good flow of haemolymph through the extremities of the limbs. The structure of these organs has been studied in a range of heteropteran species and in some auchenorrhynchan and sternorrhynchan species. Typically, the entire inner volume of the legs is divided lengthwise into two spaces or sinuses by means of a thin membrane or diaphragm. Because the diaphragm is twisted, particularly in the region of the pulsatile organ, the haemolymph flowing down one sinus spirals around the haemolymph flowing back towards the body through the other sinus. The actual driving force which keeps the fluids in continuous motion within the leg is provided by the pulsatile organ located at the 'knee end' of the tibia. These simple pumps are composed of a flap-like valve and, in most species, their own muscles. Oddly, in some sternorrhynchan groups, mainly aphids and scale insects, there is no dorsal pumping organ, its job being taken over entirely by the pulsatile organs.

Chapter 3
Bug Classification

As mentioned in the Introduction, the four bug suborders are each divided into a number of lower taxonomic groupings. So this chapter deals with infraorders, superfamilies and families. The numbers in parentheses after the infraordinal and superfamilial names that form the chapter's sub-headings indicate how many superfamilies and families respectively are currently recognized in each group worldwide. Under the level of superfamily the morphological characteristics, habitat preferences, distribution and other biological aspects of the major families are described. Small or relatively minor families are discussed together at the end of each section. To assist in identifying the various body parts, Fig. 4 on p. 22 is a detailed drawing of a typical bug.

Suborder: Heteroptera

In the past, this suborder was divided into three large groups or series called the Geocorisae, Amphibicorisae and Hydrocorisae. Broadly speaking, the Geocorisae comprised all the mainly terrestrial heteropterans, the Amphibicorisae the water surface dwelling heteropterans, and the Hydrocorisae the aquatic or sometimes semi-aquatic heteropterans. This and other classifications using the old-fashioned taxonomic groupings of division, series and section have been largely superseded during the last fifteen years by the use of seven distinctive infraorders.

Body outlines of some common aquatic and semi-aquatic bug families and terrestrial bug families are illustrated in Figs 8 and 9 respectively.

Infraorder: Enicocephalomorpha (1)
Superfamily: Enicocephaloidea (1)

Family: **Enicocephalidae**

The enicocephalids or unique-headed bugs, as they are sometimes known, comprise a group of more than 250 species of small to medium-sized, predatory bugs. In the past, they have been regarded as a member family of the Reduvoidea. The family is distributed worldwide but the majority of species are found in tropical and subtropical regions where they live on the forest floor, under litter, stones and bark and in soil or decaying wood. Some species are known only from pitfall traps and light traps.

In general they are slender, elongate, dull-coloured, membranously winged or wingless. All species have a distinctively shaped, slender head; it is constricted across the middle, behind the eyes, and then enlarged, giving the appearance of two sections. The head carries four-segmented antennae, a three-segmented rostrum and ocelli. The eyes of males, which in some species can be very large

Covering the wings almost entirely, the greatly enlarged and rounded scutellum of scutellerid shield bugs imparts a beetle like aspect. This brightly coloured species, (*Pachycoris* sp.), photographed in Trinidad, can be found from Mexico to Argentina.
Scutelleridae

indeed and occupy almost the entire head area, are generally bigger than those of females.

The tarsi of the front legs are strangely modified for grasping prey, which consists of a range of small invertebrates. The squat tarsal segment, bearing a pair of sharp, unequal claws, can be opposed on to spines arising from the inner face of the tibia. Although some species have been found in association with ant colonies where they may feed on the ant larvae, it is not fully known how they avoid being killed by their hosts.

Courtship and the laying of single eggs on the ground is preceded in many fully winged species by a swarming flight, which often takes the form of a vertical spiral and may comprise both sexes. As far as is known, these bugs are unique among the Heteroptera in their sexual swarming behaviour. Perhaps in keeping with their litter and soil habitat, in some species the females shed their wings after copulation.

Enicocephalids have very indistinct metathoracic scent glands hidden under the bases of the front wings and a pair of additional ventral glands where the thorax and abdomen join. As with many other families, there are certainly very many more species awaiting discovery and description.

Infraorder: Leptopodomorpha (1)
Superfamily: Leptopodoidea (4)

Family: **Saldidae** (Fig. 8:i)

This family includes around 260 shore bug species. Although they are found all over the world, well over half of the known species have a Holarctic distribution.

These bugs are scavengers or predatory on small organisms living on or near the ground surface. Most species live in very damp, muddy or sandy habitats and are commonly collected near fresh, brackish or salt water. Some species live in the zone between high and low tides and can survive being submerged by the sea.

Saldids, which are generally cryptically coloured brownish or black with pale markings and spots, can be anything between 2 and 6 mm (0.08–0.2 in) long, with an oval or slightly elongate body outline and large, bulging eyes. Shore bugs can run very rapidly using their relatively long legs, and jump or fly at the first signs of disturbance. Many species are good at digging and may spend some of their time below the ground surface.

Females lay their eggs inside or near the base of low-growing grasses, mosses and other plants. Once hatched, the nymphs can reach adulthood in a matter of a few weeks. *Salda*, *Saldula* and *Chiloxanthus* are typical genera.

Other families

Three additional families are placed in the Leptopodomorpha. Two predatory species comprising the **Leotichiidae** are found in the Oriental region, associated with droppings of cave-dwelling bat species. Around 30 world species of the spiny-legged bug family, **Leptopodidae**, are found mainly in the tropical and subtropical areas of the eastern hemisphere. These species are predacious and can be found on dry rocks near water or sometimes quite far from it. The **Omaniidae**, commonly known as the intertidal dwarf bugs, are represented by just four very small, beetle-like species. These predacious bugs can be found hiding in cracks in rocks and corals in some coastal regions of Arabia, Pakistan, Japan, Indonesia and Australia. A single Australian species is known only from the Great Barrier Reef.

Infraorder: Dipsocoromorpha (1)
Superfamily: Dipsocoroidea (5)

Family: **Schizopteridae**

Present in most parts of the world and particularly common in the tropics, these very small, oval or elongate-oval, probably predacious bugs have not yet been recorded from the Palaeartic region. The head of these squat, beetle-like bugs is strongly bent downwards and the eyes are large or very large. Schizopterids can jump using their hind legs. These have a roughened area at their bases which is used to engage with and strain against a spinous structure on the underside of the thorax.

Although a mere 160 or so species are known, it is almost certain that this family is very under-recorded. This is because of the cryptic appearance and secretive nature of its member species, which live among forest-floor leaf litter, detritus and soil.

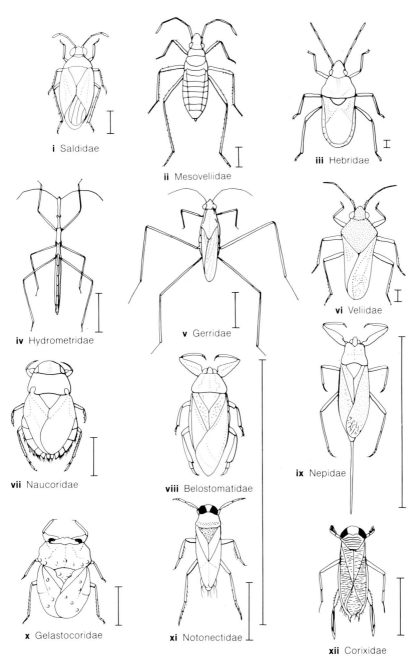

Fig. 8. Body outlines of some aquatic and semi-aquatic heteropteran bugs. Approximate body lengths are shown beside each bug.

Other families

Schizopterids have sometimes been regarded as a subfamily of the **Dipsoco-ridae**, but they look very different from the anthocorid-like dipsocorids. The head of dipsocorids is not bent downwards and appears quite pointed. The 25 world species, which are confined largely to the Holarctic region, are under 2.5 mm (0.1 in) in length. These bugs almost certainly prey on small organisms among the damp moss and leaf litter they inhabit. Dipsocorids can also be found under stones along stream margins.

The 45 or so world species now placed in the family **Ceratocombidae** were also once regarded as a subfamily of the **Dipsocoridae**. Ceratocombids, which are also very small, predacious, leaf litter dwellers, can be found in the forests of most faunal regions.

The superfamily Dipsocoroidea is completed by an additional two, insignificant families. The **Hypsipterygidae** contains only three small species known from forest leaf litter in the Oriental and Ethiopian regions, while the **Stemmo-cryptidae** has but a single species.

Infraorder: Gerromorpha (4)
Superfamily: Mesovelioidea (1)

Family: **Mesoveliidae** (Fig. 8:ii)

About 35 species of pondweed bug or water treaders are known, and species are present in all the major faunal regions. The head and eyes are quite large, the antennae are four-segmented and the rostrum three-segmented. The legs are quite long and slender, with the claws arising from the very end of the pretarsus.

The biggest genus, *Mesovelia*, contains most of the species in the family and has a cosmopolitan distribution. Mesoveliids are quite small, less than 6 mm (0.2 in), elongate and generally brownish or green in colour. Many species spend much of their lives on the floating leaves of water plants or in very wet places close to the water margin. Some mesoveliids have been found on open water, in caves and even in the damp leaf litter of forests.

Most species are wingless but winged forms do occur. The rostrum is used to penetrate the bodies of dead or dying insects on the water surface and to catch and suck out the juices of minute, live crustaceans and other small invertebrates.

Superfamily: Hebroidea (1)

Family: **Hebridae** (Fig. 8:iii)

There are approximately 150 species of velvet water bugs or sphagnum bugs, distributed worldwide in all the major faunal regions. Members of this family can be found walking on the water and on floating vegetation in marshy places, ponds and water margins, among mosses and in other wet habitats. These small, squat, semi-aquatic bugs are generally less than 3 mm (0.1 in) in length and have a dull coloration. The body is covered with a distinctive pile of water-repellent hairs. Wing polymorphism is a common feature of this group, and at certain times large numbers of fully winged individuals will take to the air. The nymphs and adults prey on small organisms such as springtails. *Hebrus* and *Merragata* are typical, common and widespread genera.

Superfamily: Hydrometroidea (3)

Family: **Hydrometridae** (Fig. 8:iv)

The common names of marsh treader and water measurer are very appropriate for the 115 or so species represented by this cosmopolitan family. The very elongate and slender body shape of these bugs makes them unmistakable. The majority of species belong to the worldwide genus *Hydrometra*.

In general, members of this family are less than 15 mm (0.6 in) long and of a dull colour. The slender head is very long indeed and bears the four- or five-segmented antennae, a three-segmented rostrum and a pair of bulging eyes that arise from about halfway along the head. The long legs are like jointed threads and enable the bug to move slowly and gracefully across the surface of the water or aquatic vegetation. Hydrometrids are normally wingless or short-winged.

Some species prefer brackish or stagnant water, and a very few have been found in rain forests. Although capable of preying on a wide range of aquatic and semi-aquatic organisms like insect larvae, springtails, waterfleas and other small arthropods, most hydrometrids attack animals that are injured or freshly dead.

Other families

The superfamily Hydrometroidea includes two other very small families, the **Macroveliidae** and the **Paraphrynoveliidae**, with only three and two species respectively. Macroveliids are found in some parts of North and South America, while the paraphrynoveliids have a southern African distribution. Members of both families are small, and live in very wet habitats where they are scavengers or predatory.

Superfamily: Gerroidea (3)

Family: **Gerridae** (Fig. 8:v)

All of the five hundred or so known species of water strider or pondskater are highly adapted to life on the water surface and occur in all regions of the world. Anything from small, peaty pools to streams, rivers, ponds, lakes and even the open oceans may provide a suitable habitat for gerrid species.

The body of these medium-sized, dark brown or black bugs, which may be up to 18 mm (0.7 in) long, can be oval or quite elongate. In common with all surface-living bugs (Gerromorpha), the body is thickly covered with a dense pile of velvety, water-repellent hairs. The legs are slender and the middle and hind pairs, which can be very long, are splayed out and equipped with unwettable feet to support the weight of the bug on the elastic surface film.

Water striders, which are the most commonly seen surface-dwelling bugs, are capable of very rapid, gliding movements and jumping. Their very acute eyes, along with their specialized ripple-sensitive body and leg hairs, enable them to locate struggling or drowning prey; these characteristics also make the bugs themselves very difficult to catch. In general, water striders sense and respond mainly to prey in front of them.

Many species are gregarious, and in some cases cannibalistic on young nymphs. Female gerrids seem to be more cannibalistic than males but, interestingly, appear to eat their own young less than those of other females.

Supported by slender legs equipped with unwettable hairs, a pair of water striders (*Gerris lacustris*) mate on the surface film of an English pond. Using his front legs, the smaller male grips the female from above. **Gerridae**

Winglessness is common, but winged forms may also occur in populations of many species when dispersal to new or less crowded habitat is necessary.

Members of the genus *Gerris* are typical and widespread. Five genera, including the well-known *Halobates*, are called ocean striders and spend all of their lives at sea, often hundreds of miles from land.

Family: **Veliidae** (Fig. 8:vi)
Veliids are commonly known as watercrickets or small water striders. They resemble gerrids in some respects, but are generally much smaller and more robust and have shorter, stouter legs. Some veliids can be up to 8 or 9 mm (0.3–0.35 in) long, but this is not by any means the norm. Some species are always fully winged, but in others there may be short-winged or wingless forms. A useful distinction is that in veliids the legs are equally spaced, while in gerrids the middle pair of legs is much closer to the hind legs. About five hundred species are known and, although they occur throughout the world, they are particularly numerous in the Neotropical and Oriental regions. *Microvelia* and *Velia* are common and widespread genera.

Like gerrids, veliids live on the water surface in a variety of habitats and prey on a variety of small, floating organisms such as trapped insects, crustacea and the eggs and larvae of aquatic insects. In some species, when a small prey item is caught by a single veliid the bug may defend it from being eaten by others; while with larger items several bugs may share the same meal.

Some species have been found in damp forests, and a very few are ocean-going. Most live in slowly flowing water around vegetation and simply walk over the surface. Those which inhabit more exposed or faster-flowing water, such as species in the genus *Rhagovelia*, have special blades or hair tufts, known as swimming fans, located in clefts or slits on the last tarsal segment of their middle legs.

On the power stroke, the hairs spread out and act like webbed feet to enable the bug to move against strong water currents.

Members of this family also use an ingenious locomotory technique known as expansion skating. The trick here, of most use perhaps as a means to escape predators, is to use salivary secretions to lower the surface tension of the water film. By releasing a drop of saliva through the mobile rostrum, the bugs can cause a fast-acting reduction in surface tension behind them which results in their being drawn very rapidly forwards over the water. In this manner a veliid can move, in a number of directions, depending on where it directs its rostrum. Veliids and other small, surface-dwelling bugs can use surface tension and particular body postures to help them climb out of the water on to plants.

Other families
The third and last family in the Gerroidea is the **Hermatobatidae**. About 10 species of these small bugs are known; all are marine surface predators living on the seas and oceans of the southern hemisphere.

Infraorder: Nepomorpha (5)
Superfamily: Naucoroidea (2)

Family: **Naucoridae** (Fig. 8:vii)
Commonly called either saucer bugs on account of their smoothly rounded, broadly oval and flattened shape, or creeping water bugs because of their habits, naucorids form a distinctive group of some three hundred species distributed worldwide. Many species look like small versions of the belostomatid family and have very similar habits. *Ilyocoris*, *Naucoris* and *Ambrysus* are typical genera.

Adapted for a sub-surface aquatic life, naucorids are streamlined and have specialized rows of swimming hairs on their middle and hind legs. The front legs are highly modified for capturing prey. The tibiae are curved and sickle-like, capable of being folded back like a jack-knife on to the enlarged femora.

Living in both static and moving water, even in hot springs, naucorids move about slowly on the bottom and climb on submerged vegetation. Prey items, which include the larvae of aquatic insects, crustacea and snails, are seized and sucked dry by means of the short, three-segmented rostrum. Supplies of oxygen, obtained from the surface, are retained in the space beneath the wings and the back of the abdomen.

Other families
Species in the closely related, monogeneric (*Aphelocheirus*) family **Aphelocheiridae** are sometimes considered to be a subfamily of the **Naucoridae** and are found only in the Old World. These bugs are very similar in looks and habits, but distinct in not having highly developed raptorial front legs for catching prey. Aphelocheirids are of great interest in that they have evolved a very efficient physical gill system or plastron. The plastron is effectively a thin layer of air trapped close to various parts of the body by means of a dense pile of special hook-tipped hairs. This trapped layer exchanges oxygen and carbon dioxide between it and the surrounding water so well that the bugs rarely need to visit the surface to breathe.

Superfamily: Nepoidea (2)

Family: **Belostomatidae** (Fig. 8: viii)

In some parts of the world these very large and handsome insects are attracted to lights during the night. For this reason they are sometimes called electric light bugs, but the name of giant water bugs is more universally applied. Somewhere in the region of 150 species are known worldwide and, although species can be found in most of the faunal regions, they are most numerous in the Americas, India and southern Africa.

Anyone who has been fortunate enough to see these fantastic bugs at first hand will know that they can be very large indeed. Some species of the genus *Lethocerus*, measuring around 150 mm (6 ins) long, are the biggest of all bugs and among the biggest of any insects anywhere on Earth.

Giant water bugs have a very streamlined, oval outline, a flattened appearance and very large raptorial front legs for seizing prey. They live in various kinds of static and slow-moving water, preferring those with muddy bottoms and plenty of water weeds. The head carries a pair of large eyes and a pair of four-segmented antennae, which are concealed in grooves. The end of the abdomen in belostomatid nymphs and adults carries a pair of short appendages which, when united, form a short, tube-like breathing siphon. The middle and hind legs are flattened and have fringes of hairs for swimming.

Species of the African, snail-feeding genus *Limnogeton* do not have their legs as strongly adapted for swimming as do species in other genera. In these bugs the legs, which are more normal in appearance, are also used for swimming but, as their prey is not fast-moving, the legs do not need to be flattened or to possess large hair fringes for rapid movement. The habit of eating snails is not confined to *Limnogeton*: species in other belostomatid genera also prey on aquatic gastropods.

Males of some species have been shown to attract females by using their bodies to generate low-frequency ripples that spread out across the water's surface. The waves, which can be produced for up to a minute at a time, increase the males' chances of mating but can also attract predatory water spiders.

The wings can be used for flight, but also serve to trap a layer of air over the somewhat hollowed dorsal abdominal surface. In the males of *Belostoma*, *Abedus* and *Sphaerodema* the surface of the folded front wings is used as an egg nursery. The female giant water bug attaches her eggs to the back of the male using a waterproof glue. The males carry the eggs until they hatch, usually in about a fortnight. In other species, egg masses are simply glued to vegetation.

Nymphs and adults are very fierce predators indeed and, depending on species and size, will attack anything from insect larvae to tadpoles, snails, frogs, fish and even small water birds. Prey-catching tactics can range from ambushing to active foraging. Victims are seized and the stout rostrum quickly injects a mixture of fast-acting enzymes to dissolve the body contents, which are then sucked out. Some species exhibit hoarding – they catch an additional item of prey while still feeding on the first.

Family: **Nepidae** (Fig. 8:ix)

About 20 species of waterscorpion have been described from all the major world regions. These bugs can be quite large, up to 50 mm (2 ins) body length, with characteristic, prey-seizing front legs and a long, slender breathing tube or siphon at the end of the abdomen. The siphon is formed from two grooved, rigid halves which unite to make a snorkel capable of being thrust through the surface film.

The family is divided into two distinctive subfamilies, the Nepinae, whose species are flattened and elongate to oval, and the slender, twig-like Ranatrinae. All the members of the family live in static or moving water ranging from bogs and marshes to slow-flowing streams and rivers. Waterscorpions spend much of their time crawling about on submerged plants or hanging stationary from the surface film by means of their siphons.

A whole range of small aquatic organisms, including insect larvae of various kinds and even tadpoles, form the diet of these predacious bugs. The adults are winged and capable of taking to the air. If disturbed or threatened, many species will pretend to be dead. *Ranatra* and *Nepa* are the two main genera.

Superfamily: Gelastocoroidea (sometimes known as Ochteroidea) (2)

Family: **Gelastocoridae** (Fig. 8:x)

Called toad bugs on account of their warty appearance and hopping mode of progress, the 85 or so gelastocorid species that have so far been described are found mainly in the southern hemisphere. These smallish – under 12 mm (0.5 in) – broadly oval bugs are mostly very cryptically coloured to blend in with their surroundings. The head is squat, broad and fits snugly into the pronotum. The bulging eyes are quite large and, as the face is flat, appear to be forward-facing. The four-segmented antennae are short and concealed from view beneath the eyes. In common with naucorids, belostomatids and nepids, the front legs are modified as prey-capturing devices.

Resting on wet sand by the side of a rain forest stream, a toad bug (*Gelastocoris peruensis*) resembles a small pebble. Toad bugs are recognizable by their squat shape, large eyes, warty surface texture and hopping movements. Peru. **Gelastocoridae**

While many species live next to ponds and streams and in other waterside habitats, some can be found in decaying wood, under stones or in leaf litter some distance from water. Adults and nymphs will jump on any suitable small organisms, mainly insects, which they encounter. *Gelastocoris* species are found in North and South America, whereas *Nerthra* species occur all over the world in tropical, subtropical and some temperate regions.

Other families

The final family in the Gelastocoroidea is the **Ochteridae**. The velvet shore bugs are a widely distributed but small group of around 35 species. In common with the gelastocorids, they live in waterside habitats where they prey on small insects, especially fly larvae. Ochterids are small and oval like the toad bugs; but, rather than being warty, they have a sparsely velvety body surface. Unusually among the water bugs, the short antennae are visible. Ochterid front legs are not designed for seizing prey. The nymphs of some species are known to spread sand grains over their bodies as a means of camouflage.

Superfamily: Notonectoidea (3)

Family: **Notonectidae** (Fig. 8:xi)

The strongly convex dorsal surface, flat ventral surface and long, oar-like and hair-fringed hind legs of these elongate aquatic bugs has given rise to the common name of water boatmen. The name is sometimes applied to corixids, but these are more usually called lesser water boatmen. A better, and less confusing, common name for notonectids is backswimmers, which describes the way they swim, with their paler, ventral surface uppermost.

More than three hundred species of notonectids are known from still, fresh water throughout the world. Species in the genus *Notonecta* are very widely distributed. Other well-known genera include *Martarega*, *Enithares*, *Buenoa* and *Anisops*.

The head of these medium-sized bugs, which fits neatly into the pronotum, carries a three- or four-segmented rostrum and a pair of short, four-segmented antennae. The large eyes cover a considerable proportion of the surface of the head.

The front legs of notonectids are of normal design and are used to grasp food. Their prey covers a wide range of organisms from larval insects to small fish or tadpoles. Some species feed mainly on small animals which drown or become trapped on the surface. These bugs use the ripples emanating from their struggling victims to locate them, and can distinguish the higher-frequency waves produced by potential prey items from the lower-frequency waves produced by their own swimming movements. In general notonectids will not attack an animal that is bigger than themselves, but the reader should be warned that they can deliver a painful stab if they are picked up and carelessly handled.

Air, obtained from the surface, is stored under the wings and on the ventral surface of the abdomen, where it is held in place by rows of specialized hairs. When the bug needs to replenish its air supply it returns to the surface where it hangs from the posterior end of the body. Backswimmers are very wary, and at any sign of danger can dive rapidly. They can also fly very well and are known to jump through the surface film when they take to the air.

Photographed from above, a backswimmer (*Notonecta glauca*) shows its underside as it hangs from the surface film of an English garden pond. This and other species in the genus prefer the quieter waters of ponds and pools where they prey mainly on a range of aquatic invertebrates. **Notonectidae**

Males of some species produce species-specific courtship sounds by rubbing roughened parts of their front tibiae and femora against a special stridulatory region at the base of the rostrum. The courtship sounds made by some males of the genus *Buenoa* can be heard at a distance of several metres. Initially the sounds made by the males are like a series of rapid clicks. As the male gets near to a female, but before he clasps her with his front and middle legs, the sound becomes more like a hum.

The use of haemoglobin as a respiratory substance in insects is very unusual indeed. In some species of *Buenoa*, living in oxygen-poor waters, the tracheal system is linked to large groups of haemoglobin-containing cells located in the abdomen. This facility allows them to exploit a habitat that would otherwise be hostile to life.

Other families
The superfamily Notonectoidea includes two other small families, the **Pleidae** (pygmy or lesser backswimmers) and the **Heloptrephidae**. These two groups, which contain around 40 and 20 species respectively, are known from most regions of the world. Like backswimmers they are aquatic, swim underside upper-most and capture prey; but they rarely measure more than 3 mm (0.12 in) long.

Superfamily: Corixoidea (1)

Family: **Corixidae** (Fig. 8:xii)

Lesser water boatmen (sometimes known as water boatmen; see **Notonectidae** above) comprise the largest family of aquatic bugs. There are slightly more than five hundred species worldwide, distributed in all the major faunal regions. Habitats range from small acidic bog pools, ponds, lakes and slow-flowing streams to brackish or very salty water. Generally slightly smaller, corixids are nevertheless very similar in general outline to notonectids: they are elongate with broad heads, short, concealed antennae and large eyes. There are, however, a number of important and characteristic differences.

In the field, the most obvious distinction is the manner in which they swim: corixids move through the water right way up, not on their backs. The dorsal surface of the body is flattened, not convex, and the three pairs of legs are dissimilar, each pair having a particular function. The hind pair are oar-like, flattened and fringed with swimming hairs to provide propulsion. The middle pair are quite slender and used as anchors to grip plants and submerged objects. The very short front pair are uniquely modified, with the femora and tibia very reduced. The single tarsal segment (the pala), which is large and equipped with hairs and peg-like structures, functions as a food scoop and, in males of some species, to grasp the sides of the female during mating.

Air supplies are carried on the slightly concave dorsal surface, beneath the wings. Many corixid species are unusual among bugs in that they feed on minute organisms such as diatoms and algal cells which they filter from the bottom detritus; others are predacious or partially so.

Males – or both sexes in many species – use species-specific sounds for mate attraction and in courtship. The sounds, which are produced by rubbing together specially modified parts of the body, may involve the genitalia and abdominal segments, the front femora and head, or the middle legs and the edges of the partner's wings.

Sigara, *Hesperocorixa*, *Corixa*, *Cymatia* and *Micronecta* are just some of the many common genera.

Infraorder: Cimicomorpha (6)
Superfamily: Thaumastocoroidea (1)

Family: **Thaumastocoridae**

Before it was realized that the members of this small family had cimicomorphan relationships, they were placed in the Lygaeoidea near the seed bugs. Around 15 species are known from South America, India and Australia. Not a great deal is known about the biology of these phytophagous bugs, which are generally less than 2 mm (0.08 in) long.

The family is divided into two subfamilies, the Xylastodorinae (three species), associated with some species of palm, and the Thaumastocorinae (12 species), which eat a wider range of host plants including *Acacia*, *Eucalyptus* and *Banksia*. *Thaumastocoris* and *Xylastodoris* are the two main genera. Some authorities consider the palm bugs to be a separate family in their own right (**Xylastodoridae**). Recent work suggests that the thaumastocorids might be better placed in the Miroidea close to the **Miridae**.

Superfamily: Joppeicoidea(1)

Family: **Joppeicidae**

The family is represented by a single, poorly known but aptly named species called *Joppeicus paradoxus*, which occurs in Egypt, other parts of North Africa and certain areas of the Eastern Mediterranean. Since its description in 1881 this very small, predatory bug has been a waif and stray of the Heteroptera. Authors have variously placed it in the **Aradidae**, the **Lygaeidae** and, most recently, within the Reduvoidea and Cimicoidea. There is now general agreement that it belongs in the infraorder Cimicomorpha and, on account of some unique morphological features, deserves a superfamily all by itself.

Limited evidence suggests that, in nature, this species is a general predator of any small insect that it might encounter within micro-habitats in litter, in caves, under the surface of bark and on various species of fig plants. In the laboratory, it has been shown that several adults may feed on the same large prey item, and that the salivary substances injected cause convulsions and are extremely fast acting.

Superfamily: Tingoidea (2)

Family: **Tingidae** (Fig. 9:i)

More than 1,800 species of lace bug occur worldwide and can be found in all the major faunal regions. Although tingids are mostly small, flattened bugs ranging from 2 to 5 mm (0.08–0.2 in) long, they are spectacularly beautiful. The dense, reticulated or net-like, raised veining of the front wings and the sometimes bizarre lateral and posterior extensions of the pitted or reticulated pronotum make these hemipterans unmistakable. Nymphs do not acquire characteristic

Resting on the head of a Creeping Thistle, their preferred host plant, these tiny lace bugs (*Tingis ampliata*) show the intricate net-like patterns and dorsal keels characteristic of the family. The flattened adults move easily through the plant's spines. Great Britain. **Tingidae**

net-like patterns until they moult to the adult stage, but some can be very spiny. The expense of a powerful hand lens or even a binocular microscope would be more than rewarded by the opportunity to see these insects close up.

All known tingids are herbivorous; some species feed on a single host species (monophagous) while others can feed on a range of related species (oligophagous). As a whole the family attacks a wide range of host plants and some species can be pests of ornamental trees, fruit and other crops, causing damage through feeding and by the transmission of disease-causing organisms. A few, such as *Teleonemia lantanae*, which eats the aggressive and serious weed species *Lantana camara*, have been used successfully in biological control programmes.

Some tingid species induce the growth of galls, inside which the young nymphs feed and are protected. Leaves which have been fed on by a number of lace bugs look finely speckled due to the bugs' habit of emptying individual cells. Eggs are laid and inserted into the tissue of the food plant, along with a secretion which hardens to form a distinctive raised bump on the plant's surface.

A number of tingid species show maternal care of the nymphs, herding them from leaf to leaf and protecting them from predators and parasites. Even more fascinating is the egg dumping exhibited by some females in a few species. This habit ensures that the other females guard and look after their nymphs along with their own (see Chapter 7).

Acalypta, *Corythucha*, *Gargaphia*, *Stephanitis*, *Teleonemia*, *Tingis* and *Dictyonota* are examples of widespread and important genera. Recent work indicates that tingids should be placed in the Miroidea along with **Miridae**.

Other families
A handful of closely related species forming the family **Vianaididae** are sometimes considered to be a subfamily of the **Tingidae**. The dorsal body surface of these small bugs may be pitted or similarly sculptured, but is not reticulate. The biology of vianaidids is not well known, but it is thought that they are probably plant feeders. All the known species live in association with ant species in South America.

Superfamily: Miroidea (2)

Family: **Miridae** (Fig. 9:ii)
Plant bugs constitute the biggest by far of all the heteropteran families. While seven to eight thousand species are already known from all parts of the world, it is virtually certain that the final total will be double this figure or more.

Mirid bugs are very variable in appearance, ranging from slender and elongate to short and broadly oval, and from cryptically coloured to brightly patterned. They generally have a delicate structure and, although some species can have a body length of 14–15 mm (about 0.6 in), the vast majority are much smaller. The presence of a four-segmented rostrum and antennae and the possession of two closed cells in the membranous region of the front wings (when present) are all good identification features.

Occurring in a large number of varied habitats from ground level to the tops of trees, these bugs constitute one of the commonest heteropteran families encountered in terrestrial studies. While many species are phytophagous, attacking all

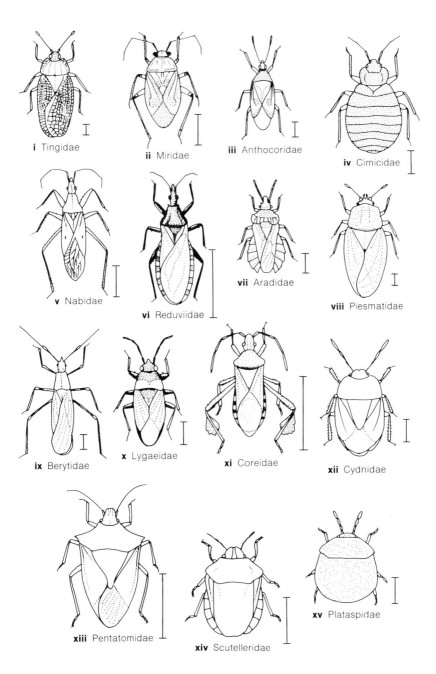

i Tingidae

ii Miridae

iii Anthocoridae

iv Cimicidae

v Nabidae

vi Reduviidae

vii Aradidae

viii Piesmatidae

ix Berytidae

x Lygaeidae

xi Coreidae

xii Cydnidae

xiii Pentatomidae

xiv Scutelleridae

xv Plataspidae

Fig. 9. Body outlines of some terrestrial heteropteran bugs. Approximate body lengths are shown beside each bug.

Plant bugs are by no means all herbivorous. The nymphs and adults of *Miris striatus*, a relatively large (10 mm/0.4 in) and strikingly marked Palaearctic species, are found on the foliage of many kinds of deciduous trees where they suck a wide range of small, soft-bodied prey items. The two closed cells in the membranous portion of the front wings, here delineated by pale veins, are typical of the family. Great Britain. **Miridae**

parts of huge numbers of plant species, many others are predatory or saprophagous. Important crops around the world are regularly damaged or destroyed by feeding mirids. In tropical regions, about 10 species attack cocoa trees while others confine their attentions to tea, sweet potatoes, tomatoes, cashew nuts, avocados, guavas, mangoes and cotton. The major species attacking cocoa trees in Africa are *Sahlbergella singularis* and *Distantiella theobroma*. In Central and South America, the major cocoa pests are species of *Monalonion*. A variety of crops in the Indo-Malayan region suffer from three fairly polyphagous species belonging to the genus *Helopeltis*.

On the positive side, predatory species are extremely valuable in the control of scale insects, aphids, red spider mites and a host of other soft-bodied arthropod pests. A few have been used very successfully as biological control agents, a well-known example being *Tytthus mundulus*, a predator of planthopper eggs. This species, a native of the Australasian region, was used at the beginning of the twentieth century to control a serious outbreak of the Sugar-Cane Planthopper, *Perkinsiella saccharicida* (**Delphacidae**), in Hawaii.

Within the family there are many fascinating specialist species which variously feed on carrion, honeydew, blood and mummified aphids, and even rob spiders' webs and carnivorous plants of their prey. Of the very large number of widespread and important genera, *Lygus*, *Deraeocoris*, *Dicyphus*, *Phytocoris*, *Psallus*, *Orthotylus* and *Plagiognathus* are random examples.

Other families
The only other family in the Miroidea is the **Microphysidae**. Somewhere in the region of 25 predatory species, generally less than 3 mm (0.12 in) in length, are known from the northern hemisphere where they live in various microhabitats among leaf litter, mosses, lichens and tree bark. Adult females are usually wingless and have a swollen abdomen, while males are of normal design. *Loricula* and *Myrmedobia* are typical of the family.

Superfamily: Cimicoidea (7)

Family: **Anthocoridae** (Fig. 9:iii)
Ranging from 1 to 5 mm (0.04–0.2 in) in length, the small, mainly predatory bugs that make up this family of some five hundred species have an elongate-oval or rectangular outline and are dorso-ventrally flattened. Flower or minute pirate bugs, as they are commonly known, live in a variety of habitats worldwide depending on species. Many can be found on flowers and vegetation, in leaf litter and under bark, while others are more specialized, occurring in association with the homes of ants, birds and mammals (including man) or even in epiphytic plants and caves.

The pointed head bears a three-segmented rostrum and a pair of four-segmented antennae. Although the majority of species are fully winged, with the membranous area of the front wings devoid of closed cells, short-winged forms do exist. Many species practise traumatic insemination: the males, using modified genitalia, pierce the body of the female through a weak spot.

Anthocorids are often termed 'timid predators', for they will not attack anything that can fight back or move very fast. Insect eggs and larvae, thrips, leaf miners, whiteflies, aphids, mites and barklice are typical prey. Some species can feed on plant material such as pollen and flowers, while others feed on the blood of birds and mammals, including man.

On account of their predacious habits, many species have been invaluable in the biological control of red spider mites, weevils, caterpillars, thrips, aphids, scale insects and other pests that damage commercially important plants. *Lyctocoris flavipes* and *L. campestris* are predators of mites and the larval stages of certain beetles and moths associated with stored produce. Among the many important genera, *Anthocoris*, *Orius* and *Xylocoris* are noteworthy.

Family: **Cimicidae** (Fig. 9:iv)
The bugs which comprise this small family of around 80–90 species, while widely distributed in most of the world's regions, are most prevalent in subtropical and tropical areas. The family had no Australian representative until two hundred years ago, when the white man brought the notorious and now cosmopolitan Bed Bug, *Cimex lectularius*.

Although the common name of bed bug is used for the entire family, this is not strictly appropriate as by no means all are found in domestic situations. All species are wingless, blood-feeding ectoparasites of birds and a range of other animals, especially bats. The two people-biting species are the cosmopolitan and widespread *Cimex lectularius* and *C. rotundatus*, the latter confined to tropical Africa and Asia.

Cimicids, which are oval and flattened in shape and dark yellowish or reddish brown, can be up to 6 mm (0.24 in) long. The legs are not modified to cling to fur or feathers, and these largely nocturnal bugs spend most of their time in the host's lair, nest, roost or other sleeping place. Several species are cave dwellers.

Copulation involves traumatic insemination, with the male penetrating the body wall of the female. The injected sperms migrate through the body fluids or through special tissues and ducts inside the female to reach the ovaries. Eggs are glued in crevices and cracks.

Species in the genus *Cimex* attack bats, man, poultry and other domesticated animals, while species of *Oeciacus* feed from swallows and martins. In parts of North America, a species of *Haematosiphon* feeds on the blood of owls, eagles and the Californian Condor. *Primicimex, Bucimex, Propicimex, Cacodmus, Loxaspis, Aphrania* and species in several other genera are associated with bats. *Paracimex, Psitticimex, Ornithocoris, Hesperocimex* and other genera feed on the blood of birds.

Repeated attempts to prove that bed bugs can act as vectors of disease, at least in man, have not supplied any conclusive data. Some bird-feeding species have been shown to transmit viruses to their hosts and, despite many negative results, it seems improbable that human-biters are totally innocent of any disease transmission.

Family: **Nabidae** (Fig. 9:v)

Relatively slender, elongate and of a dull, brown or straw-coloured appearance, damsel bugs are predatory heteropterans living in detritus and litter at ground level and on plants. Nearly four hundred species, each less than 12 mm (0.5 in) in length, have been described from all the faunal regions of the world.

The head carries conspicuous eyes, antennae with four or five segments and a slender, four-segmented rostrum. Short-winged forms are common, and in some the wings are present only as tiny flaps. Damsel bugs have thickened front legs reminiscent of some assassin bugs (**Reduviidae**); although these limbs are not properly raptorial, they can be used to control victims as they are sucked dry. A large range of small insects and other arthropods form the diet of these elegant hunters. Eggs are laid in small batches within the tissues of various plants. On hatching, the tiny first instar nymphs immediately seek out their first meal.

Originally thought to be close to the reduvoids, damsel bugs are in fact more like the cimicoids. Although they share some superficial features with the assassin bugs, the peculiar traumatic or intrahaemocoelic method of insemination found in species of the subfamily Prostemminae, together with other characteristics, places them closer to the **Cimicidae** and **Anthocoridae**.

Nabids are of great value in the control of pests in natural and agricultural ecosystems; for instance, in North America three species of *Nabis* prey on the economically important Cotton Boll Worm (*Heleothis zea*). Within the Nabinae *Nabicula, Nabis* and *Anaptus* are widespread genera, while in the Prostemminae *Prostemma* and *Alloerrhynchus* are of interest.

The **Nabidae**, together with the two species comprising a small West African family, the **Medocostidae**, may deserve a superfamily (Naboidea) of their own.

Aptly named for the greatly elevated and toothed central pronotal keel, a pair of wheel bugs mate in the rain forest. Species of the genus *Arilus*, which are found in the tropical regions of the New World, are active by day and feed mainly on lepidopteran larvae. Peru.
Reduviidae

Family: **Polyctenidae**

In contrast to the cimicids, bat bugs live permanently burrowed within the fur of tropical bat species. Slightly more than 30 species are known, almost exclusively from subtropical and tropical areas. Blind and wingless, polyctenids are highly modified for an ectoparasitic existence, feeding on their host's blood. The flattened body has numerous bristles, while the head, thorax and other parts carry comb-like arrangements of stout spines to lock on to the host's hair. Similar combs can be seen in other ectoparasitic insect groups such as fleas. Typically, polyctenids are host-specific and favour places on the host's body which are difficult for the bat to groom. Unlike bed bugs these species, especially in their nymphal stages, cannot live very long without a blood meal.

Sperm transfer is achieved not by the male coupling with the female bug's genital tract but rather, as in other cimicoids, by means of traumatic insemination. The young develop to quite a mature stage inside the body of the mother and are born as nymphs. After their birth, the nymphs have only two more moults before becoming adults themselves.

Two species in the genus *Hesperoctenes* occur in North America. Other genera include *Androctenes* and *Eoctenes*.

Other families

Three further small families complete the cimicoid roll-call. The **Velocipedidae**, with an Oriental distribution, has recently been thought to deserve its own superfamily status (Velocipedoidea). The family is represented by just four or so ground-living, predatory species, and is sometimes treated as a subfamily of the **Nabidae**. The two species comprising the **Medocostidae** are also sometimes regarded as members of the **Nabidae**. Like the velocipedids, species in this family probably catch prey, but few details of their biology are known. The webs of tropical spiders and webspinners are home to the 13 minute, anthocorid-like species known to belong to the **Plokiophilidae**.

Superfamily: Reduvoidea (3)

Family: **Phymatidae**

Whether or not the hundred or so known species of mainly tropical ambush bug are treated as a separate family or as a reduviid subfamily, they are very distinctive in appearance and behaviour. The body of these strange-looking, predacious bugs is somewhat flattened and equipped with variously shaped expansions and spines. Lying in wait and often camouflaged in flowers, ambush bugs will strike rapidly at any suitable prey, using their specially modified and highly raptorial front legs. *Phymata*, *Macrocephalus* and *Carcinocoris* are typical genera.

Family: **Reduviidae** (Fig. 9:vi)

Assassin bugs form a very large assemblage of just over five thousand highly predacious or blood-sucking species. Reduviid coloration can be cryptic or aposematic. The body shape, which is extremely variable, ranges from robust and oval such as in *Reduvius* and *Apiomeris* (subfamilies Reduviinae and Apiomerinae) to elongate and thread-like as in *Empicoris* and *Emesaya* (subfamily Emesinae). Many are masters of disguise, concealment and camouflage, coloured to blend with their substrate or coloured and physically modified to resemble their prey. Many species are very hairy or spiny, and some have strange, flange-like body expansions.

Particularly varied and abundant in tropical regions, these bugs range from 7 to 40 mm (0.3–1.6 ins) in length. The head carries a pair of four-segmented antennae which may have many subsegments, and a stout, curved three-segmented rostrum. In the majority of species, the rostrum can be used to produce sounds by being scraped along a medially located, ridged groove on the underside of the thoracic segments.

In contrast to bugs like the anthocorids, assassin bugs are not timid predators: some are capable of subduing large and well-armed insects such as bees. In at least one species studied, several nymphal bugs may cooperate in the killing of a single large prey item. Some reduviid species can be pests around honeybee hives in many parts of the world.

Victims are stabbed through a weak point in the cuticle and fast-acting, paralysing and tissue-dissolving saliva is injected. The strong front legs of many species, which are thickened or raptorial with spines and fields of special hairs forming adhesive structures, are used to grip the prey during its last frantic struggles.

The blood-feeding species of genera such as *Triatoma*, *Rhodnius* and *Panstrongylus* of the subfamily Triatominae (cone-nosed bugs) can have serious effects on man and other animals through the transmission of certain protozoal parasites. Chagas' disease (see Chapter 8), caused by the protozoan *Trypanosoma cruzi*, occurs throughout Central and South America.

Other families

The **Pachynomidae** are a southern hemisphere (except Australia) group comprising fewer than 20 nocturnal, predacious species. Not much is known of their habits, but they are probably ground-level hunters.

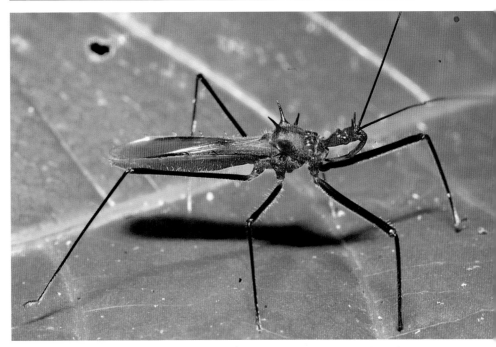

Sharp, upwardly directed spines on the head and pronotum provide additional defence for this warningly coloured, thread-legged assassin bug (*Ricolla quadrispinosa*) as it stalks over a rain forest plant in search of a meal. Peru. **Reduviidae**

Infraorder: Pentatomorpha (7)
Superfamily: Aradoidea (2)

Family: **Aradidae** (Fig. 9:vii)
Specialized primarily as fungus feeders and occasionally as sap feeders, the 1,800 or so known species of bark bug or flat bug occur in all parts of the world. The majority of aradids live on or under bark and in the crevices of fungus-infected trees. Some species have been found living among leaf litter on forest floors and on bracket and puffball fungi.

Bark bugs range from 3 to 13 mm (0.12–0.5 in) in length, have a very flattened, oval appearance and are cryptically coloured, dark or reddish brown. Their flat shape is largely dictated by the necessity of moving around in confined spaces; as a result the antennae are stout and the legs very short. The surface of the body may be covered with small spines, projections or tubercles, and generally has a roughened look due to the presence of pits and dimples. The head is distinctive in that the antennae arise from tubercle-like projections. The rostrum is very short but the stylets are very long and, when not being used to probe for fungal hyphae, are retracted into special regions inside the head.

Although many species are fully winged to enable them to disperse to new feeding sites, winglessness is common. Two of the commonest and most widely distributed genera are *Aradus* and *Aneurus*.

55

A very flattened body and lateral expansions of the pronotum and abdomen are characteristics of flat or bark bugs. This species, *Dysodius lunatus*, rests on the surface of a log in the Peruvian rain forest. **Aradidae**

Other families

Fewer than ten species, recorded exclusively from within termite colonies in tropical regions of the southern hemisphere, comprise the **Termitaphididae**. Less than 4 mm (0.16 in) in length, these strange, flattened bugs lack eyes and wings and have a broadly oval shape like a minute woodlouse. Termitaphidids are thought to be closely related to the aradids because of strong similarities in the design of the rostrum and the possession of retractable stylets. Although it is assumed that they feed on fungal hyphae inside the nests of their hosts, little information concerning their biology is currently available.

Superfamily: Piesmatoidea (1)

Family: **Piesmatidae** (Fig. 9:viii)

This family is made up of small, rarely 5 mm (0.2 in) long, oval to elongate bugs which look rather like tingids on account of their body surface pits and dimples. But they lack the tingids' intricate, net-like vein system on the front wings and their reticulated lateral body flanges. Just over 40 species have been described, and these occur mainly in the Palaearctic with a few in other regions.

The head, which carries a pair of four-segmented antennae and a four-segmented rostrum, is distinctive in that it bears a pair of short, forward-pointing, horn-like processes. The pronotum has a number of longitudinal keels or ridges.

Beet bugs, as piesmatids are commonly known, are phytophagous on a restricted range of host plants belonging mainly to the family Chenopodiaceae (oraches, goosefoots, sea beet, sea purslane and so on). Host plants in other families such as the Amaranthaceae and Carophyllaceae are also used by some species. The handful of piesmatid species occurring in Australia all eat plants in the genus *Acacia*.

In North America, the common name of ash-gray leaf bug is applied to the piesmatids, alluding either to their dull body colour or to the shrivelled and pale appearance of piesmatid-damaged leaves. The biggest and most widespread genus is *Piesma*. In the northern hemisphere, species such as *Piesma quadratum* and *P. cinereum* can be pests of sugar beet and spinach, which they damage through feeding and by the transmission of viral diseases.

Superfamily: Idiostoloidea (1)

Family: **Idiostolidae**
The four or five bug species that make up this entire superfamily have been previously regarded as a subfamily of the seed bug family, the **Lygaeidae**. Recorded only from Chile and Australia, they are found as ground or litter dwellers in Southern Beech (*Nothofagus*) woods.

Superfamily: Lygaeoidea (4)

Family: **Berytidae** (Fig. 9:ix)
Despite variations between species in body surface sculpturing or the presence of spines, all the 175 or so known species have a readily recognizable and distinctive shape. Stilt bugs, which are never longer than 10 mm (0.4 in), are very slender

Long-legged stilt bugs with characteristically swollen knees (*Parajalysus nigrescens*) clamber over a cocoa leaf. Although they are mainly herbivorous on plant sap, some species will also suck insect eggs and other small, soft prey items. Peru. **Berytidae**

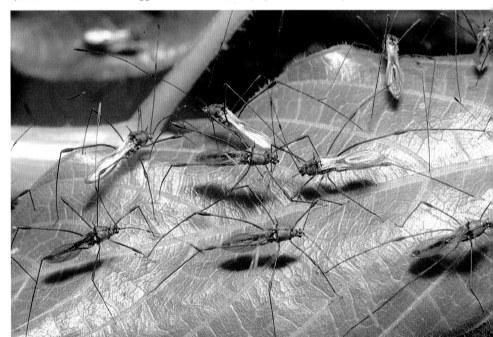

and elongate, supporting their bodies on long, spindly, thread-like legs. The apices of the femora are enlarged, making the bugs look as if they have got swollen knees. The antennae are slender and elbowed after the long second segment, while the apices of the second and fourth antennal segments are swollen or slightly clubbed.

Stilt bugs are elegant, slow-moving herbivores that feed on juices sucked from fresh plant growth. If given the opportunity, some species will also attack the eggs or the young stages of small defenceless insects. *Metacanthus*, *Berytinus* and *Neides* are typical genera.

Family: **Lygaeidae** (Fig. 9:x)

More than three thousand species of seed bug (or ground bug) have been described from all parts of the world. They are very variable in size, shape and colour. While some species may attain a body length of some 20 mm (0.8 in), the majority are smaller, at around 12 mm (0.5 in) or less.

In general outline, seed bugs are narrowly oval and elongate with tough, slightly flattened bodies. Some species may be very brightly marked with red, black and yellow, but most are dull or cryptically coloured. The head, which varies from very broad and narrow through triangular to slender, elongate and seemingly stalked, bears a four-segmented rostrum. The antennae are inserted low on the head, below the eyes. Fully winged ground bugs have five obvious veins visible in the membranous rear portion of the front wings, but many species have forms with reduced or very short wings. In many species, the femora of the front legs are enlarged or swollen and equipped with spines or teeth. The nymphs and adults of some species look very like ants.

The vast majority of species feed on the dry or mature seeds of a huge range of plant species, or on plant juices. Species of *Oxycarenus* damage cotton crops in the tropics, and the notorious Cinch Bug, *Blissus leucopterus*, can cause immense losses to grass and cereal crops in North America. While many species can be pests of crops, fruit trees, grasses and other important plants, some, such as the large-eyed and broad-headed species of the genus *Geocoris* (subfamily Geocorinae), are beneficial because they prey on the eggs and immature stages of pests such as mealy bugs, moths, fruit fly and red spider mites. A few species may feed on the blood of vertebrates.

Sound production, involving the rubbing together of the ventral surface of the hind wing over the dorsal surface of the abdomen, has been shown to play an important part in the mating rituals of many species. Of the many widespread or important lygaeid genera *Nysius*, *Drymus*, *Oxycarenus*, *Heterogaster*, *Ischnodemus*, *Oncopeltus*, *Elasmolomus*, *Blissus* and *Geocoris* are just a few examples.

Other families

The superfamily Lygaeoidea is completed by two small families, the **Colobath-ristidae** and the **Malcidae**, with around 70 and 25 described species respectively. Colobathristids are slender and come from parts of the southern hemisphere, where they can be pests of sugarcane and other grasses. Malcids are from some eastern parts of the southern hemisphere, where a few species may be minor pests of the mulberry and potato plant families. Recently, it has been suggested that these four families might be better transferred to the Coreoidea.

A bevy of warningly coloured seed bugs (*Oncopeltus famelicus*) may gain protection in numbers as they feed at a milkweed pod. The rear half of a fifth instar nymph is just visible in the lower half of the group. South Africa. **Lygaeidae**

Superfamily: Pyrrhocoroidea (2)

Family: **Pyrrhocoridae**

Although some species in the lygaeid genus *Oxycarenus* are called cotton stainers, that common name is more generally and correctly applied to members of this family. On account of their bright red and black aposematic coloration, some pyrrhocorids are also known as fire bugs or red bugs. More than three hundred species are known, the majority being confined to tropical and subtropical regions.

Very similar to some lygaeids in general outline, the cotton stainers and related species are medium-sized bugs with triangular heads which carry a long, slender, four-segmented rostrum and four-segmented antennae. They feed mainly on the fruits, seeds and sap of a range of plants, especially those of the Malvaceae. This family, comprising some nine hundred species, includes important plants such as cotton, hibiscus and mallow. Very few pyrrhocorid species have been shown to be predacious and those that are are of limited value.

Some *Dysdercus* species are very serious pests of cotton plants: their feeding damages the boll and transmits a fungus which discolours or stains the cotton fibres. Even when the fungus is not transmitted, the effect of *Dysdercus* feeding is to reduce the germination rate. Among the other important plants of tropical regions damaged by *Dysdercus* are species of *Hibiscus* and *Ceiba* (Kapok).

ABOVE: An ant-mimicking, fifth instar, broad-headed bug nymph (*Hyalymenus* sp.) finds useful additional nutrients in a bird dropping. Costa Rica. **Alydidae**

LEFT: An adult pyrrhocorid bug (*Dysdercus flavidus*) and nymphs of several different instars feed on seeds of kapok (*Ceiba petandra*). Bugs of this family are collectively known as cotton stainers because some species, when feeding on cotton bolls, introduce a discolouring fungus. Madagascar. **Pyrrhocoridae**

Other families

Previously regarded as a subfamily of the **Pyrrhocoridae**, the hundred or so species that constitute the **Largidae** are medium to large, brightly coloured bugs with very similar habits. Some are found on the ground among detritus, while others live on the aerial parts of their host plants. The known species, which occur mainly in subtropical and tropical regions, feed on ripe seeds and sap.

Some recent authors consider that both the **Pyrrhocoridae** and the **Largidae** properly belong within the superfamily Coreoidea.

Superfamily: Coreoidea (5)

Family: **Alydidae**

Previously regarded as a subfamily of the **Coreidae**, alydids or broad-headed bugs differ from coreids in being much more slender and elongate. As the common name implies, the head, which is much broader than in coreids, is more than half as broad as the rear margin of the pronotum. Another recognition feature is that the fourth antennal segment is slightly curved or bent and is longer than the third segment.

Some species look rather ant- or wasp-like, while others have slightly swollen, spiny hind femora. Nymphs of the genus *Hyalymenus*, which are found in association with ants, are particularly ant-like in appearance and even move in an excited, ant-like manner. Ant–alydid interactions are not fully understood.

A little under three hundred species are known from all parts of the world. They are herbivorous, particularly on leguminous plants (peas and beans) and grasses, from which they suck the sap and attack seeds. Although some species, such as in the genera *Stenocoris* and *Leptocorisa*, can be quite serious pests of important crops like millet and rice, the majority are of no economic importance.

Notable among the tropical crop pests in this family are species such as *Leptocorisa acuta*. The feeding activities of adult and nymphs of this bug can do immense damage to rice crops in parts of the Oriental and Australasian regions, where occasionally up to half the crop can be destroyed.

Family: **Coreidae** (Fig. 9:xi)

Although the majority of the two thousand or so known species have a predominantly subtropical and tropical distribution, species belonging to this family have been found in all the major faunal regions. Coreid species are mostly dull brownish, but can be brightly coloured or even metallic. Varying from 10 to 42 mm (0.4–1.7 ins) in body length, they have a broadly or narrowly oval outline. The head is relatively small compared to the pronotum, its greatest width being less than half that of the rear margin of the pronotum. The antennae, which have four segments, are constricted at the base where they join the head.

These bugs are always fully winged, and the membranous rear portion of the front wings has a large number of characteristic veins, with cross veins forming cells. The hind legs of some species can be very enlarged or thickened, while the legs or antennae of others, for example males of the genus *Leptoglossus*, have strange, leaf-like expansions. Coreids have well-developed thoracic scent glands, which produce mixtures of powerfully smelling defensive chemicals to repel enemies.

The common name of leaf-footed bug has been applied to the whole family and, although by no means all species feed on members of the squash plant family, Cucurbitaceae, the name squash bug has also been used in a broad sense to refer to all coreids. All coreids are herbivorous, sucking the juices from the shoots, tendrils, buds and leaves of various trees, shrubs and herbaceous plants.

Species such as those of the genera *Anasa*, *Amblypelta*, *Leptoglossus* and many others that attack crops and fruits can be very serious pests. The pods of cocoa trees in Papua New Guinea and other areas in the South Pacific are seriously damaged by species of the genus *Amblypelta*.

Family: **Rhopalidae**

Also sometimes treated as a coreid subfamily, rhopalid bugs known as scentless plant bugs can be robust or elongate and often have surface dimples, hairs and spines on various parts of the body. Slightly more than 150 species have been recorded from all parts of the world. All the known species are herbivorous, feeding on the seeds of a wide variety of herbaceous plants. A few rhopalid species can be pests of crops. *Leptocoris*, *Liorhyssus*, *Rhopalus* and *Myrmus* are examples of common or widespread genera.

Other families

Two additional small families, the **Stenocephalidae** and the **Hyocephalidae**, containing fewer than 40 and fewer than 5 species respectively, complete the

Resting between two leaves in a Peruvian rain forest, a coreid bug, *Petalops thoracicus*, displays its enlarged and banded hind legs. Its general shape, antennal banding and legs give the bug a wasp-like appearance. The presence of many parallel veins in the membrane of the front wing is characteristic of the family. **Coreidae**

Coreoidea. Stenocephalids occur throughout the eastern hemisphere where members of the only two genera, *Dicranocephalus* and *Stenocephalus*, are phytophagous mainly on members of the spurge family (Euphorbiaceae). The handful of known hyocephalids are found only in Australia, where they feed on seeds.

Superfamily: Pentatomoidea (13)

Family: **Acanthosomatidae**

Just over two hundred medium to quite large species have been described to date. Although members of the family can be found in most faunal regions, the majority have a subtropical and tropical distribution.

Acanthosomatids are often called shield bugs, but so are the species in 10 or so other pentatomoid families. In all these families the triangular or shield-shaped scutellum is large or very large; in some families it may cover a large proportion of the abdomen. Acanthosomatids are typically broadly oval or slightly tapering behind the broad pronotum. The small head carries five-segmented antennae and can appear sunk into the front margin of the pronotum.

All species are herbivorous and suck the juices from plants, particularly shrubs and trees. Some species, such as the well-known Parent Bug, *Elasmucha grisea*, show quite well-developed maternal behaviour: the females guard their egg clusters and newly hatched nymphs from the attacks of predators or parasitoid wasps.

Acanthosoma, *Elasmostethus*, *Elasmucha* and *Cyphostethus* are genera typical of the northern hemisphere. The family is often considered as a subfamily of the much larger **Pentatomidae**.

A pair of acanthosomatid shield bugs rest on the foliage of a cypress tree. This species, *Cyphostethus tristriatus*, also feeds on junipers. Great Britain. **Acanthosomatidae**

Family: **Cydnidae** (Fig. 9:xii)
Generally much less than 15 mm (0.6 in) in length, around four hundred species of cydnid or burrowing bug are known from all regions of the world. Although these bugs can be shiny brown, black, metallic or bi-coloured, all have distinctive, strongly spined tibiae. One cydnid subfamily, the Thyreocorinae or negro bugs, is sometimes elevated to the rank of family.

Their rounded, compactly oval shape and spiny legs adapt cydnids for burrowing into the ground, sometime a metre (3 ft) or more deep, where they suck root sap from various plants. Many species spend some of their lives above the ground under stones and in litter, and the nymphs of a few feed on the aerial parts of their host plants.

Males and females have special stridulatory pegs on the hind wings which are used to produce sound by rubbing them over file-like abdominal structures during courtship and mating. *Sehirus*, *Cydnus*, *Aethus*, *Geotomus* and *Corimelaena* are typical genera.

Family: **Pentatomidae** (Fig. 9:xiii)
With an estimated five thousand species, the pentatomids comprise the largest shield bug family by far and the third largest family in the suborder Heteroptera.

Characteristically very convex, rounded and shiny, adult plataspid shield bugs have an enormous scutellum which completely covers the wings. This cluster of *Libyaspis coccinelloides* in the rain forest of Madagascar includes many cryptically coloured fifth instar nymphs. **Plataspidae**

Although abundant all over the world, pentatomids are particularly diverse in the warmer regions of the southern hemisphere.

Size, body ornamentation and colour vary greatly, but most have a rounded or broadly oval outline. From the side, the back surface is slightly flattened and the underside may appear slightly convex. The scutellum, which covers up to half of the abdomen, is large and triangular, shield-shaped or rounded.

On the head are a pair of antennae which have five segments or sometimes less. The front of the pronotum may be extended at the sides to form blunt or sharp lateral points. The legs may be hairy or bristly, but are never spiny as in the burrowing bugs. The wings are well developed, and the membranous rear portion has a maximum of 12 distinct veins.

These bugs are well known for their ability to produce strong-smelling, noxious secretions from the thoracic glands in adults and from the abdominal glands in nymphs. The secretions are a complex and often species-specific mixture of volatile organic compounds designed to repel enemies. Some pentatomid bugs can produce sounds by rubbing a row of small pegs located on the inner face of the hind femur over a special ridged area on the underside of the abdomen.

Most pentatomids are plant sap suckers, and many species are crop pests around the world. The Green Vegetable Bug, *Nezara viridula*, is a very widely

Metallic colours of all hues identify fifth instar Australian Harlequin Bug nymphs as they cluster together on a food plant. This species, *Tectocoris diophthalmus*, attacks the bolls of cotton (*Gossypium* spp.) and other plants of the family Malvaceae. **Scutelleridae**

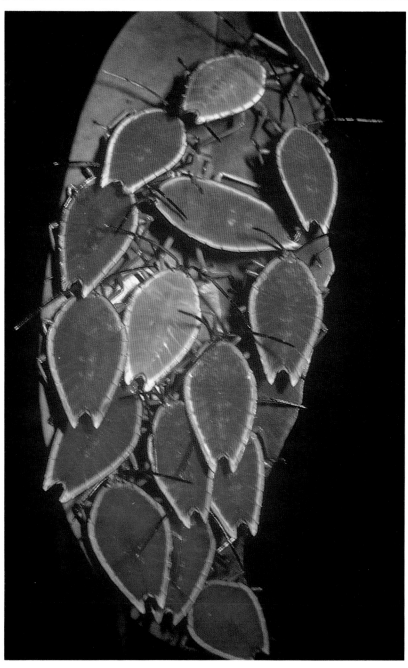

Foul-tasting and warningly coloured shield bug nymphs (*Lyramorpha* sp.) cluster together for protection on a leaf in the Queensland rain forest. Two pairs of scent gland openings are clearly visible on the back of the abdomen. Australia. **Tessaratomidae**

67

distributed species that attacks legumes, tomatoes and other vegetable crops. African coffee production can be sabotaged by species of *Antestiopsis*.

Species belonging to genera such as *Zicrona*, *Stiretrus*, *Oechalia* and *Alcaeorrhynchus* (subfamily Asopinae) are predacious, and are useful to man since they attack soft-bodied pest insects such as moth caterpillars and beetle larvae. In North America the Two-Spotted Stink Bug, *Perillus bioculatus*, is of great value as a predator of the Colorado Potato Beetle (*Leptinotarsa decemlineata*). Asopines do not hold their prey, preferring to suck the body fluids of slow-moving or otherwise defenceless creatures.

As in the **Acanthosomatidae**, the females of some pentatomids display maternal care of the eggs and young. *Podius*, *Picromerus*, *Pentatoma*, *Murgantia* and *Nezara* are a few of the very many genera. In the past, several other families such as the **Scutelleridae**, **Tessaratomidae**, **Dinidoridae** and **Urostylidae** have been treated as subfamilies of the **Pentatomidae**.

Family: **Scutelleridae** (Fig. 9:xiv)
Superficially of very similar design to pentatomids, the four hundred or so world species of medium to large-sized bug in this family can be distinguished by their very large scutellum, which covers most of the abdomen. The shape and extent of the scutellum makes these bugs look almost beetle-like. The back surface of some species is very rounded or convex, and many are brightly coloured or metallic.

In common with the pentatomids they occur in all faunal regions, but are most diverse in subtropical and tropical areas where species over 20 mm (0.8 in) in length have been found. All scutellerids are plant suckers, and some have attained pest status on account of the damage they cause to grain crops and to cotton in particular. *Eurygaster*, *Tectocoris* and *Odontoscelis* are typical genera. *Tectocoris diophthalmus*, the Harlequin Bug, is injurious to cotton grown in parts of Australia.

Family: **Tessaratomidae**
Sometimes called giant shield bugs, a few members of this family can be well over 40 mm (1.5 in) long. The vast majority of the 260 known species come from the eastern hemisphere, with only a couple of species having been recorded from the tropical regions of the western hemisphere. All species are herbivorous and some are minor crop pests. In Australia an unpleasant species capable of squirting a potentially blinding stream of defensive secretions, *Musgraveia sulciventris*, has become a fairly serious citrus pest.

Family: **Plataspidae** (Fig. 9:xv)
Around five hundred species in this family are known, mainly from the warmer regions of the eastern hemisphere. These bugs are very broadly oval or slightly elongate, and often very brightly coloured and shiny. The scutellum of these bugs is very large indeed. From the side, the distinctively convex or rounded back surface and the flat underside make them look like large beetles. In many species, males look different from females because they have forward-pointing head projections.

While most species are herbivorous, some subsist on fungi. A few plataspids are pests of leguminous crops. *Coptosoma* is a widespread and typical genus.

Other families

Another seven small, phytophagous families are here included in the Pentato-moidea. The **Urostylidae** (100 species), **Dinidoridae** (100 species), **Lestonii-dae** (3 species) and **Aphylidae** (2 species) are predominantly eastern hemisphere families. The **Megarididae** (15 species), **Canopidae** (8 species) and **Phloeidae** (3 species) are all confined to the Neotropical region.

Suborder: Coleorrhyncha

This suborder contains a single family of very unusual and ancient bugs, found mainly in Australia, New Zealand, Chile and Patagonia. In the past they have been thought of as more closely related to the Auchenorrhyncha and Sternorr-hyncha, but recent studies place them closer to the Heteroptera. The name of the suborder, which is derived from the Greek words *coleos* (sheath or scabbard) and *rhynchos* (nose or snout), refers to the fact that the rostrum is partly sheathed at its base.

Family: **Peloridiidae** (Fig. 10:i)

Peloridiids, which are less than 5 mm (0.2 in) in length, are drably or cryptically coloured greenish or brownish and have a flattened oval shape. Approximately 20 species have been discovered and, although most live among the mosses, liverworts and damp leaf litter of forest floors, a few have been found in caves.

The head is broad with laterally placed eyes, a pair of short, concealed, three-segmented antennae and a simple, four-segmented rostrum. The broad pro-notum has sideways expansions with distinctive, dimpled cells. The front wings, which are laid flat over the body at rest, have numerous characteristic cells, marked out by prominent veins, making these bugs look a little like lace bugs. Peloridiids are of no economic importance.

Suborder: Auchenorrhyncha

This suborder contains the planthoppers, leafhoppers, froghoppers, tree-hoppers, lantern bugs, cicadas and related groups. Auchenorrhynchan species can be readily distinguished from members of the Sternorrhyncha by a number of features. The most reliable difference is the way in which the rostrum clearly originates from the underside of the rear part of the head. The name is derived from the Greek words *auchen* (throat or neck) and *rhynchos* (nose or snout). In contrast, the rostrum of sternorrhynchans seems to originate from the body somewhere between the bases of the front legs, the name being derived from *sternon* (chest or breast) and *rhynchos*.

Other auchenorrhynchan distinguishing features include the possession of short, bristle-like antennae and three tarsal segments between the end of the tibia and the claw. The majority of species are fully winged and very active, and many are known for their jumping and singing abilities.

The suborder is normally divided into two infraorders, the Fulgoromorpha and the Cicadomorpha, with one and four superfamilies respectively. The body outlines of some common auchenorrhynchan bug families are shown in Fig. 10 (p. 70).

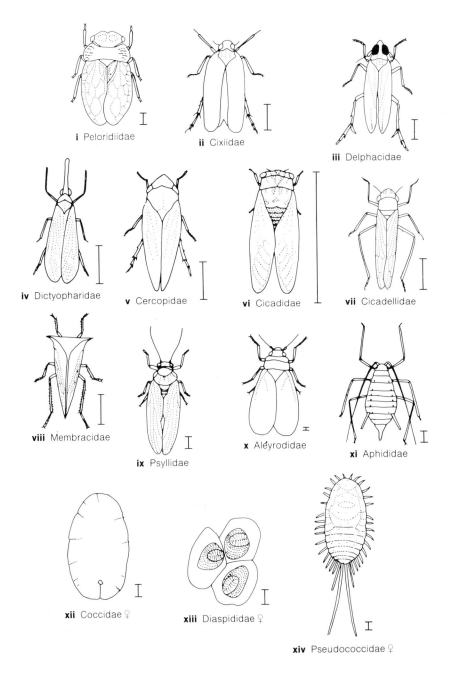

Fig. 10. Body outlines of some coleorrhynchan, auchenorrhynchan and sternorrhynchan bugs. Approximate body lengths are shown beside each bug.

Sitting on the leaf of a palm tree, a small group of adult cixiids display their large, richly veined wings. Nymphs of cixiid bugs are usually subterranean where they feed on the sap of plant roots. Trinidad. **Cixiidae**

Infraorder: Fulgoromorpha (1)
Superfamily: Fulgoroidea (20)

Family: **Cixiidae** (Fig. 10:ii)

More than 1,100 species belonging to this primitive fulgoroid planthopper family have been described from all regions of the world. Generally less than 10 mm (0.4 in) in length, slightly broadened and flattened, adult cixiids look superficially like minute cicadas. Many species jump very readily with their long, relatively spineless hind legs. The head is short and carries a pair of short, bristle-like antennae. The clear, membranous wings are held at a low angle over the body at rest, and have distinctive veins with dark hair-bearing spots along their length.

The nymphs typically live underground in the soil, where they feed on the root sap of grasses and a number of other plants. Adults can be found feeding on a variety of tree species. Some species are tolerant of brackish soil, and others have been found in association with ants. The biology of many species is not known.

Family: **Delphacidae** (Fig. 10:iii)

The common name of planthopper is typically given to the members of this large family, which numbers somewhere in the region of 1,700 species worldwide. Varying in length from 2 to 10 mm (0.08–0.4 in), most delphacids are small, brownish or greenish in colour, and with quite elongate, parallel-sided bodies. The normally short head, which may be very long in a few species, carries a pair of very short antennae. A characteristic feature of species in this family is the triangular cross-section of the hind tibia, which bears a large, articulated spur at its distal end. Males and females can look quite different and, in many species, fully winged and short-winged forms occur.

The vast majority of species are confined to species of grass and sedge as their host plants and live close to ground level throughout their life cycle. Several species are notorious pests of important crops such as rice, maize and sugarcane, and many carry a large number of plant viral diseases which they transmit from plant to plant as they feed. *Nilaparvata lugens* is the well-known Asian Rice Brown Planthopper. This species, which causes a disease of rice known as grassy stunt, is found throughout South East Asia, the Pacific, New Guinea, India and Sri Lanka. *Peregrinus maidis*, the Corn Hopper, can cause great damage to maize around the world by its feeding and through the viruses it carries. An accidental introduction of the Australian Sugarcane Hopper, *Perkinsiella saccharicida*, into Hawaii, which led to a devastating outbreak, was finally controlled biologically by the use of an egg-destroying heteropteran bug. Despite efforts to limit its spread, *Perkinsiella saccharicida*, the main vector for Fiji disease virus, is now established in many parts of the world including South America and parts of Africa. Another species of the same genus carries the Fiji disease virus in the Philippines.

In addition to those already listed, important delphacid genera include *Ribautodelphax*, *Javesella*, *Megamelus* and *Sogatodes*.

The strangely shaped head of this auchenorrhynchan bug identifies it as a member of the **Dictyopharidae**. This species, *Epiptera europea*, is sometimes called the European Lanternfly, although it is not a fulgorid. France.

Family: **Derbidae**

Derbids are generally quite small; few species reach more than 12 mm (0.5 in) in length. Just over eight hundred species occur worldwide, but the majority of these fragile-looking hoppers are confined to tropical and subtropical regions.

Many are brightly or noticeably coloured in combinations of yellow, brown and off-white. The small head carries a pair of short, flattened antennae and a pair of large or very large compound eyes. The front pair of wings are usually long and narrow and, when not in use, are held together over the body. In some species the wings may be up to three times longer than the short abdomen.

These bugs have been variously found feeding on the fungi associated with plant or wood decay, on flowering plants, on palms and on a few deciduous trees.

Family: **Dictyopharidae** (Fig. 10:iv)

Fewer than six hundred species belong to this widely distributed family of greenish or brownish bugs. One of the most recognizable features of these medium-sized planthoppers is the head, which is extended forwards into a long snout-like structure known as the cephalic horn.

Although in the majority of species the front wings are quite narrow with an arrangement of numerous veins, enclosing small cells, at their apices, some species are very short-winged. The legs are long and quite slender with the exception of a few species, where the front legs may be broad and flattened.

Grasses growing in moist conditions are the main host plants, and a very few species rate as minor pests in tropical regions.

Family: **Flatidae**

Far commoner in the tropics and subtropics than in other areas, the flatids comprise a widely distributed fulgoroid family of more than a thousand species. While temperate species are quite dull-coloured light green or brown and rarely attain more than 16 mm (0.6 in) in body length, tropical species can be very strikingly coloured and a lot bigger.

The vast majority of species can be readily distinguished by their broad, opaquely coloured, blunt-ended front wings. At rest these are held at a very steep angle or nearly vertically over the body.

The nymphs and adults of many species feed together in large groups and favour the sap of a variety of trees, shrubs and climbing plants. Nymphs are protected by long, curly threads of wax produced from the surface of their bodies. Males and females, especially of tropical species, can be quite differently coloured.

Family: **Fulgoridae**

Fulgorids range from medium-sized species a little under 10 mm (0.4 in) to giants with body lengths of 100 mm (4 ins) or more and wingspans of 150 mm (6 ins). The 750 species that constitute the family are exclusively found sucking the juices of a variety of plants in subtropical and tropical regions.

Many species are brownish or reddish, but some are very spectacularly coloured. The large front wings, and often the hind wings as well, have an intricate, net-like arrangement of veins and cross-veins.

The most distinctive feature of many species is the strange and bizarre shapes assumed by the head. In some species the forward prolongation of the head may

73

Opaque, uniformly textured and blunt-ended wings held roof-like over the body are characteristic of the **Flatidae**. Clustered together on a twig in the tropical dry forest of Madagascar, this group of *Phromnia rosea* adults resembles a spike of flowers.

Two Peanut Bugs (*Lanternaria lanternaria*), so called on account of their greatly enlarged and strangely shaped heads, rest on a tree trunk in Costa Rica. Early and now discounted stories of the luminous properties of the strange head gave rise to the common name of Lantern Bug. If the insects are disturbed, threatened or attacked, the wings can be flicked open to reveal startling eyespots on the hind wings. **Fulgoridae**

simply be long, slender, laterally toothed or bulbous, while the relatively massive, coloured and patterned heads of a few tropical species have been likened to miniature crocodiles' heads or unshelled peanuts. It was once thought that the strange heads had a luminescent function and the common name of lantern bug or lanternfly, originally applied to a few species, is now used for the whole family.

While I know of no substantiated records of fulgorid heads glowing in the dark, much stranger things can and do occur. It may be that an early traveller mistook a glow worm for a nearby fulgorid, or perhaps the head of the fulgorid had become infected with a luminescent algal or fungal species. We may never know, but at least the name is as exotic as the bug.

When a fulgorid is at rest, the possession of a strangely shaped head could confuse an enemy into attacking the rear end of the folded wings, allowing the bug to escape relatively unscathed. Many species have large, coloured eyespots on the hind wings, which can be flicked open to startle predators.

Lanternia, Phenax, Cyrpoptus and *Eurinopsyche* are examples of genera.

Family: **Issidae**

Although distributed all over the world, the majority of the thousand species in this family feed on the sap of trees and grasses in warmer regions. Squat-bodied, sombre or dark-coloured and less than 10 mm (0.4 in) in length, issids can look a bit like small beetles. In some species the head is slightly prolonged, reminiscent of weevils. The tough, textured front wings are often shorter than the abdomen, and the hind wings may be totally absent. The legs of most look normal except the front legs of some species, where the femora and tibiae are expanded and slightly leaf-like.

Other families

Another 13 families, with a predominantly subtropical and tropical distribution, are included in the Fulgoromorpha. Some species have minor pest status on a number of commercially important tropical plants such as coffee, cocoa, passion fruit and sandalwood.

More than 350 species of the **Achilidae** are found in all the world's regions; the adults feed on the sap of trees and shrubs and the nymphs are probably fungivorous. Around 350 slender species belonging to the **Tropiduchidae** are confined to feeding on understorey plant species in moist, tropical forests.

Approximately 380 species of medium to large, very moth-like planthoppers in the family **Ricaniidae** are found on plants in the warmer parts of the eastern hemisphere. Many species are brown and white and all have large, triangular wings. Some species can damage ornamental and crop plants in the Australian region. On account of the large amounts of honeydew secreted by these insects, bees often gather it. The trouble is that some species of ricaniid feed on poisonous or hallucinogenic plants such as those of the genus *Coriaria*, and the poisons are passed out in the honeydew. Parts of these plants are used for tanning, for killing flies and as dyes. In some part of the world they are used as ornamentals, and in New Zealand and other parts of the South Pacific rim there have been cases of humans being poisoned by eating honey produced by bees which gathered ricaniid honeydew from these plants.

Fewer than a hundred small hopper species belonging to the **Tettigometridae** occur mainly in the western hemisphere, where the nymphs of a few species live in ant nests. Just under two hundred species of the family **Eurybrachyidae** have been described from the Australian, Ethiopian and Oriental regions. The **Lophopidae** are represented by fewer than 125 species around the tropics and warm temperate regions of the world, where some feed on sugarcane, bamboo and other grasses. Another tropical, grass-feeding family, the **Nogodinidae**, comprises some 150 species.

Superficially similar to flatids, the 80 or so species comprising the family

Acanaloniidae are distributed throughout the western hemisphere, where they feed on the sap of grass species and herbaceous plants. With about the same number of species, the **Meenoplidae** are very small, flattened planthoppers confined mainly to the warm areas of the Ethiopian and Oriental regions.

Bringing up the rear, the last four very small fulgoroid families are the **Achilixidae** (10 species) and the **Kinnaridae** (40 species), both with a mainly Neotropical and Oriental distribution, and the **Gengidae** and **Hypochthonellidae**, both with just two South African species.

Infraorder: Cicadomorpha (4)
Superfamily: Cercopoidea (1)

Family: **Cercopidae** (Fig. 10:v)

Member species of this large family are found all over the world, especially in warmer regions. To date, roughly 2,500 species have been described. Sometimes the **Cercopidae** is divided, the subfamilies Aphrophorinae, Clastopterinae and Machaerotinae being given family rank in their own right, leaving only the Cercopinae.

'Cuckoo-spit' is a familiar sight on vegetation. Froghopper nymphs (*Philaenus spumarius*) feeding on watery xylem sap, produce vast amounts of dilute excrement which they blow into a foamy mass. The nymphs inside, which are soft and pale, are usually protected; but some birds have learnt the trick of pulling them out, and specialist parasitic wasps can probe through the foam to lay their eggs in the froghopper nymphs. Great Britain.
Cercopidae

Because of their squat, frog-like shape and amazingly powerful jumps, many species are called froghoppers. Although the majority of cercopids are dull brownish or greenish in colour and are generally smaller than 14 mm (0.6 in) in length, some can be very brightly or aposematically coloured black, orange or red, and up to 21 mm (0.8 in) long.

Some cercopids might look a bit like leafhoppers (**Cicadellidae**), but their tibiae have a round cross-section – not angular as in leafhoppers. The toughened front wings are longer than the body and held roof-like at rest, covering the larger hind wings. The strong hind legs are used for jumping, and the tibiae have a distinctive single or double circle of small spines at their distal ends.

Cercopids are plant sap suckers and, while mainly specific to one or a small number of host plants, some species are fairly polyphagous. Even if the name **Cercopidae** is unfamiliar, the strange, spume-like masses in which the nymphs are found are well known and unmistakable. This phenomenon has given rise to the alternative common name of spittle bug for the family. The traditional name of cuckoo spit is often used to refer to the foam, and sometimes the family as a whole is called cuckoo spit insects.

Although the nymphs of many species are subterranean, feeding on root sap, they still produce a frothy mass inside which they live. The froth is produced by mixing air and a special secretion with their copious liquid excrement just after it passes out of the anus. The resultant long-lasting foam is produced continuously and protects the soft-bodied nymphs from the effects of desiccation and the attentions of predators.

Needless to say, specialist birds have learnt how to pull the tiny hoppers from their froth, and some parasitoid wasps will probe into the foam with their ovipositors to lay an egg in the body of the bug. The nymphal spittle of some aphrophorine species is used by ants as a construction material; the ants also prey on the soft-bodied bugs themselves.

In some parts of the world certain species which feed on pine, clover, sugarcane and other cultivated plants have achieved minor pest status. Extensive cercopid feeding, which causes withering and stunting of a host plant and its leaves, is often called froghopper blight.

In the very widespread species *Philaenus spumarius*, the Meadow Spittle Bug, the adults exist in a large number of colour forms or morphs. Interestingly, the darker-coloured or melanic morphs seem to be commoner in urban areas, where air pollution is higher. The exact reason for this has not yet been fully elucidated but it seems likely that differential predation (where pale forms show up clearly on pollution-darkened surfaces, dark forms are less obvious to predators and vice versa in unpolluted habitats) is involved. Of the three hundred or so genera in the world, *Cercopis*, *Philaenus*, *Aphrophora* and *Clastoptera* are typical of the northern hemisphere.

Superfamily: Cicadoidea (1)

Family: **Cicadidae** (Fig. 10:vi)

Cicadas are perhaps the most easily recognised of all the auchenorrhynchan families. Ranging from just under 10 mm (0.4 in) to over 100 mm (4 ins) from head to the tips of the folded wings, many of the 2,250 described species are large and all have a distinctive broad, blunt head and large, usually transparent wings.

While most species are dull brownish, greenish or cryptically coloured and very hard to see as they sit motionless on bark, some tropical species can be very beautifully coloured with opaque or strikingly marked wings. Cicadas are most varied and abundant in tropical regions, but they also occur in warm temperate areas.

The head carries a pair of short, bristle-like antennae and large compound eyes. At rest, the two pairs of wings are held together at an angle, sloped over the body. The ends of the longitudinal wing veins are joined before they reach the wing edge, leaving a narrow, veinless margin. The hind legs are not modified for jumping, but the front legs may be larger than the others and equipped with stout, tooth-like projections.

The adults and nymphs feed on the watery sap of a variety of tree and shrub species. The female uses a stout ovipositor to lay her eggs in slits cut into the twigs of the host plant. The newly hatched youngsters fall or crawl to the ground, where they burrow deep into the soil to feed on a poor-quality diet of root sap. The nymphs, which are well designed for a subterranean life, have strongly modified, digging front legs; they moult many times and may take many years to reach adulthood. Emergences of mature nymphs from underground are often synchronized and spectacular: millions of individual adults may be present in a

Two leafhoppers feed on a leaf in the Peruvian rain forest. Although of different colours, these two belong to the same species, *Rhaphirrhinus phosphoreus*. Two droplets of honeydew can be seen at the rear end of the blue-black morph. **Cicadellidae**

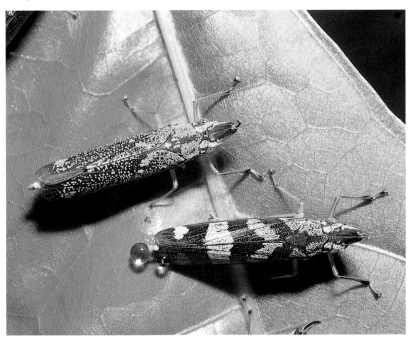

single hectare (2.5 acres). It is thought that one function of these massive emergences may be to satiate predators, who would kill and consume more if they emerged over a longer period. After the adults emerge, the empty last instar skins are left behind, clinging by the sharp claws of the front legs to the bark of trees.

Of the very many interesting aspects of cicadas' biology, their species-specific, mate-attracting songs are the most familiar. Both sexes have hearing organs at the base of the abdomen, but the males have well-developed sound-producing tymbal organs on the underside of their bodies at the sides of the first abdominal segment. A stiff membrane, protected by a cuticular plate, is rapidly clicked in and out by muscular action to produce a high-pitched buzzing sound which sets up resonance in the very large air sacs within the abdomen. The complex mechanisms of cicada sound production are not yet fully resolved and are still under investigation. Some species are physically so similar that only minute details of their songs distinguish them. Singing usually takes place during the day or at twilight, and *en masse* can be deafening. Some species can produce less spectacular sounds in other ways.

A very small subfamily, the Tettigarctinae, comprising just a couple of hairy Australian species, are sometimes treated as a separate family within the Cicadoidea. Very few species are of any significant economic importance.

Superfamily: Cicadelloidea (2)

Family: **Cicadellidae** (Fig. 10:vii)

There are probably a little more than twenty thousand species in this massive family, whose member species are found in all parts of the world, particularly the tropics. The family is by far the biggest in the order Hemiptera.

Collectively known as leafhoppers, cicadellids are generally slender-bodied and taper towards the rear end. The majority of species are less than 14 mm (0.6 in), but some tropical species may be over 20 mm (0.8 in) from head to tail. Coloration can be very diverse, and although many species exhibit mainly brown or green colour patterns, some can be brightly striped or spotted.

The long hind legs, which are modified for leaping, enable cicadellids to jump extremely well and take flight at the slightest notice. The distinctive hind tibiae have an angular, slightly flattened cross-section with one or more regular rows of small spines running down their length.

All species are plant sap suckers, most species feeding from phloem vessels, others from the nutritionally poorer xylem vessels, while a few take the contents of mesophyll cells. It has been suggested that virtually every plant species on Earth is attacked by one or more leafhopper species. Some species are very restricted, feeding from only one host plant, while others are oligophagous or polyphagous.

Very many important cultivated plants such as rice, sugarcane, maize, potatoes and cotton are damaged by the effects of their feeding, their toxic saliva and the transmission of a whole variety of plant viruses and mycoplasma diseases. Three species of the genus *Nephotettix* are major pests of rice in Japan, South East Asia, Papua New Guinea, India and Sri Lanka. *Empoasca*, *Typhlocyba*, *Macrosteles*, *Cicadulina*, *Recilia* and *Cicadella* are examples of a small proportion of the world genera which contain pest species.

All species belonging to the small family **Eurymelidae** are gregarious and attended by ant species. A few species even live permanently in ant nests. Eurymelids are only found in Australia, New Guinea and New Caledonia, where species of *Eucalyptus* are the usual host plants. Australia.

Other families

The small, related family **Eurymelidae**, which contains just over a hundred species, is restricted to Australia, Papua New Guinea and neighbouring islands, where species of *Eucalyptus* are the main host plants.

Superfamily: Membracoidea (4)

Family: **Membracidae** (Fig. 10:viii)

Nearly 2,500 species of treehopper have been described and, although species in this family are present in all the major faunal regions, their diversity and abundance reaches a peak in the tropical and subtropical areas. These bugs are never big: very few species reach a body length of more than 15 mm (0.6 in). Treehoppers are often brownish, greenish or very dark in colour, but many tropical species exhibit striking aposematic colour patterns. Treehoppers, or thorn bugs as they are also known, can be distinguished from all other auchenorrhynchans by their strangely shaped and sometimes greatly developed, backward-pointing pronotum. In some species it may cover the membranous wings entirely, or look bigger than the rest of body. The degree of pronotal development is extremely

Viewed from the front, the bizarre bifurcated pronotum of this New Guinean rain forest treehopper is clearly visible. **Membracidae**

variable, assuming any shape from a hump or simple thorn-mimicking, spine-like process to a bizarre and complex ant-mimicking structure. In some species, a large pronotal spine has been shown to defeat lizard predators.

Both as nymphs and as adults all species feed on the sap of trees, shrubs, herbaceous plants and grasses. The nymphs, which do not possess the enlarged pronotum of the adults but may have dorsal spines or lateral body expansions, feed in groups and often have complex mutualistic interactions with ant species (see Chapter 5). Ants attending young treehoppers will stimulate the nymphs with their antennae, causing the release of carbohydrate-rich excrement or honeydew from the bug's retractable anal tube.

Some female treehoppers have been shown to guard their egg masses and young nymphs from predators and parasitoid wasps. A few species can cause economic damage to plants, particularly fruit trees, but their impact is not very significant. *Umbonia*, *Centrotus*, *Gargara*, *Sphongophorus*, *Stictocephala* and *Membracis* are just a few examples of membracid genera.

Other families

The superfamily includes another three small families, the **Aetalionidae** (50 species), the **Nicomiidae** (15 species) and the **Biturritiidae**, with a predominantly Neotropical distribution. The **Aetalionidae**, whose member species are medium-sized, distinctively coloured reddish-brown or black, with pale wing veins and bulging eyes, were until fairly recently considered to be a subfamily of the **Membracidae**. The **Membracidae**, together with the last three related families, were once placed, on the basis of some shared physical characteristics, within the superfamily Cicadelloidea.

Suborder: Sternorrhyncha

This suborder is characterized by bugs which have their rostrum apparently arising from the underside of the body between the front legs. In some groups the rostrum is absent. In contrast to the auchenorrhynchans, which possess three tarsal segments, sternorrhynchan bugs have only one or two. The antennae are not short and bristle-like, but range from being quite long and thread-like to shortened or totally lacking. In some families females and the immature stages are unable to move and may not look much like insects at all.

Infraorders, favoured by many taxonomists for the preceding three bug suborders, are not generally used in this suborder. The Sternorrhyncha can, however, be neatly divided into five very distinct superfamilies, the jumping plantlice (Psylloidea), whiteflies (Aleyrodoidea), conifer woolly aphids and phylloxerans (Adelgoidea), aphids (Aphidoidea) and scale insects, mealy bugs and related families (Coccoidea).

The body outlines of a few common sternorrhynchan bug families are shown in Fig. 10. Although some species are useful to man, a great many are very serious plant pests capable of causing huge crop losses as a result of their feeding and transmission of disease.

Superfamily: Psylloidea (7)

Family: **Psyllidae** (Fig. 10:ix)
More than a thousand species of jumping plantlice have been described and can be found throughout all the faunal regions. Rarely bigger than 5 or 6 mm (about 0.2 in) in body length, psyllids may look superficially like small leafhoppers or tiny cicadas.

The head may be rounded, elongate or other shapes and carries a pair of antennae, usually 10-segmented, which may be slender or quite short. The simple rostrum has three segments. In adults it arises from the rearmost part of the head, while in nymphs it appears to come from between the bases of the front legs. The two pairs of membranous wings, of which the front pair are slightly tougher, are held together roof-like over the body. The hind pair of legs is slightly enlarged and has special modifications for rapid, efficient jumping. Although jumping plantlice are very dynamic creatures, leaping into the air and flying at the slightest provocation, they cannot fly very far or for any length of time.

All the known species feed exclusively on the phloem sap of their host plants. The majority are specific to one or, less commonly, a very small range of related plants. Some species induce the growth of galls or roll up the edges of leaves, inside which the developing nymphs gain some degree of protection. Females lay their eggs on short stalks attached to or just under the plant surface.

Psyllid nymphs are distinctively flattened, with a rounded or oval outline and noticeable wing pads. Nymphs produce wax filaments from their bodies and powder-like wax from a ring of special pores around the anus. In gall-forming

The flattened, oval nymphs of *Psylla aini*, a jumping plantlouse, protect themselves by producing masses of flocculent white wax. Here, a pale green nymph can be seen on the right with the majority of the wax still attached to shed skins of earlier stages. Widely distributed throughout the northern hemisphere, this species feeds on alder trees (*Alnus* spp.). Some species live inside galls or leaf rolls which they induce on their herbaceous shrub or tree host plants. Great Britain. **Psyllidae**

species, the copious droplets of sweet excrement or honeydew produced are coated in wax as they are expelled from the body, thus keeping the inside of the gall or leaf roll dry. Free-living species have mutualistic relationships with ant species, which, in return for their services as bodyguards, remove the psyllid honeydew as a valuable food source.

Some unusual psyllid nymphs wait until the water has evaporated from the droplets of honeydew and then use the sticky masses to form a protective shelter under which they continue to feed. The shelters or lerps, as they are known, vary in design according to species. On account of their sweet taste and rich carbohydrate content they are eaten by birds and many other animals, including man. The manna of biblical stories was certainly bug honeydew of some kind.

Quite a few species are pests of commercial plants such as cotton, cocoa, citrus and timber trees in many parts of the world. Their feeding causes stunting, blossom loss, yield reduction, yellowing of leaves and even death as a result of their toxic saliva. Some species are known to transmit plant virus diseases. *Psylla*, *Psyllopsis*, *Pachypsylla* and *Arytaina* are typical genera of the northern hemisphere.

Other families

In the past, the superfamily Psylloidea contained only one family, the **Psyllidae**. Recent work has resulted in the separation and elevation of six of the subfamilies to family status. The **Psyllidae** as discussed here, together with six other very closely related families, the **Carsidaridae** (40 species), **Calophyidae** (35 species), **Liviidae** (25 species), **Homotomidae** (75 species), **Spondyliaspididae** (300 species) and **Triozidae** (650 species), comprise a world total of just over two thousand species.

Superfamily: Aleyrodoidea (1)

Family: **Aleyrodidae** (Fig. 10:x)

Related to jumping plantlice, just under 1,200 species of whitefly are known to exist although there are certainly many more awaiting discovery. The family is represented all over the world and is especially dominant in warmer regions. Some species have become virtually cosmopolitan.

Adult whiteflies of both sexes are small, fragile and moth-like, with a wing span of around 3 mm (0.12 in) and a characteristic dusting of fine, powdery wax. The head carries the short rostrum, a pair of seven-segmented antennae and the compound eyes. The two pairs of wings, which are held flat over the body at rest and dusted with the same wax as the body, are membranous and appear white or mottled. The legs are quite long and slender. The adults and nymphs of all species feed by sucking the phloem juices of their host plants.

Reproduction can be sexual or asexual, and the eggs are laid two or three deep in curves or circles attached to the underside of leaves by a short stalk. On

Moth-like and covered with mealy wax, tiny adult Greenhouse Whiteflies (*Trialeurodes vaporariorum*) infest the underside of a tomato plant. This species, which has a cosmopolitan distribution, is a pest of house plants and greenhouse crops. Most other species are found in the world's tropical regions. Great Britain. **Aleyrodidae**

hatching, the small, mobile, first instar nymphs can be recognized by their antennae and legs, which are quite long and well developed. The nymphs of subsequent instars have smaller, non-functional appendages and do not move around. The last stage nymph does not feed, and serves as a sort of pupa in which the adult stage develops and from which it eventually emerges.

Large quantities of honeydew are produced by all feeding stages; on the plant's surface it encourages the growth of sooty moulds (*Botrytis* spp). In nymphs, the anus ends in a special opening, the vasiform orifice, located on the dorsal surface of the last abdominal segment. The droplets produced can be flicked away from the body by means of a structure called the lingula. Ants find the honeydew irresistible, and many whitefly species have mutualistic ant-relationships.

On account of their damaging feeding activities and the ability of some species to transmit plant diseases, many whiteflies have pest status. The most serious attack citrus trees, greenhouse crops and a variety of commercially important field crops. *Bemisia tabaci* is a well-known pest species occurring in all the tropical regions. This species, and others in the genus, transmit virus diseases to a wide range of cultivated plants including tobacco, cotton, tomatoes, cassava and sweet potatoes. *Trialeurodes vaporariorum*, the Greenhouse Whitefly, can be found on house and greenhouse plants all over the world. Other important genera containing pest species include *Aleyrodes*, *Aleurocanthus* and *Dialeurodes*.

Superfamily: Aphidoidea (11)

Family: **Aphididae** (Fig. 10:xi)

Plantlice, blackfly, greenfly and aphids are common names applied to this large and very important family of plant sap suckers. Gardeners in particular will be familiar with these ubiquitous and incredibly abundant small bugs and some of their habits.

In the past, all aphid species were lumped together in a single family, the **Aphididae** – some 3,800 species in all. But different texts and authorities have, at various times, elevated a number of aphids to family status. The **Anoeciidae** (30 species), **Callaphididae** (500 species), **Chaitophoridae** (140 species), **Greenideidae** (125 species), **Hormaphididae** (130 species), **Lachnidae** (350 species), **Mindaridae** (10 species), **Pemphigidae** (270 species), **Phloeomyzidae** (5 species) and **Thelaxidae** (30 species) are currently recognized as families distinct from the **Aphididae** (2,250 species). Even in this restricted sense, the **Aphididae** constitute by far the largest family and its member species are distributed all over the world, particularly in temperate regions. The description that follows refers broadly to the species contained within the superfamily Aphidoidea.

Ranging between 1 and 6 mm (0.04–0.2 in) in body length, the majority of common aphids are soft-bodied and green, although some can be black, pinkish or other hues. When present, and at rest, the two pairs of normally transparent membranous wings are held together roof-like over the pear-shaped body, which ends in a short tail or cauda. The legs are slender and can be quite long. The head carried a pair of slender antennae with up to six segments, the eyes and the short rostrum. Mouthparts and eyes may be reduced in some species and forms.

A distinctive aphid feature is the pair of tube-like cornicles or siphunculi projecting from the fifth or sixth segment of the abdomen. When the aphid is attacked, they carry defensive secretions from glands in the body to the outside. In addition, many species can secrete protective wax.

Aphids are very slow-moving and tend to feed in colonies, plugging their mouthparts into the phloem sap vessels of a huge range of plants. Some species, such as those in the **Aneociidae**, live underground, feeding from roots; while other, like the **Pemphigidae**, induce their host plants to produce galls inside which they feed. Although many are species-specific, some aphids attack a range of related plant species. Large volumes of sap are consumed and the carbohydrate-rich excrement or honeydew can fall like rain from the aerial parts of plants.

Honeydew is sweet because of surplus sugar in the diet. Nitrogenous (nitrogen-containing) compounds are present in low concentrations in plants and, as they are required for protein-building, they are a limiting factor. Within the aphid's body specialized cells called mycetocytes harbour symbiotic (mutually beneficial) bacteria whose role is to upgrade the diet by supplying certain essential amino acids. Many complex symbiotic relationships exist between aphids and ants. In return for the sweet waste product which they crave, ants protect aphid colonies from parasitoids and predators, even building shelters over them and moving them, their eggs and young like miniature cattle from place to place.

Because of their profound impact on a large number of commercially important plants, and their phenomenal powers of reproduction and dispersal, aphids have been the subject of considerable study over the years. Life cycles and reproduction may be relatively simple or very complex, involving sexual and asexual forms, the production of eggs or the birth of young nymphs and alternations of generations between two unrelated host plants (one woody and one herbaceous) at different times of the year. In sexual forms, wings and mouthparts may be entirely lacking.

In a simple, single host plant case, overwintering eggs hatch in the spring and give rise to winged or wingless, parthenogenetically reproducing (no males needed) females. These females, known as fundatrices, produce nymphs which themselves develop into parthenogenetic adult females called virginoparae. Feeding continues, and a variable number of generations exhibiting asexual reproduction are produced until the beginning of autumn, when the nymphs will develop into wingless, reproductive females and males. If the host plant has developed a very high population the aphids will already have flown off to seek out less crowded host plants of the correct species. Sexual reproduction and mating take place, and eggs are laid on the host plant.

Some 10 per cent of the world's aphid species have much more complex life cycles. These involve the colonization of two different host plants, one herbaceous and one woody species, by different generations at different times of the year.

Plants damaged by aphid attack can show a whole range of symptoms from yellowing, stunting, leaf mottling, browning and curling, lack of vigour and yield, to wilting and death. Aphid saliva is toxic to plant tissues, and many aphids transmit viruses and other disease-causing organisms. Some species, such

While continuing to feed on the sap of Meadowsweet (*Filipendula ulmaria*), a wingless, parthenogenetic female aphid (*Macrosiphum cholodkovskyi*) gives birth to a tiny, pale, first instar nymph. Many aphid species have very complex life cycles involving different host plants, winged and wingless, and parthenogenetic and sexually reproducing forms. Great Britain. **Aphididae**

as the incredibly polyphagous *Myzus persicae*, act as a vector for more than 110 different plant viruses.

Considerable money and effort are expended on the control of aphids in crops, and it is almost certain that they are the world's most damaging insect pests. It is very fortunate, given that some of our agricultural practices i.e. the planting of large areas with a single crop species (monocultures) tend to encourage pest outbreaks, that bad weather and predatory insects kill vast numbers of aphids every year. In the **Aphididae**, many genera such as *Myzus, Rhopalosiphum, Aphis, Brevicoryne* and *Macrosiphum* are common and widespread. In tropical regions *Aphis gossypii*, the Cotton Aphid, transmits viruses affecting several economically important plants such as sugarcane, papaya and groundnuts. *Lachnus, Hormaphis, Pemphigus, Anoecia* and *Drepanosiphum* are well-known genera belonging to some of the other closely related aphidoid families.

Superfamily: Adelgoidea (2)

Family: **Adelgidae**

Adelgids, or woolly conifer aphids as they are sometimes commonly known, are closely related to aphids in the broad sense. Around 50 species are known; all, except one Australian species, are confined to the northern hemisphere. Less than 3 mm (0.12 in) long as adults, soft-bodied adelgids feed solely on the needles and twigs on coniferous trees, or in galls which they induce. Unlike the situation in the aphids, the tail end of the abdomen is not prolonged as a cauda and there are no abdominal defensive cornicles.

Females may be wingless and reproduce sexually, or be winged or wingless and reproduce asexually. In the wingless, asexual females the body is covered with woolly wax. Eggs are laid – the females never give birth to nymphs. Like the wingless, asexual females, adelgid nymphs are covered with a dense, woolly wax which is secreted from glands opening on the surface of the abdomen.

In general, a complete life cycle takes two years and always involves a species of spruce (*Picea*) as the primary host plant. Secondary hosts vary according to the adelgid species and include larches (*Larix*), pines (*Pinus*), silver firs (*Abies*), douglas firs (*Pseudotsuga*) and hemlocks (*Tsuga*). Typically, there are one sexual and two asexual generations on the primary host and a number of asexual generations on the secondary host. Young nymphs spend the winter among the bases of spruce (primary host) needles. In the spring they continue to feed and become adult. These then produce eggs asexually, which hatch to produce the gall-forming nymphs. Adelgid galls on spruce, which are shaped like small, green pineapples, become hard and woody after the winged forms have escaped and dispersed to the secondary coniferous host.

A small number of generations, reproducing asexually, occur on the secondary host: the nymphs feed externally on the needles, not inside galls. Winged adults are eventually produced, and these fly back to the primary host where they give rise to wingless, sexually reproducing males and females. The eggs laid by the sexual forms hatch and, as first or second instar nymphs, overwinter among the spruce needles.

Many species are pests in softwood plantations. *Pineus* and *Adelges* are the commonest and most widespread of the eight or so known plant host genera.

Family: **Phylloxeridae**

Just under 70 species of these pale-coloured bugs, less than 3 mm (0.12 in) in body length, have been described. Although the majority of species are restricted to the northern hemisphere, three species have been accidentally introduced to Australia.

Like adelgids, phylloxerids are distinct from aphids in that they do not have abdominal cornicles or a tail-like cauda. Unlike adelgids, winged phylloxerids (also known as phylloxerans) hold their wings flat, not roof-like, over the body when at rest. The transparent wings only have three veins, which run diagonally.

These bugs are species-specific sap suckers, commonly found on deciduous trees such as oak (*Quercus* spp.), hickory (*Carya* spp.) and chestnut (*Castanea* spp.). Life cycles can be complicated, and are very similar to those seen in the **Adelgidae** except that there is no alternation of host plant species.

In a typical, simple case, overwintering eggs hatch in the spring and the young nymphs find their way to unfolding leaves, where they cause leaf galls to form. Feeding and developing, protected by the galls, they soon become adult. Within the galls these wingless, parthenogenetic females lay eggs of two types: large ones which give rise to females, and small ones which produce males. Later in the year, when mature, these sexual forms leave the galls, mate, and lay eggs destined to overwinter.

The life histories of other species can be more complex. They involve the formation of subterranean root galls and distinctive, crown-shaped leaf galls.

As well as the wingless, sexual forms, winged females can be produced which are responsible for the dispersal of the phylloxerid to other trees. The bodies of wingless, parthenogenetic females are sometimes covered with a powder-like wax. Sexually reproducing males and females have a pair of three-segmented antennae, a pair of three-faceted eyes and no wings or mouthparts.

Some species can be serious pests of pecan bushes and, more especially, grapevines (*Vitis vinifera*); the root-feeding stages can cause serious stunting of the host plant. An accidental introduction from America of the vine phylloxeran, or 'vine aphid', *Viteus vitifolii*, during the late nineteenth century saw the near destruction of European vines. The industry was spared by the ingenious grafting of European vines on to resistant American root stocks. In addition to *Viteus*, species in the genus *Phylloxera* are common and widespread.

Superfamily: Coccoidea (20)

The highly modified bugs belonging to this superfamily are often collectively known as either scale insects or mealy bugs; the names are derived from the waxy or toughened, scale-like structures under which the grub-like adult females live. There are 20 families, totalling some 7,000 species, worldwide. Seven families are very small, each containing fewer than 25 species, while three, the **Coccidae**, **Diaspididae** and **Pseudococcidae**, have more than 1,000 species apiece.

The accurate identification of families, genera and species is a technical matter that requires reference to scientific literature and microscopical examination. The following information applies in a broad sense to all members of the superfamily.

Female coccoids, although varying greatly in size (less than 1 mm/0.04 in to more than 30 mm/1.2 ins) and form, are wingless, lack legs and are generally immobile while they feed and lay eggs. A good identification feature for coccoids, although requiring microscopic examination, is that when legs are present (in nymphs and males) the normally single tarsal segment of each bears a single claw. All other bugs, have paired claws.

The body can produce a variety of waxy secretions through specialized pores and stout setae. These secretions, which may form soft, hard or woolly, scale-like or gall-like covers, protect the adult females and their eggs.

Male coccoids, which look superficially like small flies, have three pairs of legs, well-developed antennae and, although sometimes wingless, typically have a pair of reasonably developed front wings. The hind wings are very reduced, forming a pair of strap-like structures, which in flight may be mechanically joined to the rear edge of the front wings. Males have no mouthparts or functional digestive systems and rarely live for more than a couple of days. Reproduction may be sexual in some cases, involving males with elongated sexual organs capable of extending underneath the scale-like protective shield of the female. Parthenogenesis is common in many coccoids, and males are either very rare or non-existent.

The life cycles of most coccoids are much simpler than the complicated ones seen in aphids, adelgids or phylloxerans. Females may lay eggs or give birth to first instar nymphs. In a typical case, the sedentary, feeding female produces large numbers of eggs which may be kept under the scale, or within her body. On hatching or being born, the first instar nymphs, called crawlers, which have well-developed legs and antennae, become actively mobile and seek out new feeding sites. Some species have long wax filaments projecting from their bodies that enable them to be carried on the wind, while others hitch a lift on the bodies of passing insects.

Once settled down and feeding, the later instar nymphs become sedentary like the adult females and may lose their legs. Nymphs destined to become females pass through three or more feeding instars, gradually becoming adult. Males have only a couple of feeding stages, after which they pass through one or two non-feeding, pupa-like instars, protected by a wax coat, scale or pseudo-puparium secreted by the second instar nymph. When the males emerge they seek out and mate with the stationary females.

All coccoids feed on the sap of flowering plants, which they suck from the vascular tissue using long mouthparts. Although the rostrum itself is short and one- or two- segmented, the mandibular and maxillary stylets are very long and coiled inside the head or labium when not sunk deep within the host plant's tissues.

Sugar-rich excrement or honeydew is produced in large amounts. As in other homopteran groups, this has resulted in the development of many symbiotic relationships with ants and other hymenopterans.

Coccoids can be found in a variety of situations, on leaves, shoots, bark and twigs, among leaf litter and underground, sometimes in permanent association with ants. Many species are specific to a single host plant, while others can feed on a narrow or fairly broad range of host plants (oligophagy or narrow polyphagy). In general, a very wide range of plants play host to scale insects of one kind or another. Despite a few beneficial species used for the biological control of certain weeds or which produce dyestuffs, waxes, resins, medicinal, cosmetic and other useful natural products, many are very serious pests.

Family: **Asterolecaniidae**
Just over 200 species of pit scales are known to exist worldwide. These insects can be found on a variety of plant species, particularly on trees and shrubs, where the females produce on the twigs shallow pits with slightly elevated edges. Species of genera such as *Asterolecanium*, *Callococcus*, *Cerococcus* and *Frenchia* produce distinctive, gall-like swellings. The rostrum and the antennae are typically one-segmented, and the legs may be reduced or absent. The waxy, glazed, scale-like cover is renewed at each moult. Heavy infestations of pit scales can produce distortions and stunting of the host plant. Reproduction may be sexual or parthenogenetic. Several species are pests of ornamental and other trees.

Family: **Coccidae** (Fig. 10:xii)

Comprising the third largest coccoid family, approximately 1,250 species of soft scale are known and represented throughout the world. The body forms of coccids vary tremendously. The female may be exposed, with a thickened dorsal surface, or she may be covered to varying depths with pellucid or powdery wax. An easy way to distinguish coccids is the longitudinal anal cleft at the posterior end of the broadly oval body. The anus is situated at the front end of this cleft.

In many species, the nymphs and adults have well-developed legs and antennae and can move about fairly freely. Reproduction can be sexual or parthenogenetic, and in some species both occur.

A wide range of host plants is attacked, and very many coccid species are serious pests of trees (especially fruit trees), shrubs, greenhouse crops and house plants. A few species provide wax of very high quality which has been gathered on a small scale for the manufacture of candles and other purposes. *Coccus hesperidum*, the Brown Soft Scale, and *C. viridis* are widespread tropical pests of citrus, tea and fruit trees and coffee and mango respectively. Notable genera, containing many species of pest status, are *Ceroplastes*, *Coccus*, *Parthenolecanium* and *Pulvinaria*.

Family: **Dactylopiidae**

Fewer than 10 species of cochineal scale insect, originating in Central and South America, are known. These bugs feed exclusively on the sap of cacti in the genera *Opuntia* and *Nopalea*. The females have elongate, oval and convex bodies.

Some species have been introduced to Australia, parts of Africa and other regions of the world where, together with a pyralid moth, *Cactoblastis cactorum*, they have been of value in the biological control of prickly pear and other invasive cactus species. The incredibly successful control of prickly pear in South Africa was due mainly to the ravages of *Dactylopius opuntiae*. The weed, brought to South Africa from Mexico over two hundred years ago, now covers only a tiny fraction of the land it infested before these control measures were instigated. Ironically, the prickly pear, which does have some uses as animal and human food and as the food plant for the cochineal insect, is now highly regarded by the same people whose land was made virtually useless because of it, while the insect saviours are reviled. The single genus, *Dactylopius*, contains a species, *D. coccus*, which is cultivated commercially for a wax, a fat and the brilliant red natural dye cochinealin or carminic acid, which is used in cooking and cosmetics.

Family: **Diaspididae** (Fig. 6:xiii)

Armoured scales form the largest coccoid family, with more than 2,500 known species. As a family, these insects have a very wide host plant range; although adapted to a variety of conditions and found in all the world's major faunal regions, most have a subtropical or tropical distribution.

The females are distinctive in that they lack legs and (usually) antennae, and the hardened, waxy scale which they produce – composed of wax, other bodily secretions and the skins of previous moults – is totally separated from their bodies and rests like a tent over them. Some species are called mussel or oyster scales from the shell-like shape that the scale assumes as it develops.

In contrast to other coccoids, most diaspidids do not feed on the sap from

Looking more like ink spots than insects, these grass-feeding coccids are protected from enemies by a symbiotic relationship with a dolichoderine ant species. Kenya. **Coccidae**

vascular tissue but take the contents of parenchymal and other cells. Many species are serious pests of citrus and other fruit trees, greenhouse crops and house plants, and there are very few countries that do not suffer great financial losses as a result. While very many biological control programmes in different parts of the world, using a large range of parasites and predators, have been successful, around 45 diaspidid species still remain a serious problem. *Quadraspidiotus perniciosus* is the well-known and widespread San José Scale, capable of severely damaging apple and other fruit trees in temperate regions. Several pest species in this family have a pantropical distribution. The list of commercially important plants attacked by these insects is very long and ranges from pines to pineapples, camellias to coconuts and olives to oleanders. Important genera include *Aonidiella*, *Chrysomphalus*, *Lepidosaphes*, *Parlatoria*, *Tecaspis* and *Unaspis*.

Family: **Pseudococcidae** (Fig. 10:xiv)
Member species of this, the second largest coccoid family, are collectively known as mealy bugs because of the thread-like or powdery appearance of the waxy material covering the female's body and extruded from numerous strangely shaped pores and ducts. Females are oval to elongate-oval in outline, mostly less than 5 mm (0.2 in) long with clear body segmentation and, usually, well-developed legs. They can lay many hundreds and thousands of eggs or give birth to first instar nymphs. Approximately 2,000 species have been described from all parts of the world.

A large variety of hosts, ranging from grasses to trees, are attacked by these sap-sucking insects. In tropical regions, several species are widely distributed

Resting on a tree trunk in the South African savanna, a lanternfly (*Paropisoseys* sp.) displays its bright colouring. Unlike some other fulgorids, this species does not have a greatly enlarged head. **Fulgoridae**

and attack just about every cash and food crop grown, including economically valuable citrus, cocoa and avocado trees and pineapple plantations. In temperate regions, greenhouse plants are often infested. A few species are known to act as vectors for certain plant diseases.

Of the many important genera *Ferrisia*, *Phenacoccus*, *Planococcus*, *Pseudococcus* and *Nipaecoccus* are noteworthy.

Other families
The superfamily Coccoidea contains a further 15 closely related families. The ensign coccids belong to the family **Ortheziidae** and some 80 species are known. Ortheziids have long legs; curious, stalked eyes; and produce white body wax. The eggs are carried at the posterior end of the abdomen in an ovisac made of elongated wax plates.

The **Margarodidae**, often called ground pearls or giant scales, are native to the warmer regions of the world. Around 250 species are known and some are damaging to economically important plants. *Icerya purchasi*, the Cottony Cushion Scale, is a serious citrus pest. The two recorded species of the family **Phenacoleachiidae** feed on the leaves of beech, cypress and a few other trees in New Zealand.

The rain forests of the Ethiopian region are home to 15 species belonging to the family **Stictococcidae**, of which a few species may damage crops such as coffee and cocoa. The small family **Aclerdidae** is represented around the world by only 15 species, which mainly live on grasses. One or two species have minor pest status in connection with sugarcane. The 70 or so species comprising the **Kermesidae** are restricted to oak trees and related hosts in the Holarctic region.

The **Beesonidae** is made up of just three species found on certain valuable tropical trees (family: Dipterocarpaceae) from the Oriental region; this family is often regarded as being an eriococcid subfamily. The **Eriococcidae** or felted scales form quite a big family with around 500 species. Eriococcids are found in all faunal regions and vary considerably in form and habit. They live on the leaves, bark or roots of a wide range of hosts. Some induce the growth of galls on their host plants and a few are minor pests.

New Zealand and Australia are the only places where peg-top coccids of the family **Apiomorphidae** can be found. The 60 or so species are all gall formers on species of *Eucalyptus*. The **Kerriidae** or lac insects are notable for some species' production of valuable resins. The swollen, globular bodies of females produce large quantities of resinous material, which forms the covering under which they live. Just over 60 species are known from drier subtropical and tropical areas.

Just over 70 species of the family **Lecanodiaspididae** are known, mainly from Australia. The **Conchaspididae**, with some 25 member species, are confined to subtropical and tropical regions. A little more than 60 species of ornate pit scale insects belonging to the **Cerococcidae** are present in all the major faunal regions, where a few may be minor pests of fruit trees.

Palm trees in the tropics are the only known host plants of the 17 species within the **Halimococcidae**. A lone species, *Phoenicococcus marlatti*, the Red Date Palm Scale, represents the **Phoenicococcidae**. This species, which can be a pest, is distributed throughout the warmer, tropical regions of the world.

Chapter 4
Diseases and Enemies

Like any other organisms, bugs do not necessarily have an easy life – a multitude of other animals and plants depend on them for their own survival. Bugs are just one part of a complex and interdependent chain of organisms.

Factors such as the vagaries of the weather also play their part: high winds, heavy rain, excesses of temperature, frosts, natural fires and prolonged droughts can all have devastating effects on adult bugs, their nymphs and eggs. Large numbers of aphids, dispersing at high altitudes, are at the mercy of powerful wind currents and, fortunately for humans and their crops, may find themselves blown off-course out to sea or to some other unfavourable location where they will all perish.

Bugs living in small bodies of water or in ponds that have a tendency to dry up will need to disperse and, if they are able, find another suitable habitat. A late spring frost may kill large numbers of overwintering bugs, especially young nymphs and eggs. Triggered by increasing day length and rising temperatures, these bugs may have resumed normal activities after a dormant period. While many bugs have evolved protective mechanisms of various kinds to safeguard themselves from desiccation, freezing and other risks, the natural environment is hostile and sometimes unpredictable.

Mankind's increasing and damaging effects on the natural environment should also not be discounted. They are a major influence affecting not only bugs, but every other animal and plant species on Earth. The alarming rate of disappearance of natural habitats such as tropical and temperate forests, the drainage of wetlands and the relentless, destructive effects of atmospheric and water pollution present bugs and other organisms with problems against which they have no defence. Nature regulates, mankind decimates.

Natural enemies of bugs and other insects can be roughly classified under three headings: pathogens, predators and parasites (including parasitoids).

Since both parasitic and predacious animals consume the living tissues of their hosts or prey, they may be considered similar in function. In this book the term 'predator' refers to an animal (in the sense of a lion, for example) which kills and devours a number of prey items during the course of its life, each item being killed outright as it is eaten. While some parasitic species do not necessarily kill their hosts, many do. In general, an insect parasite uses one host animal in or on which to effect its complete development from egg to adult. The eggs may be laid on or in the host and the hatching larvae slowly consume the body tissues or fluids of the host from the outside or from within.

The term 'parasitoid' is generally applied to the very many species of parasitic Hymenoptera which lay their eggs in or on the eggs, nymphs or adults of the host insect. Parasitoids attacking other parasitoids within host insects are known as hyperparasitoids.

Many assassin bug species gain protection from their enemies by mimicking aggressive wasps and bees of various kinds. Here a species of *Notocyrtus* mimics a bee in the Peruvian rain forest. **Reduviidae**

Detailed records of all kinds of pathogenic, parasitic and predatory organisms are readily available for a large number of bug species of economic importance. But the enemies of the majority of bug species around the world are as yet largely unknown.

Viruses

Little or nothing is known of the viral ailments of bugs; while they probably do occur in nature, they have not attracted a great deal of research interest. On the other hand bugs themselves, especially herbivorous species, are well-known as vectors of a whole range of viruses capable of causing widespread damage to valuable crops and other important plant species. Blood-feeding species like Bed Bugs (*Cimex* spp.) and certain reduviids such as those in the genera *Triatoma*, *Rhodnius* and *Panstrongylus* are potentially capable of transmitting viruses to humans and other animals during the course of feeding.

Bacteria

Anyone who has seen the surface of an incubated agar culture plate that was touched by a human finger – or, indeed, any other object – will know that bacteria occur everywhere. The surface of any host plant or animal may be covered with these micro-organisms, which can be picked up by the bug's feet or mouthparts. Predacious bugs feeding from prey already infected with a bacterial disease may themselves become infected. The bodies of bugs infected by a pathogenic bacterium almost always turn into a dark brown or black putrefying liquid

which ultimately leaks out of any orifice or through the decomposing intersegmental membranes. Although it has been shown that bacterial diseases do not
play a very significant part in the life of bugs, it is well established that some
species of bacteria play a vital role as symbiotic organisms (symbionts) within
their digestive tracts. Man uses several species of bacteria, such as *Bacillus thuringiensis*, as biological control agents against pest insect species, although these
are mainly directed at the caterpillars of injurious moths.

Protozoa

Protozoal diseases of bugs are not at all common and are little studied. Those
that are known are mainly confined to aquatic heteropterans such as species
belonging to the **Corixidae, Nepidae, Notonectidae, Veliidae** and
Gerridae.

Fungi

Some bugs, such as the nymphs and adults of **Aradidae** and the nymphs of
Achilidae and **Derbidae**, actually feed directly on the hyphae or thread-like
growth stage of various fungal species; others are associated with the spore-
containing fruiting bodies of some fungi. But the overall balance of bug–fungus
relationships is definitely in favour of the fungi.

Like bacteria, fungi and their spores are very common in the natural environment. Many species are pathogens of bugs and other insects, and are sometimes
used very successfully as biological control agents of plant pest species. Various
factors can affect the success of a fungal species as a control agent, and while a
high density of the target species, high humidity and good rainfall generally
improve the rate of infection, variables such as the natural resistance of the target
species and its position on the crop can impede control efforts.

The entomopathogenic fungi, or mycopathogens, which affect hemipterans
and other insects all belong to the Eumycota – that is, the group containing all
the true fungi and excluding slime moulds and their allies. Within the Eumycota
four subdivisions of fungi, the lower fungi (Mastigomycotina and Zygomycotina) and the higher fungi (Ascomycotina and Basidiomycotina) contain bug-
infecting species.

The ways in which fungal species and their bug hosts interact are many and
varied. In general, fungal infections kill bugs, causing them to become dry and
stiff before their cuticle splits due to the accelerating growth of hyphae. Species in
more than 20 hemipteran families have been regularly recorded as suffering
from fungal diseases of one kind or another which may affect the eggs, nymphal
or adult stages.

Following infection, primitive fungal pathogens produce toxins which quickly
cause the death of the host. When attacked by other species, the host may survive
for some hours or days before the fungal mycelium (the vegetative stage of the
fungus, composed of a mass of threads or hyphae) spreads throughout the
haemocoel (haemolymph-filled body cavity) and its tissues. Some species
of fungus, especially those which need a long period over which to produce
their spores, cause their hosts to become 'mummified' and stuck to foliage in

characteristic positions. Here mummification is different from that seen in aphids which have been attacked by certain species of parasitoid wasp. In the latter case, the body of the aphid appears smooth, papery and light brown, with no evidence of fungal threads or spore-bearing structures.

Some of the more advanced fungi show amazing adaptations to their hosts. These fungus species, which need to ensure that the individual bugs they infect come into direct contact with other bugs, restrict their growth to non-vital abdominal segments. As a result the bug maintains its normal functions of moving around, feeding and even mating.

Fungi of the genus *Myiophagus* (Mastigomycotina) attack armoured scale insects (**Diaspididae**) and rely on their spores being washed by rainwater over the surface of leaves, where they will come into contact with other hosts. Tropical treehoppers (**Membracidae**) can be infected by a fungus of the genus *Sporodiniella* (Zygomycotina). The dead membracids, still stuck to the plant by their mouthparts, are further secured to the tree be the growth of fungal threads. The spores are dispersed by wind and rain, and may even be released in response to passing insects.

Some species in the fungal genus *Erynia* (Zygomycotina) infect aphids and leafhoppers. As in certain other fungus–bug interactions, infection may bring about strange changes in the behaviour of the victim. The affected bug may crawl up a plant stem before it finally succumbs: from a high point such as this the fungus can ensure a much wider dispersal of its spores.

The members of a large genus of widespread entomopathogenic fungi, *Entomophthora* (Zygomycotina), which are much commoner in temperate habitats than tropical ones, are particularly well known as bug destroyers. Species have been recorded from planthoppers, plant bugs, seed bugs, leafhoppers, jumping plantlice, aphids and some other families. After growing within their host's body, fungal species of this genus produce spore-bearing hyphae which break through the thin intersegmental membranes, especially those joining the abdominal segments. Bugs which have become infected with these fungi may remain active right up to the last, even when the body wall has split and spores are being released. Some bugs may adopt a characteristic position on their food plant and die *in situ* before the fungal spores are discharged, while others crawl away to die in crevices, their bodies packed with dormant spores ready to be released at a later date.

Perhaps one of the most interesting and complex of bug–fungus interactions occurs between fungi of the genus *Massospora* (Zygomycotina) and cicadas (**Cicadidae**).

Currently about 13 species of the fungus are known throughout the world and all are associated with one or more species of cicada, particularly those which are either gregarious or emerge simultaneously in large numbers. The cycle of infection begins in the soil, where the resting spore stages of the fungus await contact with the young adults of the next generation.

Generations of some cicada species emerge in cycles which may be separated by many years. However the processes that keep the spores dormant but viable in the soil for these long periods, and cause them to germinate at the correct time when the next generation of adults emerge, are as yet little understood.

The fungus affects just the rear segments of the abdomen and the internal

99

genital organs, and does not therefore interfere with the primary activities of the insect. As the fungus grows, it may occupy the whole of the abdominal cavity and cause the rear part of the abdomen to fall apart, exposing the primary infective stages of the fungus. Incredibly the cicada moves about easily, may still feed and, in the case of males, sing and try to mate with females. In this way the fungus is rapidly spread throughout a population. If older adults become infected, they behave differently from the younger adults and move back to the soil, where they die. The resting spores are released from their bodies, and the cycle of infection is completed.

Within the Ascomycotina several genera of entomopathogenic fungi, which are particularly common in the warmer regions and moist forests of the world, are associated with bugs of various families. Species of *Hypocrella* which attack scale insects and whiteflies can cause the destruction of whole colonies in a short time. Other plant sap-sucking bugs like aphids and scale insects can be infected by species of *Torrubiella*, *Hirsutella* and *Verticillium*.

A large number of entomopathogenic fungal species belong to the widespread genus *Cordyceps*, particularly common in tropical forest habitats. Species of *Cordyceps* have been recorded from bugs belonging to several different families, including shield bugs (**Pentatomidae**), assassin bugs (**Reduviidae**) cotton stainers (**Pyrrhocoridae**), damsel bugs (**Nabidae**), planthoppers (**Delphacidae**) and cicadas (**Cicadidae**), as well as scale insects, whiteflies and aphids in general.

Fungi belonging to the Ascomycotina often produce large, club-shaped, brightly coloured fruiting bodies. These bodies, which contain the spores, grow out from the body of the infected bug and may attract other insects which then act as carriers or agents of dispersal. The spores of other genera may be ejected over a short distance, or dispersed by rainwater. Other important bug-infecting genera within the Ascomycotina are *Nectria* and *Podonectria*, which attack armoured scale insets, *Beauveria* which goes for scale insects and seed bugs (**Lygaeidae**) and *Metarhizium*, which selects leafhoppers (**Cicadellidae**).

Within the Basidiomycotina the member species of a large genus, *Septobasidium*, are found only in association with armoured scale insects (**Diaspididae**). The relationship between fungus and scale insect is a very strange one and may be thought of as mutually beneficial.

The fungus grows on the bark of trees and shrubs such as citrus and tea, where it forms highly structured colonies known as 'houses' inside which the scale insects live, feed and reproduce. Only a certain proportion of the scale insects become infected by the fungus. Fungal threads grow out from the bodies of infected scales and, by joining with other hyphae of the mycelium, transfer nutrients from the fluids of the insect's body cavity to the main body of the fungus. The individual scale insects on which the fungus feeds do not become adult and do not reproduce, but they may live longer than their non-infected fellows. The spores of the fungus are picked up by the mobile, first instar nymphs, which may or may not become infected. The nymphs move away to colonize other parts of the host plant or seek out other fungal colonies in which to live.

The fungus gets its food, while the scale insects are protected from the weather and from the hordes of natural enemies such as predators and parasitoid wasps that might otherwise cause their destruction. The complex character of this particular system, and the extent, nature and range of bug–fungus interactions in general, are still far from being fully understood.

Predators

Birds and other vertebrates

Vertebrate animals such as fish, snakes, lizards, frogs, toads, birds and small insectivorous mammals are capable of eating large numbers of bugs, but the proportion of bugs in their diet is not well documented. Birds of all kinds, however are almost certainly major consumers. In a few studies, birds have been shown to be more important than all other causes of mortality put together.

Many bird species prey on any suitable insect while others may be more selective, concentrating on particular groups or habitats or on a similar size

A hungry lizard (*Anolis frenatus*) eats a cicada it has caught on a tree in the tropical forests of Panama.

range. Although many bugs are well protected by physical and chemical means against attack by higher animals, some bird species seem to be unaffected or immune to their effects. Analyses of the contents of birds' digestive tracts have shown that some species take large numbers of tough and seemingly distasteful bugs.

While aphids and scale insects might need to be eaten in fair numbers to sustain even a small bird, large bugs such as cicadas provide a worthwhile meal for many bird species and are also eaten by omnivorous creatures such as monkeys. These predators may eat the bugs whole or consume everything but the membranous wings, which are often discarded.

Some water-dwelling bugs and their nymphs form an important part of the diet of certain species of fish. In some parts of the world, the abundant eggs of water boatmen (**Corixidae**) and some other aquatic bugs are gathered from submerged vegetation by people, dried and used as a type of flour. Adult bugs also form a small part of the diet of tribal peoples.

Spiders and their allies

The Arachnida, comprising spiders, ticks, mites, harvestmen and related taxa is an example of a group containing many general predatory species. Although mainly opportunistic, spiders are known to eat bug species belonging to a wide range of heteropteran and auchenorrhynchan families.

Webs built by members of several families, such as the Argiopidae, Tetragnathidae and Linyphiidae, reveal what type of prey is being caught. This is not, however, necessarily what the spider is eating. Numerous small flying bugs such as aphids might become entangled in a web, but be of no interest to the spider as a supply of food: small or immature spiders tend to prefer small prey, while large spiders go for larger items.

Nor do all spiders catch their food in webs. A very large number of species in several families, such as the wolf spiders (Lycosidae), lynx spiders (Oxyopidae) and huntsman spiders (Sparassidae), hunt on the ground or over vegetation and rely on good eyesight, chemosensory receptors and long tactile hairs to locate their prey. Even quite large bugs like cicadas can be caught by some of these spiders. Crab spiders (Thomisidae) are often found lying in wait on foliage and in flowers, where they will ambush passing bugs. Jumping spiders (Salticidae), with their huge, forward-facing eyes, are capable of locating a prey item many centimetres distant; they will then stalk it before leaping accurately on top of it.

Related to spiders and also predatory are the long-legged harvestmen (order Opiliones), which seem to concentrate their attentions on immature planthoppers, related families and aphidoids. Also related to spiders, and to other animals placed in the class Arachnida, are the mites which, together with ticks, form the order Acari.

Mites, which comprise a very large group of very small arachnids, can be parasitic or predacious and are found on animals and plants in both watery and dry land habitats. Their life histories can be quite complex, and involve parasitic and predatory larval and adult stages.

Mite species belonging to many families around the world are known to prey on a variety of bug species, particularly those belonging to the superfamilies

Powerful jumping ability and a noxious taste has not proved too successful a protection for this cercopid froghopper (*Cercopis vulnerata*). A female crab spider (*Xysticus cristatus*) has paralysed the bug with her venom and is sucking out the dissolved body contents through the junction between the head and pronotum. Great Britain.

Coccoidea and Aphidoidea. In general, mite species prefer stationary or very slow-moving hosts, and many specialize on the egg stages of bugs. Some water-dwelling mites attack aquatic bugs such as corixids. While attached, the mites feed on the host's haemolymph; when fully engorged, they detach themselves. The various effects that parasitic mites can have on their water bug hosts range from a reduction in the number and rate of egg development and the number produced to impaired development of the flight muscles.

Diptera

The larvae of some flies, particularly those belonging to the families Tachinidae and Pipunculidae, have a parasitic lifestyle and the species attacking bugs will be discussed in the section on parasites and parasitoids (see p. 111). In addition, many species of fly in several other families are known to catch and eat bugs, their eggs and nymphs.

While gall midges (Cecidomyiidae) are better known for their widespread habit of inducing growths or galls on an incredible variety of plant species, very many species have predatory larvae which attack the eggs, nymphs and sometimes adults of aphid, scale insect, conifer woolly aphid and whitefly species. A particular gall midge species is usually restricted to one host species. The larvae are very small, and one or two may take up to a day to eat the contents of a single aphid. In some cecidomyiid species, the larvae exist as internal parasites of aphids and lace bugs, consuming the host's tissues from within.

Chamaemyiid flies (Chamaemyiidae) are predators of a range of sternorrhynchan bugs. The larvae of genera such as *Leucopis*, *Chamaemyia* and *Plunomia* prey on aphids, conifer woolly aphids, mealy bugs and scale insects. Few species attack armoured scales. Some are useful as control agents against pests and have been introduced to various countries.

Robber flies (Asilidae) are ferocious but unsystematic hunters which will tackle even large wasps and bees, stabbing them through a weak spot in the body armour with their stout, beak-like mouthparts. Species of bug belonging to many families, even quite large cicadas, have been recorded as asilid prey.

The best-known bug killers in the order are hover flies (Syrphidae). The larvae of many species, particularly those in the subfamily Syrphinae, are highly predacious on aphids, many types of scale insect, jumping plantlice, whitefly, leafhoppers and froghoppers (**Cercopidae**). Adult hover flies, which can be important plant pollinators, are not predacious and visit flowers to feed on pollen and nectar.

Females typically deposit a single egg at a time on leaves or bark among colonies of aphids or scale insects. The larvae, which are maggot-like and narrow at the front end, move about through an aphid colony and, when they touch an aphid, use their hook-like mouthparts to penetrate its body wall. Characteristically, the hover fly larva lifts the aphid clear of whatever it is standing on while it sucks out the juices. During its development, a typical larva may consume many hundreds of aphids. On account of their voracious appetite for pest bugs and ability to wipe out whole colonies, certain hover fly species are very important agents of natural and biological control.

Many other dipteran families contain species with predacious adults and/or larvae. Notable examples known to feed on hemipterans are the dance flies (Empidae), long-legged flies (Dolichopodidae), stem, grass or frit flies (Chloropidae), hump-backed flies (Phoridae), pomace flies (Drosophilidae) and dung flies (Scatophagidae).

Neuroptera

Within this order three families, the common or green lacewings (Chrysopidae), the brown lacewings (Hemerobiidae) and the dusty or powdery lacewings (Coniopterygidae) are of particular importance as predators of sternorrhynchan bugs. In general the larvae and sometimes the adult stages of these insects attack many species of bug in the superfamilies Aphidoidea and Coccoidea, as well as conifer woolly aphids, phylloxerans, whiteflies, jumping plantlice and leafhoppers.

Chrysopid eggs, which unlike those of the other two families, are borne aloft on long, slender stalks, are laid on the foliage of plants where aphids are present. The larvae, which have legs and are very active, move across leaves in search of their prey. Once located, their soft-bodied victims are quickly impaled by a pair of long, sickle-shaped, hollow jaws and their body contents sucked out. The larvae of many lacewing species are known as trash carriers, on account of their habit of attaching the sucked-out bodies of their prey on to special hooked hairs on their backs. At each moult the lacewing larva renews its disguise. This interesting habit, an insect version of a wolf in sheep's clothing, may allow the larvae to move freely and without causing their prey to flee or defend themselves.

A number of species such as those in the genus *Chrysopa* are of great benefit, and have been used in many regions of the world as biological control agents to combat aphid and scale insect pest species.

Coleoptera

Predatory beetle species occur in many families, but the best known and most useful for the control of bug pests are found in the Coccinellidae (ladybird or ladybug beetles). The attacks of the highly predacious adults and larvae of many species are probably the main reasons why plant-feeding pest insects such as leaf beetle larvae and all manner of sternorrhynchan bugs very seldom reach plague populations. The main hemipteran prey of these beetles are aphidoids, coccoids, whiteflies and phylloxerans.

Females of these distinctive rounded, convex and brightly coloured beetles lay their eggs singly or in small groups, and always choose plants where there are good colonies of prey insects. During its adult life a female can lay more than a thousand eggs. In some species the beetles may sometimes lay single eggs directly on the backs of female scale insects. The dark or warningly coloured larvae, which are often warty or spiny, are stout and soft-bodied with well-developed legs; the jaws are not large and sickle-shaped, like those of lacewing larvae.

During development a single ladybird will consume vast quantities of aphids

Impaling its victim with cruel, sickle-shaped, hollow jaws, a Green Lacewing larva (*Chrysopa carnea*) sucks out a nettle aphid's body contents. Like ladybirds, lacewings have an insatiable appetite for aphids. Great Britain.

and other pests. Pupation occurs on foliage, and the pupae of many species resemble bird droppings. The adult beetles often eat the same prey species as their larvae, and the adults of some larger species can dispose of up to five hundred aphids in a single day.

Most species do not seem to be very species-specific, but there are notable exceptions such as *Cryptognatha nodiceps*, a highly efficient predator and successful biological control agent of the Coconut Scale, *Aspidiotus destructor* (**Diaspididae**). Naturally occurring populations of ladybird beetles can save a crop from destruction, and their value to farmers is inestimable. Many species are of value as biological control agents and have been introduced all over the world to areas where particular pests pose problems.

One of the best known instances of successful biological control concerns the serious citrus tree pest Cottony Cushion Scale, *Icerya purchasi* (**Margarodidae**). In 1887 the new Californian citrus industry was all but destroyed by this species, which had been introduced by accident. The hunt was on for a suitable predator and the deliberate introduction of an Australian ladybird, the Vedalia Beetle, *Rodolia cardinalis*, saved the day. Well within two years the beetle had achieved effective control of the scale insect at an incredibly low cost. The Vedalia Beetle is now used in many part of the world where citrus crops are grown. Of the many other hemipteran species controlled in this way, Coconut Scale, Sugarcane Mealy Bug, Date Scale, Citrus Blackfly, Potato Aphid and Fir Aphid are a few examples.

While the effects of coccinellids may be spectacular, species in other beetle families can also be effective bug predators. Some pollen or sap beetles belonging to the family Nitidulidae are predators of the eggs, nymphs and adult stage of several coccid and diaspidid scale insect, whitefly and aphid species.

The gardener's friends, ladybird adults and larvae are voracious consumers of aphids. Here, a couple of mature 7-spot ladybird larvae (*Coccinella septempunctata*) devour nettle aphids. Many ladybird species are very important predators of serious sternorrhynchan crop pests. Great Britain.

In some parts of the world, a few species of Lathridiidae (minute brown scavenger beetles) feed on scale insects of the **Eriococcidae** and **Diaspididae**. Species in a few genera of the beetle family Phalacridae (shining flower beetles) attack aphids. Although some members of the Anthribidae are pests of beans and seeds, the larval stages and adults of a few (*Anthribus* and *Brachytarsus*) are predators of scale insects (**Pseudococcidae**, **Coccidae** and **Diaspididae**).

In addition to these fairly specialized predators, terrestrial beetles of other families are opportunistic bug feeders. In a variety of habitats, the adults and/or larvae of some species of ground beetles (Carabidae), rove beetles (Staphylinidae), soldier beetles (Cantharidae), click beetles (Elateridae) and soft-winged flower beetles (Melyridae) are known to prey on a wide range of hemipterans. In aquatic habitats, water bugs and their nymphs may fall prey to adults and larvae of giant water beetles (Dytiscidae).

Lepidoptera

One does not readily think of butterflies and moths as predators, but the larvae of some species in several lepidopteran families eat sternorrhynchan and auchenorrhynchan bugs. Within the Lycaenidae (Blues, Coppers and Hairstreaks) the larvae of some species in several genera are very efficient consumers of aphidoids, scale insects, leafhoppers and treehoppers. The female lays her eggs singly in or near a host colony and, on hatching, the young caterpillar begins to feed. Some species have complex interactions with ant species which tend aphid and scale insect colonies. The caterpillars can supply the ants with a highly desirable sweet substance produced from a special 'honey gland', which enables them to prey on the ants' 'herds' and even the ants' own young without being attacked.

The Australian moth family Cyclotornidae contains a strange species, *Cyclotorna monocentra*, whose first instar caterpillars feed externally on the tissues of leafhoppers. The caterpillars then build themselves a shelter and moult to the second instar. The leafhopper colonies are attended by ants and, curiously, the second instar caterpillars are taken by the ants into their nest. Here the caterpillars eat ant larvae, but are not attacked by their hosts on account of a sweet secretion they give in return.

From many parts of the world there are records of the caterpillars of a few species in moth families such as the Psychidae, Tineidae, Blastobasidae, Pyralidae, Stathmopodidae and Noctuidae being sporadic or frequent predators of various types of scale insect.

Hymenoptera

Many species of solitary hunting wasp belonging to the family Sphecidae will take hemipterans as prey and paralyse them to provision their nests. It is the female sphecid wasps which are the hunters; the males feed on nectar and take no part in the nest digging or provisioning. Although many sphecids use other insects and spiders as a food source for their developing young, many species seem to be bug specialists. Some will mix bugs with flies and other insects, while others concentrate on a particular group like shield bugs, jumping plantlice or

A female hunting wasp (*Bembecinus* sp.) drags a paralysed froghopper (**Cercopidae**) into a nest burrow where she will lay her eggs. Borneo.

aphids, and a few may confine themselves to a single prey species.

Within the family, species in eight tribes are known to catch bugs. For example, species in the sphecid tribes (a taxonomic subdivision below the level of subfamily and above that of genus) the Alyssonini, Gorytini and Psenini prey variously on cicadas, cicadellids, membracids, fulgorids, cercopids, aphidoids, coccoids and psyllids. Species in the tribe Astatini specialize in heteropterans, mainly the adults and nymphs of reduviid, lygaeid, pentatomid, scutellerid, coreid and cydnid bugs.

While many sphecids may tackle small prey, others are capable of overcoming even powerful cicada species. In Australia a large black and yellow sphecid species, *Exeirus lateritius*, is called the Cicada Killer. The same common name is given to *Sphecius speciosus*, a species with similar habits which occurs in North America.

Most bug-catching sphecids dig a nest in loose or sandy soil; it may comprise one or several cells. They leave the nest to hunt for prey which, when located, is quickly seized and stung. Sphecid venom is very fast-acting: the victim may collapse instantly and, in the case of larger prey on foliage, fall to the ground with the wasp hanging on. The paralysed prey is dragged back to the nest where it is taken down the main burrow and placed in one of the cells. The sphecid then lays an egg on the bug and seals the cell. Some sphecid species use several small prey items per cell, while others utilize a single large bug. The female will make as many trips as she needs to fill all the cells. When all are sealed, she exits and secures the main entrance. Once the sphecid egg hatches, the larva chews through the cuticle of the provisioned bug and inserts its head to suck the body juices. When the larva is fully developed, the prey item will be nothing but a shrivelled piece of cuticle.

Social wasps of the family Vespidae are general insect predators. While none are specialists on hemipteran species, small, soft-bodied bugs may be caught and masticated into a meaty paste for direct feeding to the colonies' larvae.

There can be little doubt that the nearly 9,000 species of ants worldwide constitute one of the most important groups of predatory insects. Very many are highly predacious on a wide range of insect species and other small invertebrates. Not only abundant in terms of species, ants are themselves very numerous. It has been estimated that, in some parts of the world, ant populations may reach 20 million per hectare (49 million per acre). Needless to say, this represents a large predatory force. Although there are bug species in more than 16 hemipteran families which have complex and interesting interactions with some ants, the majority of bugs serve only as ant food.

Hemiptera

While all bugs belonging to the suborders Coleorrhyncha, Auchenorrhyncha and Sternorrhyncha and the majority of terrestrial species in the Heteroptera are exclusively herbivorous, many heteropteran bugs are either wholly or partly predacious. Their diet encompasses a wide range of invertebrates including insects of all kinds, spiders and, for some species, the blood of vertebrate animals. The notable land-living families that contain predatory species are the assassin bugs (**Reduviidae**), damsel bugs (**Nabidae**), flowers or minute pirate bugs (**Anthocoridae**) and plant bugs (**Miridae**). In some habitats, mainly temperate grasslands, damsel bugs may be one of the most important groups preying on planthoppers and leafhoppers.

Although a large proportion of species contained within the **Miridae** are essentially herbivorous, many species are significant predators. Among the economically important groups of bugs on which they prey are several families of aphid, scale insects, mealy bugs, lace bugs and phylloxerans (**Phylloxeridae**). Several mirid species have been used successfully, or are under investigation, as biological control agents. Other bug families such as the **Lygaeidae** (subfamily Geocorinae) and **Pentatomidae** (subfamily Asopinae) contain predacious species which may feed to a greater or lesser extent on other bugs.

Although most predatory bugs tend to be opportunistic or non-specific in their feeding habits, attacking any insect or invertebrate of a suitable size that they chance upon, a few specialize to some degree on soft-bodied or slow-moving bug species such as scale insects and aphids of many kinds, nymphs and eggs. Some species in the **Anthocoridae** have proved particularly useful in the control of pests. The pests concerned tend to be caterpillars, thrips and other insects; but attempts have been made, sometimes successfully, to control scale insects, adelgids and some aphid species.

All water bugs, whether they are surface or sub-surface dwellers, are

A damsel bug (*Nabis rugosus*) feeds on a Sycamore Aphid (*Drepanosiphum platanodis*). Great Britain. **Nabidae** and **Callaphididae**

predacious. Certain species, particularly members of the **Corixidae, Nepidae, Gerridae** and **Notonectidae**, may take other water bug adults or nymphs as part of their diet. Among the water striders (**Gerridae**) many species will attack and eat their own kind; but this generally only happens when the victim is a young nymph, a dying adult or in some way disabled so that it cannot easily escape. Velvety shore bugs (**Ochteridae**) may take aphids as they move through their damp lake or stream-side habitats.

Insects of other orders

Predatory species which direct their attentions on bugs can be found in many other orders of insects. Members of particular families in other orders such as the dragonflies and damselflies (Odonata), grasshoppers and their allies (Orthoptera), praying mantids (Mantodea), scorpionflies (Mecoptera), earwigs (Dermaptera), barklice (Psocoptera), thrips (Thysanoptera) and snakeflies (Megaloptera: Raphidiidae) are known to include all manner of bugs in their diet. Dragonfly nymphs will catch and eat water bugs such as water boatmen and backswimmers. Adult mantids will strike at almost any insect or spider of a suitable size which passes in range; but their nymphs, especially the small first instars, subsist mainly on aphids and small leafhopper species.

In several parts of the world, long-horned grasshoppers (Tettigoniidae) will eat leafhopper species and mealy bugs. Some crickets (Gryllidae), particularly those tree-living species belonging to the genus *Oecanthus*, are well-known consumers of aphids and scale insects.

Scorpionflies, although mainly interested in flies as meals, will take small bugs. A few species of earwigs are valuable in the control of sugarcane leafhoppers, cereal aphids and citrus pests like Cottony Cushion Scale. Predacious barklice species, themselves small, include scale insects, particularly mealy bugs, and aphids in their diet.

Thrips are largely plant- or fungus-eating insects, but many predacious species are known to attack auchenorrhynchan and sternorrhynchan bugs; in some cases, they can be of great benefit in controlling natural populations of pest species. The prey of predacious thrip species includes leafhoppers, planthoppers, scale insects and whiteflies. Adult snakeflies and their larvae, which live under bark and in decaying wood, have been recorded as feeding on aphids and other soft-bodied prey items.

Parasites and parasitoids

Nematodes

Parasitic nematode worms belonging to the family Mermithidae are known to infect a wide range of hemipteran species. The young worms penetrate the host bug's cuticle and grow inside the body cavity. Normally there is one long, thread-like worm per host. When fully developed, it leaves the dying host to return to the soil, where it becomes adult.

Diptera

Within the Diptera there are a number of families, such as the Pipunculidae, Tachinidae, Cryptochetidae and Chamaemyiidae, which contain species parasitic on bugs. The small, dark-coloured flies belonging to the Pipunculidae have relatively huge hemispherical or spherical heads which are almost totally occupied by the compound eyes. Although the biologies and larval habits of most of the 600 or so world species are unknown, those that have been studied are internal parasites of bugs such as members of the **Cicadellidae**, **Cercopidae**, **Cixiidae** and **Delphacidae**. Well-known pipunculid genera include *Pipunculus*, *Chalarus* and *Verrallia*.

Female pipunculids, which have superb flying skills and excellent vision, seek out and leap on an appropriate host nymph. The victim is held tightly by the fly's strong legs and claws and carried into the air. In flight, the female bends her piercing ovipositor around to penetrate the cuticle between two abdominal segments and lay her egg. The developing larva eventually consumes all the fluids and tissues of its host. Before it pupates, it eats its way out and drops to the soil or leaf litter.

The Cryptochetidae is a small family of stout-bodied flies less than 4 mm (0.16 in) long, represented by around 25 species of the genus *Cryptochetum*. All the known species occur in the Old World but an Australian species, *C. iceryae*, was introduced to North America where it gave valuable service in the control of Cottony Cushion Scale (**Margarodidae**). The larvae of these flies are endoparasites, living within the bodies of a variety of scale insects, and the adults feed on their honeydew.

Stalking through savanna vegetation, a hungry female praying mantid makes a meal of a reduviid bug. Kenya.

The larvae of all species of flies belonging to the family Tachinidae are parasitic on insects and a few other arthropods such as centipedes. Tachinids are of immense value as natural control agents for a large number of potential pests in several orders including Lepidoptera, Coleoptera and Orthoptera. Well-known bug-killing tachinid genera include *Gymnosoma*, *Phasia*, *Trichopoda*, *Alophora* and *Subclytia*. Levels of parasitism can be quite high, and in some cases 80 per cent or more of host populations can be destroyed by these flies.

Around the world there are about 8,000 species of these medium to large, dull-coloured and very hairy flies. The family is divided into several subfamilies, each showing broad preferences for particular types of host and differences in how they get their eggs on or into the host. For instance, the Tachniniae and Goniinae tend to go for caterpillars, while other groups prefer beetle larvae. Tachinids in the primitive subfamily Phasiinae are all parasitic on adult heteropteran bugs, particularly members of the **Lygaeidae**, **Pentatomidae**, **Coreidae** and **Nabidae** and occasionally **Pyrrhocoridae**, **Rhopalidae**, **Miridae** and **Anthocoridae**. Phasiines are not known to attack bugs in the aquatic or water surface-dwelling heteropteran families.

In general, mated female tachinids, whose bodies may contain thousands of eggs, seek out their victim and lay a single egg inside or on the surface of the bug's body. When the egg hatches, usually in a short time, the first instar larva burrows inside and begins to feed on the juices in the body cavity.

As the larva grows it needs to get oxygen, which cannot be supplied from diffusion alone. Incredibly, it plugs the spiracles at the posterior end of the host's body into a special respiratory device that the victim is made to produce. The respiratory funnel may be attached directly to the air supply in the tracheal system, or to the outside.

Clinging to a barbed wire fence, a pair of robber flies (Asilidae) mate under African skies. While the female feeds on a nuptial gift of a cotton stainer bug (*Dysdercus* sp. **Pyrrhocoridae**), the smaller male copulates with her. Kenya.

Larvae in the third and last instar will also eat solid materials within the host, and finally leave through a split between the segments of the host's abdomen. The fully-grown larva pupates in the soil.

Lepidoptera

The caterpillars of strange tiny moths in the family Epipyropidae can be thought of as parasitic. About 20 or so species are confined to the tropical and warm temperate regions of the southern hemisphere. In the main, large species in the family **Fulgoridae** are the preferred hosts, but some cicadellids and cicadas have been known to serve as hosts.

Typically, the caterpillars are external parasites; they feed either singly or gregariously in small numbers on the body fluids of the adults, and sometimes nymphs, of their host bug species. Once a young caterpillar finds a suitable host it uses long, sharp mouthparts to penetrate the cuticle. When fully grown, the fifth instar caterpillar detaches itself and pupates inside the cocoon. The effects on the host are variable, depending on size and the number of parasites. At one end of the spectrum the host may show hardly any ill effects, while at the other end the host may die soon after the caterpillars leave. *Epipyrops* and *Agamopsyche* are typical genera.

Strepsiptera

This peculiar group of insects is closely related to, and was at one time included in, the order Coleoptera. Approximately 500 world species are known; all are highly specialized endoparasites of seven other orders of insects, particularly wasps, bees and bugs.

Within the Hemiptera, strepsipterans parasitize heteropteran and auchenorrhynchan bug species. The principal heteropteran families used as hosts are the **Pentatomidae**, **Scutelleridae**, **Coreidae**, **Cydnidae** and **Lygaeidae**. Among the Auchenorrhyncha, species belonging to the **Cercopidae**, **Membracidae**, **Delphacidae**, **Dictyopharidae**, **Flatidae**, **Ricaniidae**, **Fulgoridae** and a few other families are parasitized. Most strepsipterans are broadly host-specific, tending to keep within a particular bug genus, tribe, subfamily or family. The hosts of many species are, as yet, unknown.

Female strepsipterans are wingless and larva-like, lacking eyes, jaws and antennae or only having them in reduced form. They spend all their adult life within the body of the host insect in which they grew, surrounded by the cuticle of their pupal stage. To allow the strange-looking, free-living, winged male to mate, the head and thorax region of the female's body, which also provides a special genital opening, remain sticking out through between the abdominal segments of the host.

Strepsipterans do not lay eggs. The eggs hatch internally and hundreds or thousands of tiny active larvae, known as triungulins, eventually issue from the female into the space between her body and her puparial cuticle. The minute triungulins have three pairs of well-developed legs and, on exiting the brood passage, seek out a host. If successful in locating an appropriate host species, the young larva will penetrate the cuticle and begin to feed on the fluids of the body cavity. Typically only one larva will develop to maturity inside one bug host, but sometimes two or three may develop.

When fully grown, after five or six instars, a larva moves to the host's surface and cuts a small hole to the outside through which its front bodyparts protrude. The tissues heal around the cut and hold the now pupating larva firmly in place. The winged males leave the host after pupating, while the grub-like females remain where they pupated. The males, with their odd, bulging, berry-like eyes and fan-shaped hind wings (the front wings are reduced to tiny strut-like structures), fly off to seek virgin females with which to mate, after which they die.

The effects of stylopization (as parasitism by strepsipterans is known) on the host can be very varied, ranging through retarded development, loss of vigour, and damage to sexual and other internal organs. Where male strepsipterans leave a large hole in the body, death from desiccation and disease can result.

Since strepsipterans attack pest bugs such as the Asian Brown Rice Hopper (*Nilaparvata lugens*), and other species feeding on commercially important plants, they can be of considerable benefit to humans. Within the strepsipteran family Corioxenidae, species in several genera (*Triozocera, Blissoxenos, Corioxenos*) attack pentatomids, lygaeids and cydnids. In the Halictophagidae (*Halictophagus, Stenocranophilus*), stink bugs and species in a number of auchenorrhynchan families are attacked. Members of the Elenchidae (*Elenchus, Deinelenchus*) specialize in delphacids, but are also known from species in other related families.

Hymenoptera

Last but certainly not least, all manner of bugs are attacked by parasitic wasp species (parasitoids) belonging to a large number of families. Within the hymenopteran suborder Apocrita – that is, all hymenopterans except the sawflies – there are two distinct divisions or infraorders. These are the Parasitica – parasitic wasps whose larvae are parasitoids of insects – and the Aculeata – stinging hymenopterans such as the wasps, bees and ants.

Aculeata

Two families of aculeate hymenoptera are characteristically parasitic on bugs; other families use hosts in different orders, such as the Phasmatodea, Coleoptera, Lepidoptera, Embioptera and Hymenoptera.

All members of the Dryinidae attack auchenorrhynchan nymphs or adults, particularly those belonging to the **Cicadellidae**, **Delphacidae**, **Cixiidae**, **Membracidae**, **Cercopidae** and **Fulgoridae**. The adults of some species attack and kill hosts for food, others may simply obtain nourishment from body fluids taken from wounds which they inflict on them, and some short-lived species do not seem to feed at all. Around 800 dryinid species are known from tropical and temperate regions. Typical dryinid genera across the world include *Chalcogonatopus, Haplogonatopus, Gonatopus, Aphelopus* and *Anteon*.

In North America these insects are sometimes called pincher wasps on account of the strange grasping design of the female's front tarsus, a characteristic found in many but not all dryinids. Female dryinids, which may be fully winged, wingless or ant-like, locate their prey on vegetation. When they are within a range of about 25 mm (1 in) or less, they snatch their victim using their legs and

Insects from three orders interact on a plant stem in the French Alps. Aphids (*Brachycaudus cardui*) feed on their host plant and are attended by ants (*Formica* sp.), which should protect them in return for carbohydrate-rich honeydew. Despite the ants' presence, three minute female parasitic wasps can be seen. The wasps have already laid eggs in several of the aphids, which have become brown and mummified. **Aphididae**

sometimes their jaws. In those species with modified, grasping front tarsi no other hold is necessary. When holding the host bug – which, depending on size, may be firmly pressed against the surface of the foliage or held up in the air – the female stings it and an egg is inserted into its body. The positioning of the egg varies between species. In most, the egg is placed between abdominal segments; but in a few it is inserted in the thorax or neck of the host bug. The paralysing effect of the female's sting lasts a very short time, and sometimes is not even noticeable.

Immature dryinids, which feed on the host's bodily fluids and, when nearly fully grown, on the host's solid tissues, pass through five larval instars. The first instar is spent totally within the body of the host. Later on, the strange development of a larval sac bulging through the intersegmental membrane of the host gives away the presence of the parasite. Some host bugs may have more than one sac sticking out of their body, and in many cases the parasite's sac may become as big as the bug's abdomen.

As it grows, the larval sac, or thylacium as it is known, which is made up of the shed skins of earlier instars and sometimes from an over-growth of the host's own tissues, becomes dark and shiny. When mature and ready to pupate, the larva exits through a split in its covering sac and moves to lower parts of the vegetation or the ground layer where it spins a cocoon.

Some species may have more than one generation in a single year.

The host bug normally dies when the fully grown larva, having consumed a major proportion of its abdominal contents, leaves to pupate. Parasitized adult bugs may suffer some changes in the structure of their genitalia – males show female characteristics and the internal sexual organs are usually atrophied.

Closely related to the Dryinidae and sometimes regarded as a subfamily are a couple of dozen species which comprise the Embolemidae. Smaller than dryinids, embolemids do not have as broad a recorded host range. While the biology of this group is still very poorly known, the bug species parasitized by them belong to a very few fulgoroid families such as the **Achilidae**. The genera *Ampulicomorpha* and *Embolemus* contain almost all the known species.

Parasitica

Within the apocritan division or infraorder Parasitica there are many specialized wasp families whose members attack a wide range of insect host species. While some families have broad preferences, others are restricted in their host choice, and many species are ecto- or endo-parasitoids of the eggs, nymphs and adults of hemipterans. A few species are hyperparasitoids – that is to say, they are parasitoids of other parasitoids living in the bodies of bugs.

Within the very large and widely distributed family Braconidae, the majority of which attack species in the Lepidoptera, Diptera and Coleoptera, species of *Leiophron*, *Persitenus*, *Euphorus* and others (subfamily Euphorinae) are particularly associated with plant bugs (**Miridae**). *Aridelus* species are known to attack nymphal and adult pentatomid shield bugs, while species of *Holdawayella* and *Wesmaelia* have been reared from lace bugs and damsel bugs respectively.

Some euphorine species attacking mirid and other types of bug are very host-specific; others are capable of parasitizing several closely related hosts within the same family. In general, a typical euphorine female wasp will seek out and catch a second or third instar nymphal host, which she may seize and lift from the foliage or pin down. A single egg is laid by means of her ovipositor, which penetrates the host on the ventral body surface between the abdomen and thorax or at the base of a leg where it joins the thorax. The unfortunate victim seems to make a speedy recovery from the attack.

On hatching, the pale, legless larva moves freely about in the body cavity, consuming fluids and tissues. After four or five moults the larva is fully grown and will have caused the abdomen of its host to become swollen; it now escapes to the outside through a small exit which it cuts in the abdominal cuticle. Pupation takes place in a cocoon on the ground or a small way beneath it.

The host bug dies shortly after the larva has made its escape. In natural conditions the effects of parasitism can sometimes be quite impressive, with nearly 70 per cent of hosts in a particular location being attacked.

As with many other wasp groups, the host range of many braconid species is not known. It is almost certain that there are an additional 20,000–30,000 undescribed species in the family, some of which will be hemipteran parasitoids.

A common sight in a colony of aphids is the presence of strange, papery-looking, dark or pale-coloured swollen individuals stuck to the surface of a leaf. These mummified adult aphids are the result of parasitism by species of wasp belonging to the family Aphidiidae. All the known species are endoparasitoids of aphidoids, and some are of great value in the control of these ubiquitous and destructive sternorrhynchan bugs. *Ephedrus*, *Praon*, *Aphidius*, *Pauesia* and *Trioxys* are common and widespread genera typical of the family.

Before she dies, a single female wasp, depending on species, may parasitize up to several hundred aphids. After she lays her single egg inside the body of the aphid, special outer layers of cells develop on the egg. These layers take up nutrients from the surrounding body fluids of the host and the egg grows considerably. By the time the grub-like larva is mature it will have consumed all the inside organs and fluids: it then cuts a small hole on the underside of the host's body, through which it spins silk threads which stick the hollow shell of the aphid to the leaf or plant surface. Depending on the species, the wasp will either pupate inside the host's body (for example, *Praon* spp.) or emerge through the hole on the underside where it will spin a silk chamber in which to pupate (for example, *Aphidius* spp.). When the transformation to the adult stage is complete, the wasp will cut a neat, circular hole on the dorsal surface of the host and fly away.

Most of the 20,000 or so wasp species belonging to the Ichneumonidae, an enormous hymenopteran family, are parasitoids of insects that exhibit complete metamorphosis – that is, those such as the Lepidoptera, Diptera and Coleoptera that have a pupal stage. The few species that have been reared from hemipteran hosts have been present as hyperparasitoids of braconid wasps.

While the majority of the 1,000 or so small, dark-coloured wasp species belonging to the family Platygastridae attack gall midges (Cecidomyiidae), a few are internal parasitoids or hyperparasitoids of some aphidoids, pseudococcids, whiteflies and psyllids. Species in the genera *Alloptropa* and *Amitus* are specialists on mealy bugs (**Pseudococcidae**) and whiteflies (**Aleyrodidae**) respectively.

Although insects belonging to other orders are attacked, sternorrhynchan species belonging to families in the superfamilies Aphidoidea, Coccoidea and Aleyrodoidea are the principal hosts for the small, stout-bodied wasp species belonging to the Aphelinidae. This family, occurring worldwide with over 1,000 known species, is sometimes regarded as a subfamily of another wasp family, the Encyrtidae.

The life histories of aphelinids can be very complicated; in some species, such as those belonging to the genus *Coccophagus*, the males develop on the outside of the same host bug species as the females or inside a different host species. In other species of *Coccophagus* and *Encarsia*, the males may develop as hyperparasitoids of other wasp species or as autoparasitoids of the immature females of their own species. In the latter case, a virgin female locates a host which has already been parasitized and inserts an unfertilized egg which is always destined to become male.

In general these wasps, capable of very high rates of parasitism, are of great value as their hosts are almost universally pest species which do great damage to commercially important plants. Several aphelinid species are successfully used as biological control agents. A well-documented case relates to the wasp *Encarsia formosa*, a parasitoid of that widespread pest the Greenhouse Whitefly, *Trialeurodes vaporariorum* (**Aleyrodidae**). Not only do these wasps parasitize their hosts, but they can also kill without egg laying, for the females of some species feed on their host's eggs or body fluids which leak from lacerations caused by their ovipositors.

In addition to those aphelinid genera already mentioned, *Prospaltella*, *Aphytis* and *Aphelinus* are of considerable importance.

Worldwide, several thousand small or very small wasp species comprise the family Encyrtidae. Although insects in several other orders may serve as hosts, many are well-known parasitoids of nymphal and adult stages of sternorrhynchan bugs and the eggs of bugs in several heteropteran families. The majority of encyrtid wasps develop inside the bodies of their hosts and some are hyperparasitoids, the female depositing her eggs within the larvae of other wasp parasitoids inside their hosts.

The bugs attacked include species in just about every coccoid family, many aphid species, psyllids, cercopids and membracids. The eggs of shield bugs, assassin bugs and squash bugs are also utilized by some encyrtid species.

Adult wasps may feed on the carbohydrate-rich honeydew produced by their hosts or on their body fluids. Once located, a host insect, typically an adult female scale insect, is carefully examined all over by the female wasp. By means of her antennae and other sensory organs the wasp must establish whether or not it is suitable to receive an egg. In the case of hyperparasitic species, the female must penetrate the host's body and feel about with her ovipositor to locate a parasitoid larva before it too is pierced and an egg is laid.

The eggs of some encyrtids have hollow, stalk-like elongations which stay in place, partially protruding through the cuticle of the host's body. When hatched, the young larvae are thus able to obtain oxygen by keeping the spiracles at the posterior end of their body inside the funnel-shaped breathing stalk.

Polyembryony occurs in some encyrtid species which attack large hosts such as caterpillars. A single egg may divide repeatedly and ultimately give rise to tens, hundreds or even thousands of adult wasps, all emerging from the same host.

Because of their attacks on scale insects of all kinds, encyrtid wasps are of great benefit to the human race. Many species have been used very successfully as biological control agents against a number of damaging pests. Of the very many common and widespread genera, *Anagyrus*, *Blastothrix*, *Habrolepis* and *Comperiella* are noted bug enemies.

Over 3,000 species of wasp worldwide are currently placed in the large family Pteromalidae. Pteromalids are generally small, and most have beautiful metallic coloration. In the main, these wasps are parasitoids of Lepidoptera, Coleoptera, Diptera and Hymenoptera. The larvae can be parasitoids or hyperparasitoids, solitary or gregarious, and can feed inside or outside their host's bodies. Species belonging to a few pteromalid genera are parasitoids of scale insects, while others are predacious on the eggs of planthoppers and scale insects. Many species, although they may be reared from aphidoids and coccoids, are in fact hyperparasitic on the larvae of other parasitic wasp species inside the host bug's body.

The Eulophidae is another large and diverse family of small, often metallic-coloured wasps, some of whose 3,000 or so member species are predators or parasitoids inside the eggs or nymphs of bugs. Within the Hemiptera, the bugs affected by these wasps include several families in the Coccoidea, the **Aleyrodidae, Psyllidae, Cicadellidae, Delphacidae, Membracidae** and a very few heteropteran groups. Notable eulophid genera containing species with bug hosts are *Aprostocetus* and *Euderomphale*.

Most of the specialized egg parasitoids belong to the Mymaridae, a family of worldwide distribution containing in excess of 1,300 species. As in many other parasitic wasp families, there are probably many undescribed species and the host range will eventually prove to be much larger. The genera *Polynemus*, *Alaptus* and *Gonatocerus* are widespread and, although some species parasitize beetle, fly and barklice eggs, the majority are destructive to bugs' eggs.

These very small or minute wasps, which are the smallest of any insects on Earth, have an exceedingly delicate appearance and, as a result, are often known as fairyflies. Some species, with a body length of 0.2 mm (around a thousandth of an inch), are smaller than some single-celled protozoan organisms. The wings of fairyflies are not conventional but consist of narrowly elongate, hair-fringed struts. The air is so dense a medium in relation to the wasps that they row through it rather than fly.

Interestingly, the females of some species enter water and swim down to locate the submerged eggs of aquatic insects. All known species are egg parasitoids and, although a very wide range of insect hosts is used, the eggs of sternorrhynchan and auchenorrhynchan bugs and, to a lesser extent, heteropteran bugs are a favourite target. Hemipteran families that contain species known as mymarid hosts include all manner of scale insects and aphids, leafhoppers, planthoppers, spittle bugs, whiteflies, plant bugs and lace bugs.

In general, female mymarids do not live very long and do not contain a very large number of eggs. Typically, very fresh host eggs are preferred and, after the female has assessed their quality by feeling and tapping the eggs with her antennae, she will insert a single egg of her own into each of the available host eggs. The larva hatches and consumes the egg's contents before pupating inside the now empty shell.

Some species of the widespread genera *Anagrus* and *Paranagrus* are of great value in the control of serious pests such as the Sugarcane Leafhopper. Many other species exert an important control over a variety of potential bug pests.

Some species belonging to two other wasp families, the Trichogrammatidae and Scelionidae, are known to attack bug eggs. Within the Trichogrammatidae, species of the genera *Oligosita* and *Paracentrobia* are noteworthy. Some scelionids of the genera *Teleonomus* and *Trissolcus* attack a range of freshly laid hemipteran eggs. The minute females of some species in the genera *Limnodytes* and *Tiphodytes* can swim through water using their wings and lay their eggs in the eggs of pondskaters (**Gerridae**). In order to avoid superparasitism many scelionid species, such as those of *Trissolcus* which attack pentatomid shield bugs, draw their ovipositor over the top surface of the parasitized egg. The mark left, which may be physical or chemical, deters other females when they examine the host egg for suitability.

Chapter 5
Bug Defences

From Chapter 4 it might be thought that the Hemiptera are a rather helpless group of insects, barely able to protect themselves from destruction. Nothing could be further from the truth, for they make use of myriad physical, behavioural and physiological defensive strategies.

These defences include kicking, jumping or rapid escape flight, as seen in many planthoppers, leafhoppers, psyllids and other auchenorrhynchan families. Cryptic camouflage and warning coloration are used by bug species in many families. Mimicry of inanimate objects such as thorns or dangerous insects such as ants, wasps or bees is a common approach. The production of special irritant, toxic or repellent secretions is characteristic of Heteroptera; while the use of pheromones to cause rapid dispersal of colony members under threat and to bring the colony all together is widespread.

Physical protection from predators can be afforded by spines (as, for instance, in treehoppers), tough cuticular armour (shield bugs) or waxy coverings (many sternorrhynchans). When attacked, bugs may stab out with their rostrum (try

A pair of bizarre-looking coreid bugs *Phyllomorpha laciniata* superbly camouflaged against the flower heads of their *Paronychia* host plant, seem well hidden from predators. The strongly leaf-like, spiny lateral expansions of the abdomen and pronotum represent the oddest modifications seen in the entire family. Israel. **Coreidae**

Often living high in the rain forest canopy, treehoppers belonging to the genus *Sphongophorus* have a greatly enlarged and strangely shaped pronotum which, in some species, can be much bigger than the rest of the body. This species, *S. guerini*, resting on a vine stem in Trinidad, has two antler-like projections. **Membracidae**

handling a reduviid or notonectid bug in a rough manner) and can inject toxic salivary juices. If seized, some species, particularly mirid bugs, can shed their legs quickly, and some coreid species may have odd, brightly coloured, leaf-like tibial expansions to distract a bird or other predator's attention from the body. As already discussed, many bugs have evolved mutualistic relationships with ants, which act as personal bodyguards. Finally, although not a great deal of detail is known, some bugs can mount a sort of immunological response involving the encapsulation and destruction of parasitoid eggs laid within their bodies.

Chemical defences

In many groups chemical defence systems are patchily distributed, but within the Hemiptera their presence is characteristic of the suborder Heteroptera, including many of the aquatic and semi-aquatic species.

Some years ago I was beating the foliage of oak trees in a wood near Oxford to collect nymphal plant bugs (**Miridae**). An adult shield bug, *Pentatoma rufipes* (**Pentatomidae**), was shaken from the leaves and I put it in my pooter before sucking up the many species of mirid rapidly escaping from the beating tray. Although I was aware of a strong, but not unpleasant, taste and smell, collecting fervour drove me on. But the effects of a mere ten minutes' exposure to that stink bug's scent gave me a vicious headache which lasted for eight hours and caused my throat to become inflamed and swollen for two days. I had become a victim of chemical warfare; despite its efforts, the shield bug responsible is now on a pin.

Mimicry of bees and wasps is not confined to heteropteran bugs. Here a black and yellow marked, rain forest-dwelling leafhopper (*Lissocarta vespiformis*) holds up its transparent wings in a very wasp-like pose. Peru. **Cicadellidae**

Heteropteran chemical defence centres on specialized scent glands in the metathorax of adults and the abdomen of nymphs. Particular groups of bugs may have different sorts of main predators, such as ants, birds, reptiles and fish, and their defensive secretions have evolved to target the appropriate creature. The compounds may work as vapours or as soluble liquids, to be sprayed into the eyes or mouth of an attacker or wiped by the bug on to the surface of the attacker where they may penetrate beneath the cuticle or skin. Indirect or accidental predation may be prevented by scent – for instance, the smell of grass-feeding bugs may put off grazing sheep, cows and horses.

Recent studies have shown that these secretions may also contain components which function variously as short-range aphrodisiacs and sexual attractants for mate location and courtship, aggregation, dispersal or alarm signals, or self-applied antifungal treatments. Some of the gland products are chemically very similar to the alarm pheromones of ant species and their effects may well be directed towards these major predators, causing them to scatter in panic. The use of scent secretions as an antibacterial or antifungal agent has been suggested in a number of bug species, particularly those in aquatic families where the need for antiseptic conditions on the bug's surface might be greater.

A few bugs, such as certain species of the **Reduviidae**, have additional glands in other locations. Brindley's glands, for instance, are found under the dorsal surface of the first abdominal segment; a few shield bugs and cotton stainers, among others, have ventral glands on the underside of the abdomen. In some species these additional scent glands are responsible for the production of sexual

Only the yellow-green colour of the adult female gives away the presence of this group of fantastically camouflaged bugs (*Coriplatus depressus*) resting on the lichen-covered bark of a tree deep in the Peruvian rain forest. Nymphs and a male, copulating with the female, are barely visible. **Pentatomidae**

odours or pheromones. There is good evidence that bugs make their own scent utilizing a number of biochemical metabolic pathways and to some extent may obtain precursors of the scent compounds from the sap of their food plants.

Nymphs

In immature bugs, the sac-like dorsal abdominal glands are found beneath the surface of the cuticle on the dorsal surface of the abdomen. The glands open to the outside by means of ostioles or scent gland openings, which may be single or paired, and are placed in a body mid-line between the dorsal abdominal segments or tergites (Fig. 11: iii). There are never more than four ostioles and they may occur between the tergites of segments three and four, four and five, five and six, and six and seven.

The number, type and location of the ostiole vary between families or subfamilies, and can be used as a rough classification of nymphs found in the field. For example, plant bugs (**Miridae**) have a single nymphal gland opening located between tergites three and four, while shield bug nymphs have three paired openings between tergites three and four, four and five, and five and six. Some bugs such as dipsocorids (**Dipsocoridae**) and species in a few other families possess the maximum number of four ostioles, although here one or more of the glands and their associated ostioles are very much reduced or rudimentary. Other species, in families such as the **Gerridae**, **Notonectidae**, **Belostomatidae** and **Gelastocoridae**, may have no nymphal glands or openings at all.

Under cover of darkness, this Trinidadian millipede has been caught by the assassin bug *Brantosoma notata*. This bug is aposematically coloured and short-winged. Although tropical millipedes are able to produce highly repugnant secretions to protect themselves from attack, many predacious bugs seem to be immune to their effects. **Reduviidae**

Fig. 11. (i) View of the underside of an adult heteropteran bug's thorax, showing location of metathoracic scent gland openings. *(ii)* Magnification of the surface sculpturing of the 'evaporative' or scent-retentive area around the gland opening. *(iii)* Heteropteran nymph with three dorsal abdominal gland openings. (**Lygaeidae**)

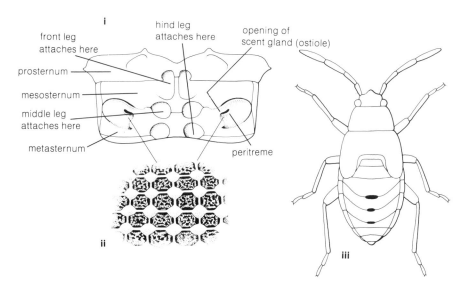

A black and white, weed-feeding, largid bug (*Arhaphe cicindeloides*) runs across gravel-strewn ground in Arizona. Species belonging to the subfamily Arhaphinae have a characteristically swollen head, a constricted pronotum and short wings. The dark body colour and pale marks on the wings make it an excellent mimic of mutillid wasps (velvet ants), which are well known for their powerful venom. USA. **Largidae**

Typically, the nymphal glands are constructed as simple invaginations of the intersegmental membranes. The inner surface of the gland sac is lined with thin cuticle to act as a reservoir for the substances produced by the secretory cells which surround it and form the wall of the sac. The cells empty into the gland sac through microscopic cuticle-lined ductules. As the sac fills up, its contents may be expelled by the contraction of special muscles which flatten the sac and open its neck. The secretions pass along the neck of the gland sac leading to the ostiole and thus to the outside of the body.

Nymphal glands may not all be the same size or equally active, and species which have more than one gland may produce different secretions in different places. For instance, in some nymphal cotton stainers the first two abdominal glands produce odours which encourage aggregation, while those of the third gland are responsible for defence and alarm-raising.

In chemical terms, the secretions of dorsal abdominal glands are mainly variants of unsaturated carbonyl compounds and alcohols with a short to medium carbon chain length. While the nature of the secretions varies from family to family, relatively few species have been studied in detail. Nymphal seed bug (**Lygaeidae**) secretions contain 4-oxo-alk-2-enals, alk-2-enals and alkanes.

Shield bug nymphs can produce in addition octenals, hexenals, tridecane and benzaldehyde.

The nymphal glands, which are usually only active during the nymphal instars, are lost or become atrophied when the last moult takes place; their function is then taken over by the adult metathoracic glands. There are, however, exceptions, and in some bugs one or more of the nymphal glands may continue to function in adult life.

.Adults
On reaching the adult stage, heteropteran bugs are defended by special paired thoracic glands within the posterior or metathoracic segment. They open to the outside of the body through small apertures on either side of the metasternum between the middle and hind pairs of legs (Fig. 11:i). All species in the **Aphelocheiridae** and **Nepidae**, and some in the **Notonectidae**, **Gelastocoridae** and **Belostomatidae**, lack metathoracic scent glands.

Although within the suborder there is considerable variation in structure and arrangement of gland components, the system is typically composed of large masses of tissue which make up the main glands. These tissues do not form the inner lining of the gland reservoir as in nymphal abdominal glands, but are separated from the reservoir or sac by a duct through which they empty their products. Smaller glands in the reservoir wall are believed to secrete the enzymes which act on the products of the main glands to change their chemical structure to that of the final ejected substances.

Two brightly-coloured, leaf-footed bugs mate on a leaf in the rain forests of Costa Rica. The foliar expansions of the tibiae might serve to confuse predators into attacking there rather than at more vulnerable parts of the body. *Anisoscelis* sp. **Coreidae**

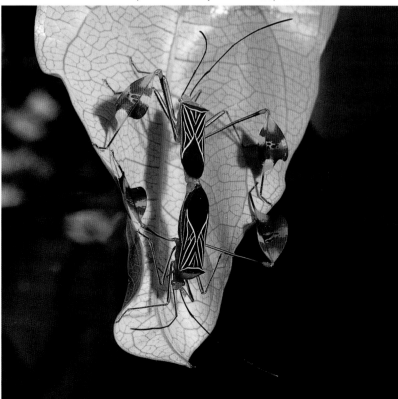

This fifth instar, alydid bug nymph (*Hyalymenus* sp.) assumes a very ant-like appearance as it moves across foliage in Trinidad. The swollen rear portion of the abdomen clearly shows a pair of slit-like scent gland openings. **Alydidae**

In some species the paired glands may have their own separate lateral reservoirs, or they may both empty into the main median scent reservoir. When the bug is attacked, disturbed, handled or responding to some other stimulus, the contents of the median reservoir are discharged by indirect muscular action and the natural elasticity of the reservoir through ducts leading to the scent opening or ostiole. The scent gland apparatus has a valve system operated by special muscles which, when contracted, pull on a cuticular lever to open the scent duct. The secretions, which in some species can be directed at an attacker or predator with some force in a stream or spray, leave through the ostiole and run along a furrow-shaped channel called the peritreme.

Land-dwelling bugs may have a large area of specially modified cuticle surrounding the ostiole and peritreme; this is known as the scent accumulation area or evaporative area. The structure of the cuticle in this region as revealed by scanning electron microscopy is a complex three-dimensional system of pleats, folds, furrows and strange mushroom-shaped bodies (Fig. 11:ii). Its function, it has long been thought, is to enhance the dispersal and thus evaporation of the scents over a greater area. However, recent findings suggest that its main purpose may be to prevent the scent compounds from damaging the bug. The openings of the metathoracic spiracles (breathing holes) are very close by, and the strange sculpturing of the cuticle surrounding the ostiole and peritreme may hold the scent and prevent its spread into these sensitive areas. In many bugs, the droplets of scent that are produced in response to a particular stimulus may, if needed, be drawn back into the scent reservoir for reuse.

The metathoracic secretions produced by adult bugs are generally more complex and varied than those produced by nymphs and fall into several major chemical categories such as the aliphatic aldehydes (=alkanals), aliphatic alcohols (=alkanols) and dicarbonyl compounds. The final product of these

Capable of producing noxious and repellent, volatile secretions from dorsal abdominal glands, these three fifth instar coreid nymphs are well protected from attack as they sit on the leaf of a climbing plant in the Brazilian cerradão (scrubby savanna). **Coreidae**

glands, which to the human nose may range from disagreeably acrid to pleasantly fruity, can consist of complicated mixtures, the separate components of which may have different functions. Hexyl acetate, geranyl acetate, ethyl acrylate, hydroxybutanals, benzyl alcohol, butyric and hexanoic acids, sesquiterpenes, monoterpenes, phenolics, ketones, hydrogen peroxide and very many others are just part of a long and steadily growing list of organic compounds produced by adult bug stink glands.

Function: specific examples
The metathoracic scent gland secretions of adult pygmy backswimmers (**Pleidae**) contain large amounts of hydrogen peroxide and a few other compounds. Pleid bugs are known to leave the water and quickly spread the gland secretions over their ventral body surfaces, using their legs. The secretions, which unlike those having a primarily defensive role, have no noticeable smell and are bactericidal. In particular they help to keep clean those parts of the cuticle which function as an air store when the bugs are submerged.

In contrast to the secretions of pleids, those produced by adult water boatmen (**Corixidae**) are strong-smelling and released as a defensive strategy when threatened. But these bugs show similar secretion-grooming behaviour to that seen in pleids, and their secretions too have strong antibacterial properties. Corixids will either rise to the surface or climb a little way out of the water, and the metathoracic gland secretions are spread in a matter of a few seconds by means of the legs, one side of the body being treated at a time. As in pleids, it is thought that the secretions prevent the growth of micro-organisms among the dense fields of water-repellent hairs which retain the bubbles of air essential to underwater living. Adults of some corixid genera and the nymphs of all species do not, however, behave in this way.

Some species need to aggregate for feeding or mating, or to disperse rapidly in response to danger; this may be triggered off by metathoracic scent gland secretions. Waving a piece of filter paper covered with the body fluids of a crushed or damaged bug over a feeding group of bugs of the same species will cause a very speedy evasive response. Sometimes the scents of closely related species will also function as alarm pheromones and cause dispersal.

The metathoracic glands of some bugs are sexually dimorphic, suggesting a sexual role. In many species of shield bug and leaf-footed bug secretions from dorsal abdominal glands or specialized patches of cuticle on the underside of the abdomen act as powerful species-specific sexual pheromones to attract females and, in some cases, other males. The smells given off by copulating bugs can prove an irresistible lure for other males, which will even attempt to mate with one or other of the mating pair. In coreid bugs these glandular regions are ventral, between the seventh and eighth abdominal segment. The sexual odours are typically a variety of aromatic alcohol compounds and esters. Interestingly, some of these compounds are constituents of perfumes and flavourings such as vanillin, oil of roses, geranium and cherries.

The production of sexual attractant odours is probably widespread and it is known that bugs belonging to other heteropteran families such as the **Miridae**, **Lygaeidae**, **Pyrrhocoridae** and **Cimicidae** produce chemicals to attract males or females. In many cases the nature of the pheromones and the exact place on the body where they come from are not yet known.

When bugs are crop pests there is an obvious advantage in being able to isolate and chemically imitate sexual pheromones. Once the chemical structure of the odour has been identified, traps can be designed with in-built odours to attract large numbers of bugs before they mate and lay eggs. On the other hand, some bugs such as the predatory shield bugs belonging to the pentatomid subfamily Asopinae are extremely valuable in killing pests, and the use of their sexual pheromones could enhance their impact as biological control agents. The identification of several bug sex pheromones has already been achieved, and in time many more will give up their secrets to gas chromatograph and mass spectrometer.

Evolution, however, can turn the tables on the best-laid plans of bugs, and it is known that certain parasitic flies (Tachindae) and a number of hymenopteran parasitoids in several families use the defensive scents and sexual odours of nymphal and adult bugs as cues to locate and thus parasitize them or their eggs. Recent findings have revealed that shield bugs and leaf-footed bugs, when snared in webs, are not just eaten by the spiders. Very small flies belonging to the family Machilidae are attracted by the defensive gland secretions of the trapped bugs and fly in to share the meal. This and other fascinating inter-relationships are probably quite widespread.

In heteropteran bugs, chemical defences against predation are not just confined to the metathoracic and abdominal glands. Many species of insect which feed or gather openly are distasteful to birds and other insect-eaters and advertise the fact with bold black, red and yellow warning coloration. One of the best-known examples is the Monarch Butterfly *Danaus plexippus*, whose aposematic (warningly-coloured) caterpillars take up and isolate (sequester) poisonous cardiac glycosides (cardenolides) from their milkweed (*Asclepias* spp.) host plants and store them in their bodies. These compounds are very unpalatable and generally make the birds vomit; high doses can even be fatal.

The trick of sequestering toxic compounds from plants is also used by bugs. Some rhopalids (**Rhopalidae**) make toxic cyanogenic glucosides from cyanolipids sequestered from their host plants (Sapindaceae). The toxins are present in the bug's body fluids, which can be released in small amounts through intersegmental membranes. Many seed-feeding lygaeid bugs such as the red and black Milkweed Bug, *Oncopeltus fasciatus*, are able to store just below the dorsal surface toxic cardenolides obtained from their host plants. The ability to sequester plant chemicals such as cardiac glycosides and pyrrolizidine alkaloids as defensive compounds is shared by nearly 30 lygaeid genera.

Unpalatable bugs are invariably brightly coloured, so that after a few unpleasant encounters predators learn to avoid them. Sequestered plant compounds may not necessarily have the same effect on all predatory animals. Toad, lizard and bird species attacking chemically protected bugs vary in their responses; some may reject the bugs rapidly, while others may find them palatable.

The nymphs of some lace bug species (**Tingidae**) possess specialized hairs and spines on their antennae and dorsal surfaces. These hairs are capable of secreting a repellent chemical cocktail of hydrochromones and diketones which is very efficient at deterring birds. Secretory hairs and spines also occur on the nymphs

Closely related to treehoppers, a cluster of adults and nymphs of *Aetalion reticulatum* are attended by a species of stingless bee (*Trigona* sp.). This species, recorded from many host plant species in South America, is attended by several species of bee and ant. The females show maternal care of their egg masses and will use their legs to scrape off parasitic wasps. At the bottom of the picture, a bee can be seen removing honeydew from the rear end of an adult bug. Peru. **Aetalionidae**

of some other heteropteran families such as the stilt bugs (**Berytidae**) and plant bugs (**Miridae**), and in nymphs and pre-adult stages of some whiteflies (**Aleyrodidae**). The substances produced through these hollow spines, presumably from glandular cells within the body, are often very sticky, and the droplets formed may protect the bugs from parasitism or predation.

Of one thing we can be certain – only a small part of the heteropteran biochemical store cupboard is fully understood. Many more surprises, a large number of novel compounds and some fascinating interactions await discovery.

Bodyguards

Ants are important, highly effective and even specialized predators of a great many insect species, including bugs. But at the same time complex and often mutualistic relationships have evolved between them and a long list of auchenorrhynchan and sternorrhynchan species and a few heteropteran species.

Among the heteropterans, ground-living nymphs and sometimes adults of a few broad-headed bugs (**Alydidae**), and damsel bugs (**Nabidae**) can look very like ants, and presumably gain protection from some predators on this account. In the **Coreidae**, many species have nymphs which are very ant-like and probably suck body fluids from their ant host's young. Similarly, the plant bug family (**Miridae**) contains many ant-mimicking species in several genera. Here the sometimes incredible similarity between the bugs and the particular ant species with which they associate enables them to prey on their host's larvae and pupae. The host ants obviously do not recognize the bugs as alien and usually allow them to feed unimpeded. The situation is probably very complex, with the involvement of special odours to fool the ants. Other predacious, ant-mimicking mirids use their resemblance to gain ready access to colonies of aphids which might be protected by ants.

New cases of interactions between heteropteran bugs and ants are being found all the time. A few plataspids (**Plataspidae**) and leaf-footed-bugs (**Coreidae**) are known to provide food for ants in return for protection from predators and parasites. The ants use their antennae to stimulate the bugs, especially the nymphs, to release droplets of sugar-rich excrement (honeydew). Undoubtedly many more heteropteran–ant interactions remain undiscovered.

It is among the auchenorrhynchan and sternorrhynchan families that some of the most complicated ant relationships are found. Many of these interactions, known collectively as trophobioses, are based on the seemingly simple principle of reward (usually honeydew) for services rendered (usually protection). In many cases the reward gained far outweighs the cost of providing the service. The relationships can be very specific, involving just a single ant species and one bug species, or slightly broader, with one ant species associating with more than one bug and vice versa.

The interaction between the two partner species can range from occasional and non-essential to constant and critical to the survival of the bug species. In some cases, the ant species too may depend on honeydew as its main food source. The sight of ants attending colonies of aphids or scale insects is common; anyone out for a walk or working in the garden will be able to observe them.

The plants, too, play an important role. Phloem sap-sucking sternorrhynchan bugs within the superfamilies Psylloidea, Aphidoidea and Coccoidea, and species in auchenorrhynchan families such as the **Fulgoridae**, **Cixiidae**, **Membracidae**, **Cicadellidae** and **Cercopidae**, exhibit varying degrees of ant trophobiosis. These bugs consume vast quantities of watery sap from which they extract the nutrients they require. The most essential components of their diet, present in low concentrations in the food, are those containing nitrogen. Carbohydrates in the form of sugars of all kinds are present in abundance, and, as most of this is not required, it passes out of the anus in solution. Almost all the dry weight of honeydew is in the form of sugars.

Many bugs have evolved means of firing or somehow propelling the honeydew

Many treehopper species have complex and interesting mutualistic relationships with ants. Here a Brazilian species, *Gelastogonia erythropus*, is attended by a small ant species. In return for sweet honeydew, ants will fiercely defend their hosts from enemies.
Membracidae

away from their bodies, for as it dries it becomes very sticky and could pose serious problems. The honeydew can either fall to the ground or be dropped on foliage, sometimes in vast amounts. These species that have become associated with ants show an array of adaptations: some have special anal hairs which hold the honeydew until it is removed, others will only release the honeydew when stimulated by the ants, and yet others which can eject their honeydew will not do so if ants are present.

In return for this rich reward, which may be laced with other attractants and valuable amino acids, the ants act as bodyguards. They can be ferocious, and when protecting colonies of their particular aphid or scale insect will attack anything, predator or parasitic wasp, that comes near. Evolution has produced a few very specialized aphid and scale insect predators such as lacewing larvae which are able to fool the ants by disguising themselves physically or chemically in various ways. Some root aphid species (**Anoeciidae**), which depend on ants to excavate underground chambers next to roots and to protect them, can still be parasitized by specialized wasps. Using antennal contact and leg rubbing, the wasps mimic the ants' behaviour and may produce chemicals to control the ants' aggressive tendencies.

The range and complexity of these bug–ant relationships can be quite awe-inspiring. When aphid colonies are attacked by a predator, individual aphids may kick out at the foe and release defensive secretions from their abdominal siphunculi or cornicles. These secretions are sticky and also contain specific alarm pheromones which alert the rest of the colony to the danger and, in many cases, attract large numbers of the aphids' bodyguards.

Some bugs, which have evolved to become almost totally dependent on ants for protection, have a reduced ability to protect themselves physically, chemically or in other ways. The ants may provide additional services to ensure their survival. They may protect the host plant from generalist herbivores by catching and biting or throwing insects such as caterpillars from the leaves. Their presence may also prevent the build-up of sooty moulds such as *Botrytis* which grows on honeydew and can reduce photosynthesis by blocking out sunlight.

Bug colony size and reproductive potential increase, and the numbers parasitized decrease, when the bugs are attended by ants. Some of the most advanced relationships involve the ants treating their colonies of bugs much as a farmer looks after livestock. In some instances, ants attending colonies of root aphids will take their charges into their nest during the colder months to protect them from frosts. When spring comes, the ants take the young nymphs to suitable plant roots where they can feed. Some mealy bug species (**Pseudococcidae**) are kept in the ants' nest. When feeding on foliage they are protected, and if danger threatens they either clamber on to the ants' backs or are carried to safety in the ants' jaws. Some ant species may build carton-like shelters over their bug colonies, and move their herds from plant to plant. A few may perform a culling operation to regulate the numbers in a bug colony if they get too large. Special ant secretions regulate the developmental processes within the colony, for instance by slowing down the production of winged aphids. Ants may be partly responsible for the spread of plant-borne virus diseases by moving aphids from plant to plant, and they may also reduce the efficacy of parasitic wasp species used in biological control efforts against pest bugs.

But ants are not the only insects which take honeydew from colonies of sap-sucking bugs. Stingless bees belonging to the genus *Trigona*, other bee species, social wasp species and a few beetles and flies will feed on honeydew; but not all the relationships are trophobiotic. Wasps such as those of the genus *Polistes* can be highly attracted to scale insect honeydew, and when other food such as plant nectar is in poor supply they will compete very strongly with other insects for the sweet substance. While it is true that some of these non-ant honeydew harvesters such as the wasps and bees do protect the bugs from attack, some do not give anything back and can be regarded as straightforward thieves. As with the biochemical defences of the Heteroptera, much remains to be learnt about these highly evolved symbiotic relationships.

Soldiers

Aphids, sometimes disparagingly described as small bags of haemolymph on legs, may seem defenceless without their ant protectors; but even here there are surprises. For a long time the only insects thought to show sociality in varying degrees were social wasps and bees (Hymenoptera) and termites (Isoptera). So the discovery, some 20 years ago, of a special solider caste in species belonging to the aphid family **Pemphigidae** was of great interest. In essence these species operate a division of labour, with a reproductive caste and a worker (or soldier) caste which does not reproduce.

First instar nymphs of the Sugarcane Woolly Aphid (*Ceratovacuna lanigera*), for example, serve as colony defenders. These nymphs, born of wingless adults, will attack predators such as hover fly larvae with their sharply pointed frontal horns. In addition, the young nymphs secrete from their abdominal cornicles droplets which are spread on the attacker's body. The secretion contains an alarm pheromone which causes the adult aphids in the colony to back away and calls up many more of the sterile soldier nymphs.

Several gall-inhabiting aphid species have a first instar soldier caste whose job is to protect the rest of the colony. In these species, the soldiers may have distinctively thickened or lengthened legs which are used to kick and pierce. Experiments and field observations have shown that the soldiers are well able to keep at bay predators such as anthocorid bugs and herbivores such as moth caterpillars. They will kill eggs or larvae of a wide range of insects, and will even attempt to pierce human skin.

The fighting techniques used by soldier castes vary from species to species. Some use their hind legs to tear cuticle, others have sharp horns, and many use their short, stout rostrum to stab the attacker. The soldiers will attack most things alien or likely to be a threat to the colony, and while they are not capable of killing ants it is interesting that ants are rarely associated with species which produce a soldier caste.

The presence of a soldier caste has now been established in many aphid species, and the phenomenon is probably quite widespread. Soldier castes have already been found in the genera *Pemphigus* and *Colophina* belonging to the **Pemphigidae** and *Ceratoglyphina*, *Pseudoregma* and *Ceratovacuna*, which are placed in the closely related **Hormaphididae**.

Although soldiers may spend much longer in the first instar and be able to feed, in the vast majority of species they do not live past the first instar and are thus effectively sterile. In the aphid *Pemphigus spirothecae*, spirally shaped galls are formed on the leaf petioles of the host plant, Black Poplar (*Populus nigra*). Unusually, the soldiers that survive their first instar develop into wingless adults and give rise parthenogenetically to both more soldier first instar nymphs and normal first instar nymphs. The latter will ultimately become the winged generation whose job it is to produce the sexual forms.

Waxes and resins

Many sternorrhynchan bug species feeding gregariously in exposed positions on their host plants protect themselves by secreting wax in the form of threads, sheets, powders or resins, which form a scale-like covering. The waxes have many roles, such as protecting eggs or surrounding droplets of honeydew and thus preventing them from fouling the colony. Wax maintains a stable microenvironment around the insect, freeing the bug from temperature and humidity fluctuations and to some extent protecting it from rain, parasitoids and predators. Species which live inside galls or are tended by ants do not produce copious body wax.

Wax-secreting species occur in all the sternorrhynchan superfamilies – the Psylloidea, Aleyrodoidea, Adelgoidea, Aphidoidea and Coccoidea. The nymphs of many psyllids produce large quantities of white waxy material, while the nymphal and adult stages of whiteflies are covered with scaly or powdery waxes. Some aphids such as the woolly aphids (*Eriosoma* spp., **Pemphigidae**) have reduced defensive abdominal cornicles but are well endowed with wax glands all over their body surface. The well-known Woolly Apple Aphid, *Eriosoma* *lanigerum*, is easily recognizable by the tangled masses of white wax that it sec-retes. In the **Adelgidae**, wingless females and nymphs of conifer woolly aphids, or pine and spruce adelgids as they are also known, live on the bark, needles, cones and twigs of their host trees under tufted masses of white wax threads. The closely related phylloxerans do not produce threads of wax, but may have a dusting of powdery wax.

The wax and resin producers *par excellence* are coccoids. These bugs may be covered with anything ranging from sparse waxy threads to complete, dense and impenetrable tangles. Species belonging to the **Coccidae**, **Pseudococcidae** and **Diaspididae** are of particular note, and many yield commercial quantities of these valuable materials in a very pure state.

In general, the wax is produced from special glands located underneath the cuticle in the epidermal layers. The number of glands may vary from a few tens to tens of thousands on a single insect. The glands may be made up of just a few or many individual secretory cells, arranged around a common reservoir. Their products are carried to the outside via microscopic ducts.

Scanning electron microscopy has revealed that the threads produced can assume very varied and intricate shapes. Within the Coccoidea, the final wax

A wax body covering and long, white, waxy tail filaments protect these young flatid nymphs (*Phromnia rosea*) living in the tropical dry forests of Madagascar. **Flatidae**

covering may take the form of short, hollow or solid curls with a circular cross-section. Other species may produce curls of wax with a crescent-shaped or curved cross-section or large, shapeless masses. Some species produce very delicate, solid threads less than 0.1 microns in diameter, which can themselves be formed into hollow cylinders; others make ridged wax ribbons, solid cylinders, macaroni-like or even more complicated extrusions with a diameter of up to 7 microns (a micron is a thousandth of a millimetre).

Some specialized predatory insects, like ladybird larvae and a few parasitic wasps, are able to home in on coccoids by using some odour component of the waxy covering of their prey or host species. Even more complex is the behaviour of certain lacewing larvae which live among and prey on mealy bug colonies: the larvae gather the mealy bug's waxy covering and use it to build up a protective cover on their own backs. A similar habit is practised by aphid-feeding lacewing larvae, which stick the sucked-out bodies of their victims on to hooked dorsal hairs. The disguise may help them to move about, camouflaged in the colony, or protect them from predators such as birds.

The actual chemical composition of the secretions varies from family to family and species to species. In most cases, waxes and resins are the major constituents with minor amounts of triglycerols, fats, proteins and terpenes. In the Lac Insect, *Kerria lacca*, nearly 80 per cent of the secretions are resins, whereas in some species of ground pearl (**Margarodidae**) the secretions are pure wax. The structure of the wax covering and the type and distribution of the pores on the body surface are very useful in identifying many sternorrhynchan families, genera and species.

After producing long filaments of ultra-pure wax from special glands and pores in their bodies, the nymphs of this whitefly species, living in the Queensland rain forest, are totally obscured from view. Australia. **Aleyrodidae**

Chapter 6
Food and Feeding

Within the class Insecta, the habit of sucking has arisen several times. Although the end result is the same – that is, the ability to take liquids – the mouthparts of other insect groups show a range of structural sucking modifications. Butterflies and moths suck nectar through a characteristic proboscis. Bees suck nectar through a highly modified, tongue-like structure. In fleas, prolongations of parts of the mouthparts form a sucking tube and in parasitic lice, which also feed on blood, there are three slender stylets. Nectar-feeding and blood-sucking flies of various kinds display an assortment of mouthpart modifications to allow piercing or stabbing and sucking.

Bugs, however, are often described as the 'perfect suckers' because the hemipteran rostrum is uniquely adapted for the ingestion of liquid foods. Bugs' diet consists of liquids like plant sap, insect haemolymph or blood or solid food which has been predigested outside the body before being ingested. The only exception to the liquid food rule may be found in some species of corixid, which can ingest very small, solid particles of algal debris.

Gripping tightly to a plant stem in the Brazilian cerradão, a pair of warningly coloured adult coreid bugs (*Pachylis pharaonis*) drive their mouthparts into the plant's tissues to suck sap. **Coreidae**

Despite some controversy, the evidence available makes it likely that the earliest bugs of some 250–280 million years ago were plant feeders and land-living, as most still are today. On common sense grounds, the structure and backwards-directed rostrum seems to be much better adapted for a sap-sucking insect rather than a carnivore. Whole new groups of plant-eating bugs such as the aphids arose around 100 million years ago, and these must already have been pre-adapted to feed on the newly evolved Angiospermae or flowering plants.

Heteropterans' ability to bring their rostrum forwards may well have been a particular adaptation to reach and feed on particularly nutritious or inaccessible plant parts, which then made it easier for them to feed on other things such as soft-bodied, slow-moving insects. Being a herbivore is not a particularly easy job for an insect and, as will be seen later, eating plant sap can be a difficult and sometimes risky business.

All bug species belonging to the suborders Coleorrhyncha, Auchenorrhyncha and Sternorrhyncha (the Homoptera of some authors) are herbivorous, feeding on the sap or cell contents of vascular plants (those with xylem phloem transport systems). With somewhere in excess of 300,000 vascular plant species worldwide, there would seem to be no shortage of food for these bugs. A few species feed on non-vascular plants such as mosses and fungi, and the primitive peloridiids (**Peloridiidae**) are believed to feed on mosses and liverworts. While the suborder Heteroptera contains many predacious species, mixed feeders and a few specialist blood feeders, here too the majority of species are herbivorous.

There are two common ways for herbivorous bugs to feed. They can take liquid from the phloem vessels of roots, stems and leaves, which is what most auchenorrhynchan and sternorrhynchan bugs and a few heteropterans such as the **Cydnidae** do, or from xylem vessels in the case of **Cicadidae**, **Cercopidae** and some **Cicadellidae**. Alternatively, they can puncture and flush out the contents of individual cells either singly or in groups; this latter feeding method is used by members of the **Lygaeidae**, **Pyrrhocoridae**, **Miridae**, **Tingidae**, some of the pentatomoid and coreoid groups and most species in the **Cicadellidae**. Predacious bugs penetrate the cuticle of their prey through a weak spot, and then use their stylets and saliva to macerate the internal tissues before they are sucked out.

Rostrum

The unique feeding apparatus of hemipterans has contributed greatly to the success of the order as a whole. Between the suborders there are differences in design, in the way in which it operates and in its position on the head. But the description that follows is generally applicable to all bugs.

With the exception of non-feeding male scale insects and the sexual forms of a few aphids, whose mouthparts are vestigial or totally lacking, the rostrum is made up of a number of elongate components (Fig. 12:i). The outer covering of the rostrum is the labium, which can be anything from a long three- or four-segmented tube, typical of the Heteroptera, to a short, non-segmented stump as seen in some scale insects. The dorsal surface of the base of the labium, where it joins the head, is covered by a narrow, shortish or quite elongate labrum.

The dorsal surface of the labium (actually presented as the ventral surface, as

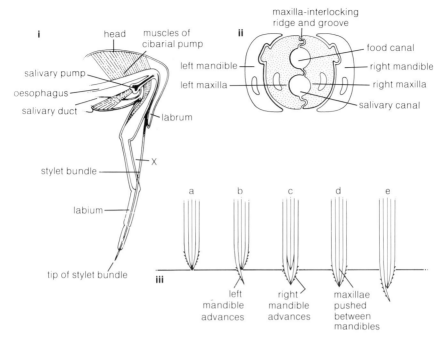

i head muscles of cibarial pump ii maxilla-interlocking ridge and groove

salivary pump

oesophagus

salivary duct

left mandible

left maxilla

labrum

food canal

right mandible

right maxilla

salivary canal

stylet bundle

labium

X

tip of stylet bundle iii

a b c d e

left mandible advances

right mandible advances

maxillae pushed between mandibles

Fig. 12. (i) Diagrammatic section through a bug's head. *(ii)* Cross-section through stylet bundle at X. *(iii)* Stages in the insertion of a bug's stylet bundle into food source. The process may be repeated many times until the required location is reached.

it lies folded backwards underneath the body) is grooved for most of its length and surrounds the long, toughened feeding stylets. The function of the labium is mainly to protect the slender stylet bundle and to act as a guide as the stylets are pushed into plant or animal tissues. Since hemipterans have no maxillary or labial palps, the labium also provides the bug with sensory information. The labial apex is equipped with a variety of chemo- and mechano-sensory receptors designed to respond to plant or prey surface texture and chemistry.

In most bugs, penetration to any great depth by the stylets is not necessary and the labium is about the same length as the stylets. When feeding, the middle segments of the labium can be folded back on each other, allowing the stylets to slide through and be clamped by the end of the last labial segment. This facility means that, if needed, the mouthparts can extend to somewhere approaching their actual length into the plant or animal tissues. In use, the stylet bundle is thus anchored only by the top and bottom segments of the labium. A few species can penetrate a little deeper by being able to completely disengage their stylets from the last labial segment. In other bugs the stylets are very much longer than the short labium and can be withdrawn looped or coiled inside the head or within a specially expanded segment of the labium. In these species, a special part at the end of the short labium acts as a clamp. The stylets, which can be introduced a bit at a time by means of serial contractions of muscles acting on levers attached to bases of the maxillary and mandibular stylets, are held firmly in place by the labium between thrusts.

141

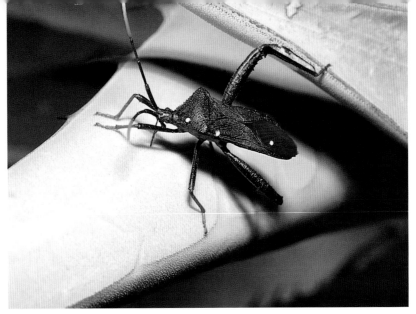

With the first two segments of the rostrum folded back, and its leg braced against a leaf margin, this coreid bug (*Acanthocephala* sp.) achieves deeper stylet penetration through the leaf of an *Agave* plant in the Chihuahuan desert of Mexico. Three tiny mites can be seen clinging to the bug's back. **Coreidae**

The stylet bundle itself is made up of the mandibular and maxillary stylets, which take the form of two pairs of exceedingly slender, tapering, thread-like structures. Like all cuticular structures they are shed and renewed at each moult. The outer pair, the mandibular stylets, can be free, simply enclosing the maxillary stylets, or closely connected to longitudinal ridges on the outside surfaces of the maxillary stylets. These fine ridges fit into special grooves running the length of the inside faces of the mandibular stylets, giving support and allowing the two pairs to slide freely on each other. The way these connecting grooves and ridges work is similar to the sealing mechanism of a zip-lock plastic bag (Fig. 12:ii). The sharp ends of the mandibular stylets have saw-like serrations, teeth and sometimes barbs. In predacious species, whose stylets can be very long, the mandibular stylets may be sharply barbed and toothed to cut and shred the prey's tissues. The end of the stylet bundle may reach deep into recesses of the victim's body.

In general, the ends of the mandibular stylets are the first bits of the mouthparts to penetrate tissues, and they can be pushed in alternately or, in some cases, at the same time (Fig. 12:iii). In heteropteran bugs maxillary glands in the head, opening near the base of the maxillary stylets, produce secretions that lubricate the stylets and may also, in predacious species, have a toxic function. Typically, the maxillary stylets are pushed in as a single unit behind the advancing mandibular stylets until they reach the required location for feeding.

The maxillary stylets are of a very special design – not only do they have external ridges that slide in grooves on the mandibular stylets, but they also contain the salivary and food canals (Fig. 12:ii). The inner faces of the maxillary stylets are complexly folded into longitudinal ridges and grooves which firmly unite the two and provide two very fine, parallel channels, the food canal and the salivary canal, running along their entire length.

A close-up of this cicada as it clings to a tree trunk in the Peruvian rain forest clearly reveals that the bug is feeding. The ridged green portion at the front of the head is occupied by the powerful muscles of the cibarial sucking pump. **Cicadidae**

Less than 12 mm (0.5 in) from head to tail, and supported on slender, thread-like legs, a water measurer bug (*Hydrometra stagnorum*) stalks slowly across the floating vegetation of an English pond in search of food. When a suitable, small prey item such as a waterflea or immature insect is located, the bug uses its rostrum to spear the victim. **Hydrometridae**

Often smaller in cross-section than the food canal, the salivary canal carries from the salivary glands in the anterior part of the thorax digestive enzymes and other secretions having a variety of functions. Heteropterans normally have a pair of glands, while in the other groups there may be two or more pairs. Each gland may have numerous lobes, and there may be additional accessory glands. Salivary secretions from the various glands join a single duct just before reaching the salivary pump in the head. From here they are forced down the salivary canal of the maxillary stylets and into the plant or animal tissues.

Bug saliva is a complex mixture of enzymes (to break down complex carbohydrates, proteins and fats into simpler molecules), toxins, lubricants and other substances. The exact composition of the saliva varies from bug to bug, according to its diet. Herbivorous bugs need enzymes such as pectinases to break down plant cell walls, while carnivorous heteropterans may need powerful toxins to subdue their prey.

Of the heteropteran families that have been studied, species of water bug belonging to the **Belostomatidae**, **Nepidae**, **Notonectidae**, **Naucoridae** and **Hydrometridae** and terrestrial families such as the **Enicocephalidae**, **Reduviidae** and **Nabidae**, are known to produce toxic saliva, containing powerful enzymes (proteinases, hyaluronidases and phospholipases) similar to those in snake venom. An injection of saliva from some species causes the virtually instantaneous paralysis and death of the prey. Reduviids, especially those which tackle large or dangerous prey like wasps or bees, tend to make the first stab near the victim's head or neck, thus ensuring that their toxic saliva has maximum effect in the shortest possible time. Belostomatids produce incredibly powerful venoms capable of rapidly subduing vertebrates such as fish, frogs and small birds. The salivary secretions of blood-feeding bugs (**Cimicidae** and some

Powerful, paralysing and tissue-dissolving saliva has enabled this large assassin bug quickly to overcome a grasshopper. In this case, the grasshopper's warning coloration, distastefulness and powerful hind legs have proved inadequate defences. Peru. **Reduviidae**

Reduviidae (Triatominae)) may contain anticoagulants to prevent clotting.

Within the saliva of gall-forming bug species in the **Psyllidae** and the **Pemphigidae** there may be some plant growth-modifying substances which are responsible for causing the leaf roll deformations inside which they live. Such compounds, including the plant growth hormone indoleacetic acid, have been recorded from bug saliva, but the exact nature of their action with respect to gall formation remains unknown.

In plant sap-feeding bugs such as aphids, the site of the phloem vessels in the plant may be some way from the surface. The stylet bundle therefore has to wander between the tough-walled cells of the plant's epidermis before reaching a suitable feeding site. The stylets are protected, and their movement through the plant tissues rendered easier, by the formation of a proteinaceous sheath made by the hardening of special salivary gland secretions which are produced throughout penetration. A salivary sheath or short plug is also formed by species belonging to some plant-feeding heteropteran families in the superfamily Pentatomoidea.

The very apex of the food canal in the maxillary stylets is, in effect, the bug's mouth, through which all its food must pass to begin the journey through the digestive tract. In the head, at the end of the food canal, the action of powerful muscles operating the sucking or cibarial pump draws the liquid or predissolved food up the stylet bundle and passes it into the pharynx. Bugs feeding on the sap in phloem vessels do not require very strong cibarial pumps. As their diet is under slight pressure, once they have their stylets in place they do not need to change their feeding site or suck that hard: the plant does the work for them.

In some aphids and scale insects the stylets can be very long; to reach the correct feeding site, deep penetration taking many hours of effort may be required. Sternorrhynchan bugs like aphids, which feed *en masse*, may, by acting as a 'metabolic sink', actually encourage the plant to send more nutrients to the leaves which are infested than to other parts of the plant.

Digestive system

The insect digestive system is essentially a long, open-ended tube with special regions for the production of enzymes, the absorption of nutrients and the elimination of wastes. The digestive system of bugs is similar in many ways to that of most other insects, being divided into a fore, mid and hind gut. The mid gut is often further divided into two or more distinct sections, of various designs and with different functions.

Because the diet is entirely liquid, the fore-part of the gut does not need to be dilated into a crop region for grinding or storage. The front or anterior part of the mid gut in many auchenorrhychan bugs may, however, be very enlarged.

The last or posterior mid gut section in many herbivorous heteropteran bugs (**Lygaeidae, Coreidae, Pentatomidae** and **Pyrrhocoridae**) has sac-like pockets or outgrowths called caeca, which harbour symbiotic bacteria and yeasts. In these groups, their exact function is not yet clear, but some studies have shown that without them the nymphs grow very slowly or die young. Blood-feeding **Cimicidae** have their symbiotic bacteria contained within special bodies in the haemocoel (body cavity) called mycetomes. As with triatomine

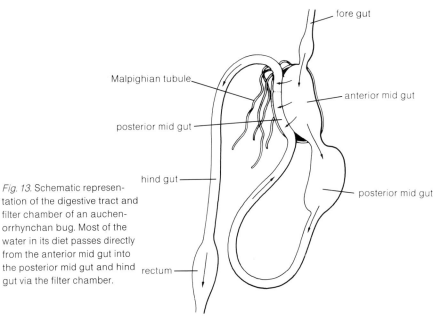

fore gut

Malpighian tubule

anterior mid gut

posterior mid gut

hind gut

posterior mid gut

Fig. 13. Schematic representation of the digestive tract and
filter chamber of an auchenorrhynchan bug. Most of the
water in its diet passes directly
from the anterior mid gut into
the posterior mid gut and hind
gut via the filter chamber.

rectum

reduviids, whose symbionts are located inside the mid gut, the bacteria are believed to be responsible for providing the bugs with the B vitamins that are lacking to their blood-based diet. Auchenorrhynchan and sternorrhynchan bugs are universally well known for their bacterial and yeast symbionts, which are contained inside special cells called mycetocytes. The mycetocytes, which may be aggregated into bodies known as mycetomes, are free in the body cavity and are not associated with the gut as in pentatomorphan heteropterans.

These symbiotic micro-organisms have a large number of varied functions. They occur in a number of insect groups, particularly those whose diet is nutritionally incomplete or imbalanced. Researches have shown them to be important in the recycling of nitrogen, and in providing their hosts with vitamins, certain essential amino acids absent from the diet, and certain lipids such as the sterols, which insects are unable to manufacture for themselves. Sterols are very important chemicals, vital, in addition to other functions, to the production of the insect moulting hormone ecdysone. Substances like this must be obtained direct from the diet or through symbiotic organisms.

In all auchenorrhynchan and sternorrhynchan bugs and the **Cimicidae**, these vital symbiotic micro-organisms are transferred to offspring internally – in other words, the symbiotic organisms are either released from mycetocytes and move to the ovaries, or else entire mycetocytes are transferred to the ovaries. In other bugs (the Heteroptera apart from the **Cimicidae**) it is done by the mother spotting on to the eggs drops of her excrement containing the symbionts. When the first instar nymphs emerge from the egg they immediately feed from the egg's surface or become infected with the micro-organisms in some other way.

Waste disposal

Like all other animals, insects need to get rid of nitrogenous wastes which would eventually poison their body tissues. In most animals, the removal of the waste

A group of young shield bug nymphs, standing face towards the eggshells from which they have recently emerged, collectively resemble a poisonous caterpillar. First instar nymphs rarely feed on plants; instead they ingest symbiotic bacteria, vital to their digestive systems, that their mother smeared on the eggs as she laid them. Peru. **Pentatomidae**

products of metabolism requires them to be dissolved in water. But for terrestrial insects loss of water is critical, and so a different system is required.

At the junction of the mid and hind gut are a number of special ducts called Malpighian tubules. In the Hemiptera, heteropteran and auchenorrhynchan bugs tend to have four tubules, while in the Sternorrhyncha coccoids tend to have two and aphidoids none. The function of these tubules is to extract the waste products from the body cavity fluid or haemolymph in which all the internal organs are bathed. The soluble wastes are converted to insoluble uric acid granules, which do not need water for their expulsion from the body. Valuable water and salts are then reabsorbed by the hind gut and rectum before the excrement is voided.

Aphids survive without Malpighian tubules because the job of producing nitrogenous waste is done by the cells of the mid gut and a special organ known as the fat body. In addition, aphids and some other sap-sucking species never have a problem with water loss as they consume vast quantities of liquid food almost continuously. In these cases, ammonia is the preferred waste product. Although the ammonia is toxic, it is kept so dilute by the watery component of the diet that it never becomes a problem.

In some scale insects the mid gut is a closed sac with no physical connection to the hind gut. In this case the contents of the mid gut are completely digested, after which the waste products are extracted from the body fluids by the Malpighian tubules and passed through the hind gut where water is reabsorbed. In essence this is not really any different from that which normally happens except

148

that, as there is no solid, indigestible matter in the diet, there is no need for anything to pass between the mid and hind gut.

Another interesting modification of bugs' guts, seen in many sap-sucking groups such as the **Cicadidae**, **Cercopidae**, some **Cicadellidae** and virtually all the coccoid families, is the filter chamber. In simple terms, large amounts of watery food can bypass the mid gut entirely and pass straight into the rectum to be voided. The process allows the material passing through the mid gut to be processed more efficiently than would otherwise be possible, and gets rid of water in as short a time as possible. The manner in which the filter chamber is arranged concerns the close and intimate association of epithelial tissues from the rear of the mid gut or front of the hind gut with those of the fore gut (Fig. 13). In some cases, the Malpighian tubules too are involved in the formation of the filter chamber.

Diet

Herbivores

Sap-sucking bugs obtain carbohydrate in abundance, but protein-building, soluble nitrogen compounds are in much shorter supply in plant sap. No more than 4 per cent of the dry weight of plant tissues consists of nitrogen, whereas in insect tissues it may be up to 15 per cent. It is vital for insects to obtain the amino acids, fats, vitamins and minerals that they require to grow properly, and there are two options open: to eat a lot more, or to grow at a slower rate.

Many herbivorous heteropteran bugs are adapted to locate and feed selectively on particular plant parts, such as the embryos of seeds, pollen, fruits and buds, which offer greater nourishment. The value of the plant as a food resource may, however, vary according to the time of year – young, actively growing tissues are generally more nutrient-rich. Auchenorrhynchan and sternorrhynchan bugs, on the other hand, are restricted to taking sap from the vessels of the plant's vascular system. The sap of phloem vessels, fed on by the great majority of herbivorous bugs in all the suborders, usually contains very little nitrogen; xylem sap, fed on by cicadas, froghoppers and some leafhopper species, is even worse. Some bugs which specialize on this diet may take many years to complete their nymphal development.

Apart from the poor quality of a plant diet, herbivorous bugs have other dietary problems with which to contend. Normally the eggs are laid on the host plant, so there is no need for the young nymphs to seek out the correct food; but adult bugs which have moved or migrated may have to seek out their preferred plant. Most herbivorous species may be very restricted in their choice of food, perhaps being able to feed from one species (monophagous), while others may be able to eat a number of closely related species (oligophagous) or, less commonly, a wide range of host plants (polyphagous). Within the Aphidoidea, for example, nearly all the known species are very specific about their choice of host plant.

Plants have evolved a variety of physical and chemical protections against phytophages, and many bug species have had to evolve mechanisms to overcome

Clinging to a plant stem in the Brazilian cerradão, a shield bug sucks sap through slender mouthparts. The mandibular and maxillary stylets, sheathed by the segments of the labium, are not visible. **Pentatomidae**

them. The two processes of plant defence and insect attack are maintained in a sort of evolutionary balance. Problems can occur, for instance, when an alien bug is accidentally introduced to a country where a particular plant species, which proves to be a suitable host, has no defences against the alien. Wild plant species, which may have a natural physical and biochemical resistance to certain kinds of insect attack, may lose some of their protection when selectively bred by humans for better yield, faster growth, improved seed set and other character-istics.

Among plant defence mechanisms, leaves may have thick, waxy cuticles, tough leaves, dense hairs, spines and sticky glandular hairs, known as trichomes, to trap and snare small insects such as aphids. The sharp-hooked leaf hairs of beans (*Phaseolus* spp.) can pierce the cuticle of aphid and leafhopper species.

Trichomes, for instance on tomato plants (*Lycopersicon* spp.), are not just sticky: the fluid, once released from the swollen hair tip by a passing aphid's or white-fly's leg, can also be toxic. Some plant trichomes are thought to release aphidoid

Female cones of the strange South West African desert plant *Welwitschia mirabilis* provide a food source for nymphs and adults of *Probergrothius sexpunctatus*. The nymphs have three clear, dark-margined dorsal abdominal stink gland openings. The plant obtains its moisture from the air. Namibia. **Pyrrhocoridae**

alarm pheromones. Many modern potato (*Solanum* spp.) varieties show a reduction in the number of sticky, glandular hairs on their leaves. This has led to increased aphid attack and, consequently, increased use of pesticides. Wild potato species are much better equipped with glandular hairs, which are most effective in trapping and killing a number of aphid and leafhopper species.

The nature of a plant's surface may greatly influence whether or not a bug species will settle and attempt to feed or move on. An aphid, leafhopper, psyllid or any other herbivorous bug species uses surface chemistry to identify its correct host plant; a bug landing on a plant to which it is not adapted will be repelled. But while some of these plant characteristics may provide an initial barrier to eating it, once the bug's stylets have penetrated the tissues other defences may be brought into play.

A large number of plants produce secondary defensive compounds, known as allelochemicals, which are present in the tissues, phloem sap and, to a much smaller extent, xylem sap. These substances are produced as a result of the

Death of a damselfly. Attracted by ripples sent out by insects trapped or dying on the water's surface, pondskaters quickly locate potential prey items. Here, two adult *Gerris lacustris* have seized a Common Red Damselfly (*Pyrrhosoma nymphula*). The bugs have inserted their stylets deep into the victim's body through the soft, intersegmental membranes that join the toughened body parts and are injecting paralysing and tissue-dissolving saliva. Great Britain. **Gerridae**

plant's metabolic processes. The compounds include all manner of alkaloids, flavonoids, glycosides, furanocoumarins, oils, phenols, prussic acid (hydrogen cyanide) and other repellent, toxic and digestibility-reducing organic substances. These allelochemicals need not be present in the plant all the time, and may only be produced in response to insect attack. Many of these compounds are of great value to humans and have important pharmacological (for instance quinine, cocaine and morphine), agricultural (derris and pyrethrin, for example) and other uses. Others, arguably of less practical value but certainly sought after, include caffeine, tannin and nicotine.

Some plants go so far as to manufacture imitation insect hormones, known as phytoecdysones, which are designed to interfere with the insect's growth and moulting. Even more sneaky is the production, by some plants, of what are known as suicide substrates. These compounds are themselves harmless but, when ingested and inside the bug's gut, become altered through the digestive process to form highly toxic compounds. In response, many insects have evolved enzyme systems to detoxify the compounds, while some become specialist feeders on particular plants, even using the smell or taste of the plant's defensive compounds as a host-finding cue. It has already been seen that some bugs may sequester plant defensive compounds for their own defence.

Voracious consumers of aphids, ladybird larvae and adults can sometimes themselves fall victim to predacious bugs in several families. Here a freshly emerged 2-spot ladybird (*Adalia bipunctata*) is being sucked dry by a mirid bug (*Deraeocoris ruber*). Great Britain.
Miridae

Carnivores

Predacious bug species occur only within the heteropteran suborder. Carnivory is almost the rule in water bug families, but is less common among the terrestrial bugs. Under water, the **Nepidae**, **Belostomatidae**, **Naucoridae** and **Notonectidae** are the main predatory families. On the surface film, the main ones are the **Gerridae**, **Veliidae**, **Hydrometridae** and **Hebridae**. On land, predacious bugs can be found everywhere from bare ground to the aerial parts of plants. In the mainly herbivorous superfamilies Pentatomoidea and Lygaeoidea, species in two subfamilies, the Asopinae and the Geocorinae, belonging respectively to the **Pentatomidae** and **Lygaeidae**, are predacious. The vast majority of species placed in families within the Cimicoidea (the **Anthocoridae** and the **Nabidae** being the biggest families) and Reduvoidea (**Reduviidae**) are highly predacious. Some predatory species, such as those in the **Cimicidae**, **Polyctenidae** and species in the reduviid subfamily, Triatominae, have become specialized to feed on the blood of a wide range of vertebrate animals including reptiles, birds, humans and other mammal species. Within some families, typically the plant bugs (**Miridae**), species can exhibit a wide range of mixed, herbivorous and predacious, feeding strategies.

It might be thought that, nutritionally speaking, predacious bugs have an easier time of it, as their food is a richer resource and similar in composition to the tissues of their own bodies. There are, however, other problems. Their prey might not be nearly as abundant, it can be mobile and more difficult to catch, and, like plants, it may fight back physically or chemically. Here, too, bugs show a fascinating range of adaptations.

Many heteropteran bugs are opportunistic in their feeding, and some three dozen species in more than 10 families are known occasionally to take sustenance from a wide range of fresh or dried animal carrion, dung and bird droppings. Of particular note are species belonging to the **Alydidae**, **Coreidae** and **Lygaeidae**. The habit is probably much more widespread than is currently recorded. Some anthocorid and mirid bugs are capable of piercing vertebrate skin if given the opportunity, but the blood they might take is by no means an essential part of their diet.

The type of prey a bug chooses to eat will be largely dependent on its size in relation to the bug, and on the type of habitat (land or water) occupied by the predator and its prey. A variety of prey-capturing modifications can be seen in many families. Front legs can be thickened and raptorial for grasping; the rostrum may be short, stout and curved for downward stabbing, or longer, straight and capable of being held out horizontally for spearing prey.

Two basic approaches, with variations, can be adopted by predatory bugs. Aggressive hunters like many assassin bugs actively stalk and pounce, or else sit in wait to ambush and subdue their victims. Damsel bugs are intermediate between aggressive and timid. They often use a single front leg to tap their prey gently before inserting their stylets. Timid terrestrial predators include such bugs as anthocorids and asopine pentatomids, while on the water's surface hebrids

Nestling camouflaged in the flower of a hedgehog cactus, an assassin bug (*Apiomeris* sp.) waits for its next meal. The sucked-out carcass of a bee, the bug's last meal, lies below. New Mexico. **Reduviidae**

and hydrometrids fall into this category. Timid predators will not use their legs at all to hold prey. Instead they prefer to attack very small or slow-moving insects, larvae, eggs and pupae, approaching them with their rostra held out in front. Some anthocorid bugs feed to a large extent on the larvae of leaf-mining moths and flies, and first have to probe through the plant's epidermal layers to reach their prey. Blood-feeding bugs tend to use stealth and often live in close proximity to their host's living or sleeping areas.

Some bugs may have a broad prey range, feeding on all manner of suitable, soft-bodied invertebrates, while others may be very restricted in what they eat and, through the course of evolution, become highly specialized in the way they catch it. Damsel bugs, for instance, are in the main fairly catholic in their choice of prey, but many species show a marked preference for leafhoppers, aphids or seed bugs.

Some intriguing examples of prey specialization can be seen in several bugs belonging to the families **Reduviidae**, **Nabidae**, **Plokiophilidae** and **Miridae**, which are all associated in some way or other with spiders, psocopterans (barklice) or embiopterans (webspinners) and their webs. The reduviid

Crawling across a leaf in Mexico's Oaxaca state, a predatory shield bug (*Oplomus dichrous*) has found its next meal. Shield bugs belonging to the subfamily Asopinae are very beneficial in controlling pests such as moth caterpillars and beetle larva. So-called timid predators, these bugs rely on stealth and fast-acting salivary toxins to subdue their sluggish prey. **Pentatomidae**

subfamily Emesinae contains a number of genera (*Eugubinus*, *Ploiaria*, *Emesa*, *Stenolemus* and *Empicoris*) whose elongate, thread-legged member species feed on insects caught in spiders' webs or on the spiders themselves. These slender, slow-moving bugs never get trapped in the spider silk; obviously they either avoid the sticky spirals or walk very carefully.

Web-inhabiting bugs show a variety of adaptations which enable them to occupy this feeding niche. Spider predators such as those in the genus *Stenolemus* may have specially modified antennae which are used to send and receive vibrational signals through the web. When the bug moves on to a web, it causes the web to sway in a manner that simulates wind motion. The spider young or adults do not seem to realize their impending doom until the raptorial front legs of the bug strike out.

Species belonging to the appropriately named damsel bug genus *Arachnocoris* also live among the webs of spiders, but in this case they simply feed on trapped insects. The **Plokiophilidae** is a very small, southern hemisphere family of some 15 or so tiny, flattened bugs. The species contained in the main genus, *Plokiophiloides*, are all found in the webs of spiders, where they feed on trapped insects but will sometimes kill small prey items on their own. The very few known species in the other plokiophilid genus, *Embiophila*, live in association with webspinners; they suck out the eggs and young stages of their hosts.

Highly unusual among plant bugs, the very small species belonging to the mirid genus *Ranzovius* are found only on the irregular, sheet-like webs made by certain spider species. The bug, which feeds on a range of small snared insects which the spiders have disregarded, seems to be able to move about without attracting its host's attention. At the first sign of disturbance, however, the mirid will quickly make its way off the sheet and hide itself among surrounding vegetation.

Without doubt some of the most interesting prey-capturing techniques are found in assassin bugs. Many adult and nymphal reduviids have special hairs on their bodies which secrete sticky substances. In the nymphs of many genera, the dorsal body surface hairs are used to hold debris or the sucked-out bodies of their prey as a camouflage, enabling the bugs to move freely among their prey.

In the adults of some species the tibiae of both front legs and sometimes the middle legs have a special region on the inner surface, known as the fossa spongiosa. The main purpose of these structures – pads made up of tens of thousands of individual hollow hairs – seems to be to give the bug a good grip for efficient prey capture. The bug may also gain some advantage when climbing smooth or steep surfaces and, in a few species, when mating. In some species the fossa may be confined to the end of the tibiae, while in others the area covered by the special pads may be much more extensive. The gripping power is dependent on the broad and often fanned shape of the hair tips and the oily secretions they produce.

Reduviids may produce a lot of sticky secretions on their front legs and use them to catch small insects in the manner of flypaper. Other assassin bugs, particularly those belonging to the subfamily Apiomerinae, go one step further and collect certain resins from plants which they spread over their front legs. These resins are very attractive to insects, and to bees in particular. Assassin bugs in the genera *Amulius* and *Ectinoderus*, among others, are very good at attracting

A bee-killing assassin bug (*Velinus malayus*) sucks the body fluids and dissolved tissues of a small, stingless bee of the genus *Trigona*. The bug may have attracted its prey by the use of odoriferous resins on its front legs. Malaysian rain forest. **Reduviidae**

stingless bees of the genus *Trigona*. They use resins obtained from pine and copal-producing tree species; having covered their front legs with the gum, they lie in wait to catch a bee lured by the odours.

While it has been clearly established that many assassin bugs use self-produced or sequestered plant odours to lure and catch prey, little work has been done on the nature or chemical composition of the scents. It is likely that, where the bug is close to a nest entrance, bees are caught not because they were attracted to scents but rather because they were trying to attack or drive the bug away.

An ingenious and very efficient means of catching prey has evolved in some assassin bugs belonging to the genus *Ptilocerus*. These small reduviids, which have very hairy legs and antennae, are found in the Oriental region and use chemical lures to trap and prey on dolichoderine ants. The source of the lure is a special ventral abdominal gland whose secretions seep out on to a modified, raised portion of the third abdominal segment. Brightly coloured yellow hairs on this

Barely discernible on account of a thick covering of debris stuck to its sticky dorsal hairs, an assassin bug nymph (*Salyavata variegata*) goes fishing for termites (*Nasutitermes*) in a Costa Rican rain forest. Incredibly, these bugs use the bodies of freshly killed termites as bait to lure others out of nest openings. When in range, the bug seizes his victim and sucks it dry. Interestingly, the bugs are not so keen on the soldier caste, preferring the workers.
Reduviidae

section act as a reservoir for the secretions. The bug moves about on the ground in the vicinity of an ant trail. When an ant comes near, the bug raises the front part of its body to expose the underside of the abdomen. The ants are very attracted by the secretion and begin to lick the hairs. Unfortunately for the ants, the secretion also paralyses them; as soon as the bug senses the onset of paralysis, it inserts its rostrum to feed. The trick of luring prey in this manner is probably more widespread within the **Reduviidae** than is presently known.

Even more amazing is the use of tools by some assassin bugs. Many species in the reduviid subfamily Salyavatinae prey on termites, and most species occur in the tropical and subtropical regions of the Old World. Species of the genus *Salyavata*, however, are found in the neotropics. Like many reduviid nymphs, those of *S. variegata* disguise themselves heavily by sticking debris to glandular hairs on their backs. What distinguishes them from other reduviid nymphs is that they go fishing for their prey, using the sucked-out bodies of previous victims as bait. The nymphs dangle the bait in front of holes in the termite nest. When the workers come out to investigate they often grasp the lure, and are then seized and eaten by the assassin bug.

Chapter 7
Mating and Egg Laying

A bug, having survived all the myriad dangers that lurk in the natural environment to become adult, has one last task to accomplish before it dies – that of reproducing. The great majority of insects, including bugs, reproduce bisexually and use the process of cell division (meiosis) to produce the sex cells or gametes. Males produce sperm, while females produce eggs or ova. The eggs are fertilized by sperms stored inside the body of the female. A very few, unusual species of scale insect such as the Cottony Cushion Scale are hermaphrodites, a single individual being capable of producing eggs and sperm. There may be anything from one to many generations in a single year.

Heteropteran and auchenorrhynchan bugs always reproduce bisexually. The resultant eggs are laid (ovipary) on foliage, bark or litter, or inserted into plant tissues. In some bugs, such as giant water bugs, the eggs may be laid in strange places. Female belostomatids lay their eggs on the back of the male, which acts as a mobile guard and ensures that they are kept moist and well oxygenated.

Among the sternorrhynchan bugs, particularly in the Aphidoidea, reproduction can be much more complicated. It may involve more than one host plant; and parthenogenesis (reproduction without the need for males to fertilize females) may be alternated with sexual reproduction at different times of the year. Eggs may be laid externally or hatch inside the body, after which the female gives birth to live, first instar nymphs (ovovivipary).

The process of evolution acts through the genetic material. The genes dictate how successful an organism is going to be; success is, in essence, how many offspring are produced to carry the genes into future generations. The bug species we see on Earth today can be regarded as very successful. From the time they arose they adapted to changing conditions, and they are still here millions of years later. To put it simply, if chance mutation produces an individual whose genetic make-up renders it more able to compete for food or mates, its chances of leaving those genes behind in the form of offspring are increased. Natural selection through the survival of individuals carrying successful genes has moulded all aspects of bug biology.

The vital importance of reproduction, which involves, particularly for some female bugs, a substantial investment of resources, is reflected in the many parental care strategies that have evolved within the Hemiptera. While it may be important for a female bug to find a suitable partner, it is also important for the male to be sure that his sperm cells and not someone else's are the ones used to fertilize the eggs that result from the pairing. The ways in which males try to achieve this assurance of paternity include territorial combat, mate guarding, and prolonged or repeated copulation.

Attracting a mate

The initial job of finding or attracting a mate may be achieved in a number of ways. In some bugs males locate females at particular sites. The males of some aphids will gather at female oviposition sites; some male seed bugs, shield bugs and coreids may find their respective females at feeding sites on favourite host plants; while others, such as cicadas, may use certain conspicuous tree trunks. The formation of large groups of feeding and mating individuals are common in pentatomid bugs.

Despite the presence of these known meeting places, a male and female may appear to meet each other in a chance encounter. For many bugs the chance of meeting the right mate can be greatly enhanced by species-specific communication. Information about the gender, sexual state and location of the sender may be imparted by acoustic means, via the air, water or solid objects or by chemical means through pheromones.

From subterranean burrower to forest singer, a cicada emerges under cover of darkness from its last nymphal skin. This species, *Venustria superba*, lives only in the rain forests of north-eastern Queensland, where its unusual, frog-like call can be heard late in the afternoon. Australia. **Cicadidae**

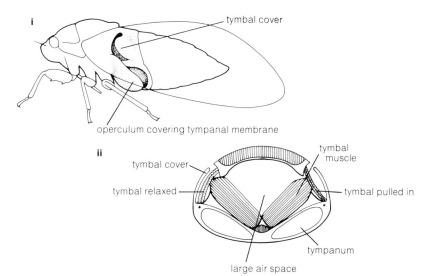

Fig. 14. (i) Location of the tymbal (sound-producing) and tympanal (hearing) organs on one side of a cicada. (ii) Schematic cross-section through cicada at base of abdomen.

Acoustic signalling is found in many hemipteran families, and serves a variety of purposes from defence, alarm raising, species spacing within a particular habitat and aggregation to mate attraction, courtship and copulation. In the Heteroptera, species belonging to the **Corixidae**, **Notonectidae**, **Veliidae**, **Pentatomidae**, **Alydidae**, **Nabidae**, **Reduviidae** and **Lygaeidae** do so. Among the sternorrhynchan bugs only a few species – some aphids and psyllids – are known to make faint noises. In the Auchenorrhyncha, the **Cicadidae** are the loudest and by far the most spectacular of all insect singers.

The sounds produced by male cicadas originate from special organs known as tymbals located on each side of the first abdominal segment (Fig. 14). The tymbals are a pair of stiff, drumskin-like cuticular membranes which can be rapidly clicked in and out by means of a large tymbal muscle attached beneath each. The tension of the 'skin' can be altered by other muscles. The noise is amplified by a pair of large resonating air sacs which fill up most of the abdomen.

The frequency of the songs is governed by the area of the tymbal, the speed of tymbal muscle contraction and the physical characteristics of the air sacs in the abdomen. In tropical forests a chorus of freshly emerged cicadas can be heard more than a mile away, and up close it can be painful to the human ear. When two or more species are calling simultaneously a little experience will enable the listener to distinguish the different songs.

The hearing organs or tympanic membranes, which are present in males and females, lie on the underside of the abdomen, protected by a cuticular flap called the operculum. In singing males, much of the sound produced is radiated out of the tympanic membranes, which are often much larger than those of the female. In mixed species groups, the females generally have no difficulty in picking out the appropriate song as their hearing organs are tuned to be responsive to that particular frequency.

Until well into this century it was thought that other auchenorrhynchan bug

In the Chihuahuan desert of Mexico, a pair of small, squat ambush bugs (*Phymata erosa*) take time out from capturing prey to begin the courtship rituals which will lead to copulation. The strongly modified, raptorial front legs are clearly visible. **Reduviidae**

species did not produce sounds. It is now known that bugs such as planthoppers (**Delphacidae**), leafhoppers (**Cicadellidae**), froghoppers (**Cercopidae**) and treehoppers (**Membracidae**) are capable of doing so. Apart from their use in mating rituals auchenorrhynchan bug songs are also used in male-to-male aggression. Although the sounds they make tend to be much quieter than those of cicadas, the organs that produce them are essentially similar to those of other auchenorrhynchan bugs.

Many species cannot be heard easily by the human ear. Rather than vibrating air molecules to transmit the energy of the song, the sounds that these small bugs produce are generally transmitted by mechanical vibrations through their legs to the foliage on which they rest. It is possible that some heteropteran bugs may also be able to sense substrate-borne vibrations to enhance mate location. Water bugs such as gerrids can attract mates by sending out pulsed surface ripples with their legs.

Song, particularly the calling or attraction songs used to signal to potential mates, can be very complex and highly species-specific. On reception of a male song females can reply with a less complex song encouraging the males to move towards them. Different songs take over once the pair are together and as an immediate prelude to courtship and copulation. In some species the female hardly sings at all, while in others serenades originate from both sexes.

The production of very loud, general or otherwise obvious signals can be a costly and sometimes risky operation for the sender. The noisy acoustic signals employed by male cicadas might enable predators as well as females to locate them. To counter this, cicadas tend to be very cryptically coloured and cease singing at the slightest disturbance. No doubt the smaller auchenorrhynchan bugs can be found by predators homing in on the vibrations they set up. Chemical signals too can be subverted in various ways. Shield bug males emitting sexually attractive pheromones may attract a number of rival males of the same species.

Bugs which defend a territory for access to females may have to oust rival males. This happens in several coreid bug species, where the males command a perch on particular plants where the females come to feed. In species such as *Acanthocephala femorata*, where inter-male combat occurs, the males have large, expanded, spined or toothed hind legs which are used to kick out in an attempt to dislodge the rival from the plant. The simple kick response can also be directed at other bugs, predators and parasites. Wrestling involves one or both males trying to squeeze the abdomen of the opponent, using their large hind legs like nutcrackers. Males of the same size and strength have been known to fight in this way for some time, but generally the larger of the two bugs will win and the smaller one will retire unscathed.

Gerrid bug males also command breeding territories on the surface of water and compete for these areas and receptive females. The size of territory held by a male is dependent to a large extent on his own size – larger males hold bigger territories than smaller males. The obvious advantage to any territory-holding male is that he will be able to mate successfully with more females than a non-territory holder.

Copulation and sperm transfer

When a receptive female and male bug finally meet, the next stage of the proceedings may involve some sort of courtship. The males of some seed bugs (**Lygaeidae**) may bring a nutritious seed as a nuptial gift for the female to feed on while copulation – the joining of the external genitalia and sperm transfer – takes place. The offering of nuptial gifts is common in some other insect groups, but unusual in the Hemiptera. In many species, a complex pattern of varied chemical, acoustic and behavioural signals, the exact details of which are known for very few species, may occur during and just after copulation.

The reproductive organs are contained within the rear portion of the abdomen. The eggs are fertilized internally by the sperm, which is introduced by the male's aedeagus or penis via the female's vagina. Sperm is deposited in or near a sperm-storage organ known as the spermatheca – some species have more than one – and is subsequently used to fertilize the eggs. Sperm cannot be stored indefinitely, and many bugs mate repeatedly to maintain a fresh supply.

The reproductive system of the female

A pair of bug ovaries is made up of a very variable number of ovarioles, each producing a supply of follicles in varying stages of development (Fig. 15). The

Males of many coreid bugs, like this specimen of *Nematopus indus* resting on a leaf in the Peruvian rain forest, have enlarged, curved and heavily spined hind legs. In some species, these modifications are used for defence and in territorial combat for access to females.
Coreidae

number of ovarioles in the Heteroptera varies from two to eighteen, but seven or eight is a common number in many families. In the other subfamilies there may be anything from two or three to many tens of ovarioles. A follicle comprises the developing egg together with surrounding nutrient cells and those cells which will produce the final egg shell or chorion. Each of the ovaries is joined by its own lateral oviduct to a main or common oviduct, which leads in turn to the single vagina or genital chamber. The spermatheca or sperm store, which can assume a huge variety of shapes and sizes, is normally a pocket-like outgrowth from the dorsal wall of the vagina. Additionally there are a number of accessory glands, which may be involved in the production of glues and waterproof cements to stick eggs to plants and other surfaces.

The reproductive system of the male

A pair of bug testes is composed of connective tissue enclosing a number of testis follicles. Within each of the follicles, large numbers of very small, motile, sperm cells develop inside cyst-like clumps of cells. When the developing cyst reaches the end of the follicle it breaks down to release the sperm cells. Each testis is joined by means of a duct known as the vas deferens to a common ejaculatory duct (Fig. 15). This common duct takes the sperm to the external genitalia where it opens at the end of the penis.

There may be a number of accessory glands or swollen portions of the vas deferens which serve as seminal vesicles (sperm storage sacs) or which supply lubricants and other fluids vital to the survival of the fragile thread-like sperm cells. Before the common ejaculatory duct enters the aedeagus proper there may be a sperm pump to force the seminal fluid along. Finally, separated from the sperm-conducting tubes there may be other fluid-containing pouches, glands and structures responsible for the inflation of the aedeagus.

The male external genitalia are located on the ninth abdominal segment, which forms a boat-shaped genital capsule. This capsule carries the penis or aedeagus, which can be toughened or soft and inflatable. The aedeagus is itself flanked by a pair of claspers or parameres. The parameres, which can be very variable in shape and size, are used to grasp parts of the female bug's external genitalia as the aedeagus is inserted deeply into the genital chamber or vagina.

The three-dimensional structure and the way in which bugs' external genitalia lock together can be exceedingly complex and varies from group to group. As a general rule the genitalia are so designed that mating between individuals of even very closely related species is physically impossible, and the structure of the male and female genitalia are often used to identify bugs.

Copulation

The act usually begins with the male bug on top of the female and holding her back with his front legs; however, the final positions taken by mating bugs can be quite different. Water bugs tend to maintain their original position, but in many bugs the male and female copulate side by side, parallel or at an angle, in other tail to tail, and sometimes tail to tail with the male on his back or underside to underside. These contortions may involve not only the whole body but also physical rotation of the genital segments.

Once firmly locked in place, sperm transfer can begin. Normally the job is effected in a matter of seconds but, oddly, the male and female may remain coupled for very long periods and move around freely, feeding and sometimes flying. The normally smaller male has no choice but to be dragged wherever the female wants to go, but there is method in his madness.

In many cases, especially if there is a shortage of available, receptive females, prolonged copulation prevents other males from mating and thus increases the number of eggs that will be fertilized by him. If the male was to leave the female

Fig. 15. Schematic representation of hemipteran internal reproductive organs.

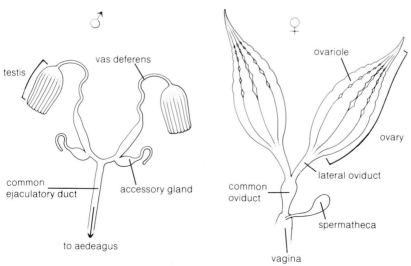

alone after insemination, another male's sperm might displace his. The sperm in the spermatheca is used on a last-in, first-out basis and this phenomenon, known as sperm precedence, effectively means that the last male to copulate will fertilize the lion's share of the eggs laid. The proportion of existing sperm displaced by the last male to inseminate can vary from as little as 20 per cent to over 90 per cent. So, although the actual transferring of sperm from male to female may only last a matter of seconds, copulations lasting several hours or even days are common in the Hemiptera.

Post-insemination strategies do not always require the male to remain locked with the female. Many male bugs may simply guard their mate until just before or even after she lays the eggs. It is thought that, during the spectacular simultaneous emergences seen in many cicada species, the females mate only once while the males can mate several times. Further matings are prevented by the successful male, who uses a seminal plug to block part of the female's genital apparatus.

In certain groups of bugs, males do not inseminate the female by introducing the aedeagus into the genital tract. Instead, sharp parts of the male's external genitalia are used to penetrate the body wall of the female or in some species the wall of the vagina. This strange process, known as traumatic (or haemocoelic) insemination (or fecundation), is found in all species belonging to the **Cimicidae**, **Plokiophilidae** and **Polyctenidae** and some species in the **Anthocoridae** and **Nabidae** (subfamily Prostemminae). These families and two other, very small families, the **Velocipedidae** and the **Medocostidae**, about whose biology very little is known, belong to the superfamily Cimicoidea. In adult females there is no proper spermatheca but some, which do not exhibit haemocoelic insemination, may have other seminal sacs to store extra sperm.

Although the result is the same in cimicoid bugs, the way in which the male

Locked tail to tail, a pair of broad-headed bugs (*Hyalymenus* sp.) mate on foliage in Trinidad. The male, with enlarged hind legs, is facing to the right. The female appears to be probing a fruit with her rostrum as copulation proceeds. **Alydidae**

introduces his sperm into tissues of the female's body cavity varies from family to family. In the simplest case, male prostemmine nabids such as those of the genera *Alloeorhynchus*, *Prostemma* and *Pagasa* introduce their aedeagus through the normal genital opening in the female. Copulation in these bugs usually takes place with the male's and female's undersides opposed. When in place, a spine at the tip of the aedeagus penetrates the wall of the vagina and the sperms are then released and pumped into the haemocoel. In some nabids there may be a special pocket to receive the sperm; it subsequently bursts to release the sperm into the haemocoel. Although some of the sperms are destroyed by the females' immune system, the majority migrate towards the ovaries where they accumulate around the bases of the ovarioles. Fertilization of the follicles occurs by means of the sperm getting under the surrounding layer of cells.

In the **Cimicidae**, **Polyctenidae**, **Plokiophilidae** and most **Anthocoridae** the process of insemination is even more bizarre and complicated. Although the details of the process may differ slightly between families and genera, males never actually use the female genital tract. Instead, using a specially shaped, sharp clasper or paramere, they directly penetrate the cuticle of the abdomen between two segments. The aedeagus then pumps sperm in a dense mass through the hole. The cuticle of the female is physically punctured in a variety of locations according to species.

Lying immediately beneath the site of the wound, which heals after insemination, there may be a special mass of tissue called the mesospermalège. In some genera there is a cuticular lined pocket, called the ectospermalège, to take the male's piercing clasper and aedeagus. Together, the ectospermalège and the underlying mesospermalège are known as either the organ of Berlese or Ribaga's organ. These organs may be dorsal or ventral, to one side or in the body mid-line, but all serve to receive the male's ejaculate.

The sperms migrate through the tissues of the spermalège and are conveyed either into the haemocoel or by special conductive tissues or cells to secondary sperm stores called seminal conceptacles. These conceptacles function effectively as spermathecae, and are located at the base of each of the lateral oviducts.

In the **Anthocoridae**, the males of some species (*Anthocoris* and *Orius*) copulate by introducing the aedeagus into a special opening between the seventh and eighth segments on the underside of the abdomen. The sperm are pumped into a centrally located sac which acts as a store and conveys it through special tissues to the bottom of each of the lateral oviducts. In these bugs, therefore, the male's sperm is never actually free inside the fluids or cells of the body cavity.

Male bugs can make mistakes when picking a partner for copulation. In some species males will attempt to mate with nymphs, males, non-receptive females, females of the wrong species and even inanimate objects of the right size, shape, colour or smell. Freed from the necessity of actually coupling with specific three-dimensional female structures, it is not surprising that adult males of those bugs practising haemocoelic insemination frequently engage in homosexual activity.

Homosexual copulation has been observed in cimicids, plokiophilids and many anthocorid species. In the anthocorid species *Xylocoris maculipennis* homosexual rape is fairly common and is indistinguishable from normal sexual activity. The male punctures the cuticle of the other male in the normal manner and his injected sperms migrate through the haemocoel to the testes and seminal vesicles of the 'victim'. This process may seem like a waste of sperm, but nothing could be further from the truth. When the raped male next copulates with a female he will not just be passing on his own genes but those of the rapist. The rapist can thus inseminate females himself in the normal way and other females by proxy.

Egg laying and guarding

When an egg is laid it passes down the lateral oviduct from the ovary into the common oviduct, and from here to the outside through an external egg-laying structure or ovipositor (if there is one). An ovipositor is present in heteropteran and auchenorrhynchan bugs; it may be quite long and elongate or short and flattened. In most heteropteran bugs the ovipositor consists of two pairs of valves; in most auchenorrhynchans, the ovipositor has three pairs. The vast majority of female sternorrhynchan bugs do not have a valved ovipositor (Aphidoidea and Coccoidea), but psyllids have a small ovipositor made of three pairs of valves protected by two special plates. In those species that lay their eggs inside plant tissue, such as the **Miridae**, the ovipositor may be enlarged and its apex equipped with minute saw-like serrations to enable the female to cut through the epidermal tissues of their host plant.

When present and well developed, the ovipositor can be clearly seen lying in a slit on the underside of the female's abdomen. Bugs in other groups with reduced or rudimentary ovipositors, or none at all, simply lay their eggs directly on surfaces. At some point during their journey from the ovary to the end of the vagina, typically in the common oviduct, the passing eggs are fertilized by sperm released from the spermatheca.

Bug eggs may be laid singly or in groups, glued to surfaces or inserted inside foliage in terrestrial habitats or under water. Like all living tissue they need oxygen, and to achieve the necessary exchange of gases, minute holes or aeropyles are present. In aquatic eggs, the aeropyles are protected by a finely structured, mesh-like layer which acts as a physical gill or plastron. The layer of air, held in place by the upper layer of the egg shell, absorbs oxygen from the surrounding water and carbon dioxide is given up in solution. In other species there may be a number of elongate respiratory horns.

To assist the hatching of the tiny first instar nymphs the egg's shell may have lines of weakness along which it splits easily, or a cap-like lid known as the operculum. The hatching nymphs may assist themselves to leave the egg by using special spines, ridges or temporary egg bursters on their heads. In heteropterans there are usually five nymphal instars before the adult stage is reached (Fig. 16), whereas in auchenorrhynchans and sternorrhynchans the number of nymphal instars may vary from three to eight depending on the group concerned.

The eggs of bugs may be protected by being laid in the tissues of plants or in crevices and cracks under bark. The eggs of species which lay in exposed positions on the foliage of plants, or in chambers in soil, may be vulnerable to predators. In many bugs the female, or less commonly the male, parent may invest considerable energy in protecting their eggs and nymphs from attack by predatory insects such as anthocorid bugs, ladybird and hover fly larvae and

LEFT: Moving slowly forwards over a leaf in the tropical dry forest of Costa Rica, a cryptically coloured, female shield bug cements a neat double row of green, barrel-shaped eggs to the surface of a leaf. **Pentatomidae**

RIGHT: On close inspection, this thin red line is made up of many, very small, first instar, shield bug nymphs which have just broken out from their eggs. South Africa. **Pentatomidae**

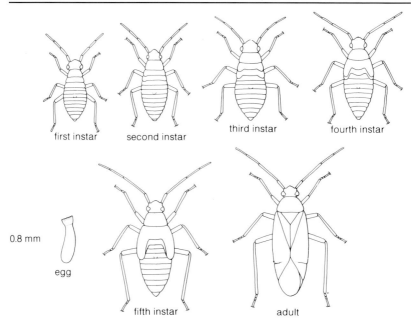

first instar   second instar

third instar

fourth instar

0.8 mm

egg

fifth instar

adult

Fig 16. The egg, nymphal stages and adult of a typical heteropteran bug. The egg is actually only the length of the adult's last hind tarsal segment. (**Miridae**)

parasitoid wasp species. Female brood guarding is well known in treehoppers (**Membracidae**) and aetalionids (**Aetalionidae**); several pentatomoids, mainly shield bugs (**Pentatomidae** and **Scutelleridae**); leaf-footed bugs (**Coreidae**); and some species of assassin bug (**Reduviidae**), burrowing bug (**Cydnidae**), bark bug (**Aradidae**) and lace bug (**Tingidae**).

When dealing with the often complex repertoire of behaviours shown by these and other bugs towards their offspring, it is all too easy to use terms like 'maternal instinct', 'caring' and 'protecting' in a way which implies that the insect knows or has a choice in what it is doing. But what we see may be simply a genetically based, automatic response on the part of the adult bug, or an action brought about by alarm pheromones or other behaviour-releasing triggers. It is known, for instance, that in some species the smell of a crushed nymph will evoke aggressive responses from the adult female. While bugs undoubtedly defend their brood extremely vigorously against all manner of threats, care must be exercised when interpreting these activities.

Species belonging to very many genera (*Leptocentrus, Platycentrus, Platycotis, Polyglypta, Acanophora, Umbonia, Membracis, Guayaquila, Sextus* and others) in several membracid subfamilies exhibit maternal care of eggs and nymphs; indeed, the habit may be considered characteristic of the family. In a few species the male will take a minor role in sharing the duties of guarding with the female.

Defensive strategies include vigorous wing fanning, buzzing, rapid movements, physical contact and butting. Overall protection may be greatly increased in those species attended by ants, and there may be subtle interactions

To protect them from enemies, an almost beetle-like female shield bug (*Pachycovis* sp.) straddles the clutch of eggs she has glued to a leaf in the Panamanian rain forest. Some of the eggs are dark-coloured and very nearly ready to hatch. **Scutelleridae**

When danger threatens, young shield bug nymphs (*Cocoteris* sp.) crowd together under the body of the female for protection. At their next moult they will be too big and have to defend themselves. New Guinean rain forest. **Pentatomidae**

Mimicking plant thorns, a cluster of treehoppers (*Umbonia spinosa*) cling to a plant stem in the Peruvian rain forest. The females of this and many other treehopper species exhibit maternal care. **Membracidae**

between ant and treehopper in the decision about where she lays her eggs. Females of some species may add their own eggs to egg masses defended by another female. The advantages may be mutual, in that the non-guarding female has her eggs looked after for free while the guarding female's eggs may be partly protected by the additional eggs placed in a more vulnerable position around the outside. Once hatched, the young nymphs continue to be protected and are often herded into groups by means of the female's legs. The females of some species provide ready-made feeding sites close together by slitting the plant's surface with their ovipositors.

In most species the female loses interest in her brood once they have reached the third instar, while in others her protection may be continued in some degree until the nymphs reach adulthood. In some membracid genera, the females have been shown to desert their egg masses to lay another mass elsewhere. They do, however, show a marked tendency to desert a small egg mass rather than a large one. Various complicated crèche systems occur and there are undoubtedly many more surprises in store, particularly in the tropical forests where these fascinating bugs are mainly found.

Within the Heteroptera, some very interesting phenomena occur. It has been known for a long time that some lace bugs species (*Corythuca* spp. and *Gargaphia* spp. of the **Tingidae**) guard their eggs and nymphs, and herd nymphs from place to place in response to changing food quality or threats such as predatory bugs and spiders. The cost to the female, especially in those species which guard

Taking their first steps, tiny assassin bug nymphs, freshly emerged from their egg clusters, will soon disperse to seek their first meal. Brazil. **Reduviidae**

from egg until adulthood, is in the potential number of eggs she can lay. If she protects, she can lay fewer eggs, but the important point is that the survival rate of those few eggs is much greater than that of unprotected eggs. This being so, there is a great selective advantage to be gained from guarding.

What has been found out concerning a species of Nearctic tingid, the Eggplant Lace Bug (*Gargaphia solani*), is intriguing. These bugs may lay several clutches of eggs in a single year, gluing them to the undersides of host plant leaves (*Solanum* spp.). A certain proportion of the adult females in a population may never look after their own eggs; instead they find the first suitable foster female, who may be laying her own eggs at the time, and they add their eggs to the egg mass. This phenomenon has become known as egg dumping. As a result, not all females in a population rear their own offspring. Occasionally females may add their eggs to another's and then guard the whole mass by ousting the other female; in other cases the foster female may reject the other female and drive her away.

Egg dumpers, freed from the arduous task of many weeks' guard duty, can lay a lot more eggs. If all the lace bugs egg dumped there would be nobody to look after any of the eggs, but it has been found that there are always some females who will guard even if they do not have to and, conversely, there are females who always seem to egg dump. Research has subsequently shown that young females, with great potential as reproducers, are the ones who tend not to look after their young and prefer to dump their eggs on someone else. Older females, which have

Displaying paternal care, unusual among insects, a male assassin bug (*Rhinocoris tristis*) sits guard over his mate's regular array of columnar eggs to defend them from predators and parasitoids. Just visible on the midrib of the leaf, two tiny parasitic wasps of the family Trichogrammatidae wait their chance to lay their own eggs inside the bug's eggs. The male reduviid will chase them away or try to stab them with his rostrum. Kenya. **Reduviidae**

much less potential as reproducers, are the ones who tend to act as efficient guards and have eggs dumped on them.

It is not yet clear to what extent egg dumpers and the guarding females are genetically related. The proportion of the population using either strategy may be greatly influenced by available food resources, population density and environmental conditions.

While it is usually the job of the female to protect the brood, in several species of **Reduviidae** and **Belostomatidae** the males take over the role. Such behaviour is probably much more widespread than known at present. There have been some unconfirmed reports of paternal care in a very few species belonging to the **Gerridae**, **Aradidae** and **Coreidae**. Males of some species in the reduviid genera *Rhinocoris* and *Zelus* behave similarly.

In *Rhinocoris*, the male is carried on the back of the female while he copulates with her. The female then lays a batch of eggs, each just under 2 mm (0.08 in) long, which she glues in a regular, tight cluster to the leaf of a plant. The male stands by and, when the female has finished laying, takes up his position astride the egg mass. Over the course of the next few days the female will mate several times with the guarding male and lay additional egg batches. Sometimes, other females with whom the brooding male has not mated will also add their own contribution to the egg mass. During the time that the male is guarding he will chase off parasitic wasps and other dangers; he does not generally feed unless easily caught prey comes his way.

When the eggs have all hatched, the male loses interest and moves away. In contrast to this, newly hatched *Zelus* nymphs do not disperse straightaway and the male may provide some additional protection until they do. The male may not always be completely successful in defending his progeny – when he is guarding a large egg mass those on the outside may fall victim to minute parasitic wasps such as those of the family Scelionidae.

The most famous case of sexual role reversal in bugs is found among the **Belostomatidae**. The females of many species, such as those belonging to the genera *Belostoma* and *Abedus* (Belostomatinae), take a major part in courting and competing for available males, on to whose folded front wings they glue their eggs (Fig. 17). The cost of this brooding service may be quite high to the male. While carrying a large and heavy egg mass he is less mobile and less able to catch prey; as he cannot use his wings, he cannot move away from the pond in which he lives. Given the high cost of his protection, it is quite important that the eggs the male bug is looking after are indeed his: there would be no point in putting himself at risk for another male at the expense of his own genes.

Like many other hemipterans, female giant water bugs can store sperm from

A single adult female Egg-plant Lace Bug (*Gargaphia solani*) seems to have her work cut out as she tends a large mass of nymphs. It is probable that not all the nymphs are hers; some may have hatched from eggs dumped into her egg mass by other females. Mexico.
Tingidae

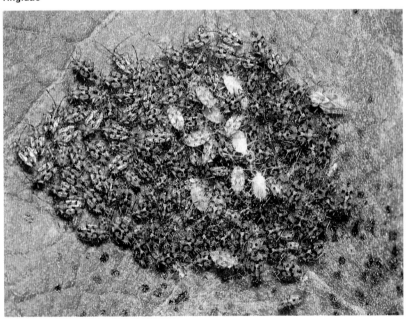

previous matings inside special organs known as spermathecae in their bodies. As previously mentioned, due to the widespread phenomenon of sperm precedence the sperm from the last mating is generally going to fertilize a much larger proportion of the eggs laid by the female than the sperm of an earlier mating. It is therefore understandable that males will only allow the females to glue eggs on their backs once they have mated with them. The male further enhances this assurance of paternity by letting the female glue no more than a few eggs at a time before he copulates again. When all the eggs are laid, the female leaves the male to look after their brood.

In other giant water bugs (Lethocerinae), where the egg masses are glued to emergent vegetation, it is still the male bug which protects them and prevents them from drying out by carrying water from the pond to moisten them. As with the back-brooding species, egg masses which are not properly aerated or moistened will not hatch. In some species of *Lethocerus*, the males may have to protect their egg masses from other females and the older nymphs of other broods, which can be highly cannibalistic. When few non-brooding males are available, females will try to take over brooding males by pinching them with their powerful front legs and using their beak. The male may fight back, but if he is driven off the egg mass the female may destroy all the eggs. After the eggs are killed, the female may then copulate with the male and lay her own eggs.

Fig. 17. A female *Abedus* giant water bug (**Belostomatidae**) glues additional eggs on to the dorsal surface of her mate's folded front wings.

Chapter 8
Bugs and People

Insects, whether reviled or revered, have always been very important to the human race. They played a major role in mythology, religion, art, health and food production, both positive and negative, in the past, and continue to do so today. Among the insects the Hemiptera are, without doubt, one of the most important orders as far as their impact on mankind is concerned. Bugs have been present on Earth for a lot longer than humans and have long since become an indispensable component of the unique web of life that, despite our concerted and misguided actions of the last hundred years, still persists on this planet.

While the vast majority of the 82,000 or so bug species that have been described to date have no direct effect on man and his endeavours, there are a couple of thousand which cause damage to a huge range of commercially important plants through feeding and the transmission of viruses and other disease-producing organisms. The whole of the suborders Auchenorrhyncha and Sternorrhyncha and many of the Heteroptera feed only on plants. Blood feeders such as triatomine reduviids can bring about illness, great suffering and early death.

There are, however, also many useful bug species. Predacious species of all kinds keep a large number of insect pests under control, and some of these have been incredibly useful as man-managed agents of biological control against both insect pests and weeds.

Blood feeders

There are many reported cases of bugs biting people with unpleasant results. Although the word 'bite' is used in this context bugs cannot, of course, bite in the true sense; instead, their mouthparts pierce or stab through the skin's surface.

Species in all the predatory bug families and a few in some of the phytophagous families, such as the **Membracidae**, **Cicadidae** and **Cicadellidae**, have occasionally bitten people. But when phytophagous bugs probe skin, they are simply trying to obtain moisture. The most important bugs, and those which have evolved specifically for the ingestion of vertebrate blood, are found in the **Cimicidae** and **Reduviidae** (Triatominae) (Fig. 18).

Reaction to bug bites can vary enormously from mild itching to local tissue destruction, allergic reactions and shock. The bites of reduviid bugs and some of the larger predatory species can produce excruciating pain, pronounced swelling and numbness, nausea, dizziness, headaches, chest pains and a marked reduction in heart rate and blood pressure. In some rare cases, involving very sensitive individuals in extreme shock, death may occur as a result of respiratory failure, oedema of the lungs and other body parts. Reduviid bugs in the genus *Platymeris* are known to spit or eject saliva from the end of their rostrum. The author was once bitten on the hand by a triatomine bug nestling in a palm tree; it

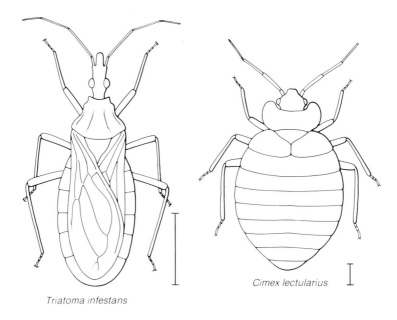

Triatoma infestans

Cimex lectularius

Fig. 18. Two serious human blood feeders. Approximate body lengths are shown beside each bug.

caused severe swelling and pain which lasted for forty-eight hours.

Bed bugs have a long association with people and their dwellings. Writings concerning their bloodthirsty activities go back to the days of the Ancient Greeks. Originally confined to the warmer parts of the world, the bed bug has now become virtually cosmopolitan. During the early part of this century its widespread occurrence in temperate and cool temperate regions was probably caused by the regular heating of dwellings. But *Cimex lectularius* – from the latin words *Cimex*, meaning a bug, and *lectularius* meaning of a bed or couch – is not nearly as common in Great Britain nowadays. Only a few thousand cases of infestation are reported every year.

In the past, various curative potions for ailments ranging from kidney problems to malaria, and remedies against snakebite and leeches, have used whole or crushed bed bugs. They probably became intimately dependent on human blood when early man settled down to live in caves with fires for warmth during cold spells. There is good evidence that cimicids were probably once confined to bat species; but, having found a regular and increasingly common food supply, they may have transferred their feeding activities to humans.

Adult bed bugs are flattened, reddish brown, wingless, nocturnally active insects with a body length of 4–6 mm (0.16–0.25 in). During the day the bugs hide in bedding, mattresses or cracks in floors, walls and other structures. Eggs are laid in cracks and crevices in rooms where people sleep, and they hatch in one or two weeks depending on temperature. There are five nymphal stages, and during each instar the young bugs may feed more than once. The entire life cycle, which is affected by temperature and food supply, can take anything from two to ten months.

Hosts are located, at least at close range, by body temperature; but odours and carbon dioxide are almost certainly also involved. The adults can live for several months and sometimes longer than a year without a blood meal. When they feed, adult bed bugs can consume more than five times their own weight in blood in a matter of 15 minutes after which they hide away.

Infestations are normally associated with poor hygiene and poverty. In the past, insecticides of various kinds have been very successful in controlling this bug, but in some parts of the world the insects have become resistant. Bed bugs have been suspected of acting as vectors for several human viral and bacterial diseases, including viral hepatitis, but no positive evidence has been found. Recently there has been concern over the possible transmission of human immunodeficiency virus (HIV) by bed bugs. Using highly infected blood to feed a tropical species of man-biting bed bugs (*Cimex hemipterus*), researchers have shown that, while the virus could be detected in the bugs many days after feeding, the virus particles did not multiply and were not passed out with the bugs' excrement. Transmission could not be proved, and it was concluded that infection by this means was impossible or highly improbable. But, as in many other areas of research, we simply do not know enough at present to be absolutely sure.

Chagas' disease, prevalent in Central and South America, is caused by the microscopic protozoan organism *Trypanosoma cruzi*, carried by triatomine reduviid bugs of many species. Members of the subfamily Triatominae, comprising just over 100 species, are found mainly in the Neotropical and Oriental regions of the world. The disease organism and the bugs that carry it have been present in Central and South America for a long time and, before the arrival of people, infection was confined to a variety of other mammalian species, birds and some marsupials. At the beginning of this century a Brazilian doctor, Carlos Chagas, first recognized and described the disease in humans and investigated the life cycle and other aspects of the protozoan and its insect vectors. Recent estimates indicate that up to 18 million humans may be affected by this disease, and that 90 million more are at risk.

Triatomine bugs vary greatly in their host preferences and the extent to which they have become adapted to living in domestic situations. At one end of the spectrum, some species are never found anywhere but in the wild and live in a whole range of habitats and microhabitats such as the crowns of palm trees, the nests of certain birds and the burrows and homes of animals such as armadillos, opossums and rats. At the other end some species, notably of *Triatoma*, *Panstrongylus* and *Rhodnius*, have become intimately associated with humans, their houses and domestic animals. The three most important species in this regard are *Triatoma infestans*, *T. dimidiata* and *Rhodnius prolixus*. A further 18 or so species, belonging to the three genera mentioned above, can act as vectors for the disease but are more local in distribution. The disease is much more common in rural areas, where houses may harbour up to 1,000 bugs.

After passing through five nymphal instars, the adults reach a length of about

25 mm (1 in). During daylight hours they hide in thatch or in cracks and crevices in walls. They emerge to feed at night, biting sleeping people especially on the face and around the mouth – hence the common name of kissing bugs. An adult triatomine bug can ingest anything up to 10 times its own weight in a single blood meal. The risk of infection from a single bite is low but, since people may receive a dozen bites a night and thousands in a year, the risk of infection by *Trypanosoma cruzi* is considerable. When they feed, the bugs leave excrement behind on the skin; transmission of the protozoan occurs when people scratch their bites.

As many as half a million people may contract Chagas' disease annually and of these some 45,000, mainly children, may die in the early critical phase. Those who survive are infected for life. The parasite, circulating in the bloodstream, infects, multiplies and ultimately destroys muscle and nerve cells all around the body, particularly in the heart and digestive system. The medical problems associated with it range from general weakness to serious problems of the alimentary tract, cardiac arrhythmia, heart failure. Death may result. Drugs are available, but they are expensive and to have any effect must be given soon after infection occurs. The disease can also be contracted by the transfusion of already infected blood.

Recently, many South American countries have banded together to combat this scourge by mounting a multi-million-dollar insecticidal spraying programme. Using a chemical cocktail of synthetic pyrethroid insecticides, every human habitation in infected areas will be sprayed to control triatomine bugs, particularly *Triatoma infestans*. It is hoped that, due to the relatively long life cycle of these bugs and the simultaneous use of several insecticides, resistance will not develop.

Plant feeders

The world's human food production is based on a mere handful of plant species. Many are grasses, grown in vast uniform stands (monocultures) and, in developed countries, largely sustained through the use of huge quantities of fertilizers and pesticides. The domestication and improvement of these species has in many cases led to their becoming a better nutritional resource (for both humans and insects), but with fewer chemical and physical defences against herbivores. Monocultures contain far fewer beneficial insect species, which might control the numbers of pests, than are present in more complex habitats.

Phytophagous insects in general and many bug species in particular are superbly suited to using these crops as food plants. Many bug species only became pests when their preferred food plant suddenly became abundant, and many others have switched from wild plant species to cultivated ones. On account of their phenomenal reproductive powers, pests like aphids and scale insects can adapt very quickly to take advantage of new opportunities and develop resistance to man-made insecticides. It is therefore not surprising that nearly one-fifth of the world's crop production is eaten by insects.

In the Hemiptera, all the sternorrhynchan superfamilies, the Psylloidea, Aleyrodoidea, Adelgoidea, Aphidoidea and Coccoidea, contain notable plant-damaging species. While the worldwide economic damage and losses that plant-

Stylets thrust deep into vascular tissue, a large colony of Rose Aphids (*Macrosiphum rosae*) feed on rose sap. The back surface of the abdomen carries a pair of long, dark siphunculi or cornicles, through which a defensive fluid can be secreted. Because of their phenomenal powers of reproduction and the transmission of plant diseases, many aphid species are very serious pests. Great Britain. **Aphididae**

A recent introduction to Great Britain, *Pulvinaria regalis* attacks lime, horse chestnut, plane, sycamore, maple and other tree species. Very many coccid species are serious pests. Here a group of adult females with their white woolly ovisacs form part of a dense colony on a lime tree. **Coccidae**

feeding bugs can cause is immense, the vast majority of species are not pests. Of the several thousand species of aphid, probably no more than 150 are notorious crop pests. Similarly, of the 2,500 known species of armoured scale insect (**Diaspididae**) in the world, fewer than 150 are of economic significance and of these perhaps fewer than 50 could be called serious pests.

This is not to underestimate the impact that these insects have on world crop production. The effects do not have to be obvious – like the death of the plant. Under the intensive agricultural systems practised in many parts of the world today, with fewer and fewer growers producing increasing quantities of food for more and more consumers, there are economic thresholds. With any commercial crop, the cost of production must be taken into account. Reduction in yields by only a few per cent, caused by bug feeding or disease transmission, could result in financial disaster.

Broadly speaking, aphids and scale insects are the most damaging and widespread of all bug species, responsible for almost incalculable economic losses worldwide. Their feeding causes physical damage and metabolic disorders, and directly infects the plants or makes them prone to a plethora of viral, rickettsial, mycoplasmal and fungal diseases.

The viral diseases that are transmitted to plants by aphids probably do much more damage than the aphids' theft of nutrients, and aphid pest species are capable of transmitting a number of different viruses to their host plants simultaneously. These diseases can be acquired by probing already infected plant tissues, and are then carried in the bug's rostrum. Some of the viruses can survive in the bug's mouthparts for only a short while; others may last longer. Many other disease-causing viruses, rickettsias and mycoplasmas can actually multiply within the bodies of their bug vectors, and are passed to the bug's offspring by means of transovariole infection in the female's body. To become infected with this type of organism an aphid has got to feed for some time from an infected plant, not just probe the tissues.

The streaking or breaking of colour in flower petals, thought by some people to be attractive, is caused by bug-borne viral infection. In the seventeenth and eighteenth centuries, before people knew about viruses, flowers affected in this

Hardly looking like insects at all, these flattened, oval female scale insects produce from the rear end of their body a waxy mass inside which they lay their eggs. Just visible, and equipped with functional legs, a number of minute first instar nymphs, called crawlers, ensure dispersal. Many coccoid species are pests of citrus and other valuable tropical crops. Brazil. **Coccidae**

way were highly prized and great but fruitless efforts were made to encourage the phenomenon.

Planthoppers (**Delphacidae**) are a cosmopolitan group of auchenorrhynchan bugs, many of them confined to grasses. Unfortunately a large number of the world's important crops, such as rice, wheat, sugarcane, sorghum and maize, are grasses. Delphacids, like other phloem sap-sucking bug species, damage the plants by taking nutrients, reducing yields, causing a characteristic yellowing of the leaves and acting as vectors for plant viruses.

Leafhoppers (**Cicadellidae**), which feed by emptying the contents of plant cells, cause a characteristic spotting or stippling effect, while others feed in phloem vascular tissue and cause browning, wilting, stunting, curling and death of affected parts. Leafhopper saliva is toxic to the plants, and phloem-feeding species are notorious vectors of plant viral diseases. As a group, leafhoppers are the next most serious vectors of plant diseases after aphids. But strains of major crop plants such as cotton, potatoes, beans and alfalfa are being developed which are resistant to damage by leafhoppers and some of their associated virus

A male and female *Anasa varicornis*. mate on a leaf. Some species in the genus can be pests of squash plants and cucumbers. Trinidad. **Coreidae**

diseases. These successful hybrids have been obtained by crossing the cultivated varieties with available wild plant stock which showed a natural resistance to attack. However, the bugs are evolving as well. Many pest bugs species are now resistant to certain insecticides, and in time they will adapt to whatever natural or man-made obstacle is put in their path.

Biological control of bug pests using bacteria, fungi, predators and parasites can be very successful. Of the 500 or so control programmes directed against auchenorrhynchan and sternorrhynchan species (mainly aphidoids and coccoids), just over 40 per cent have resulted in the pest being controlled satisfactorily. Integrated pest management, employing a whole variety of different techniques and incorporating biological control, may hold out some hope for the future.

Useful bugs

The tissues of insects are very nutritious; besides forming a vital part of the diet of innumerable animal species, they have been used as human food in the past and continue to be used by many tribal peoples today. While beetle larvae, caterpillars and locusts are the insects that spring to mind in this connection, some of the Hemiptera can provide a valuable source of protein and fat.

The honeydew of sap-sucking auchenorrhynchan and sternorrhynchan bugs such as cicadas, planthoppers, leafhoppers, psyllids, aphidoids and coccoids is very rich in sugars. Some species produce vast quantities of this sweet excrement, which builds up on foliage and can be scraped or licked off. In a few psyllid species the immature stages retain their excrement, which dries and accumulates as a thick, variously shaped and sculptured covering called a lerp. Species belonging to the psyllid subfamily Spondyliaspinae are well known; their lerps are gathered by native Australian peoples who prize them as a delicacy. Honeydew in all its forms is eaten in many parts of the world, either on its own as a sweet, or to make a sweet or even alcoholic drink.

A variety of coccoid waxes and resins have proved useful to human beings for the production of cosmetics, folk medicines and candles. The two best-known examples are the resinous secretions of the Lac Insect *Kerria lacca* (**Kerriidae**), from which shellac is made, and the colouring agent cochineal, which is obtained from the bodies of species belonging to the genus *Dactylopius* (**Dactylopiidae**).

The Lac Insect is cultivated commercially on fig, banyan and other tree species in the Oriental region, particularly in India, Burma, the Philippines and Thailand. The resinous material, which forms encrustations up to 15 mm (0.6 in) thick around the bodies of the insects, is gathered by scraping it from the twigs. It is then melted, dried and dissolved in raw alcohol to produce shellac, which is used in the manufacture of high-quality varnishes. Around 33,000 Lac Insects are required to make a kilogram of shellac (15,000 to the pound). Shellac has been used in the Old World for thousands of years, and now foreign exports contribute very significantly to the economies of the countries where it is still produced.

Cochineal is obtained from the bodies of female *Dactylopius coccus* insects. They are harvested by brushing them from their prickly pear cactus host plant, after which they are killed by drying them in the sun or boiling them in water. The

While many species in the genus *Ceroplastes* are of significant economic importance as pests of cultivated plants, the wax produced by a few species, particularly in the Oriental region, is used commercially. Brazil. **Coccidae**

dead bugs are then dried and ground up to extract the valuable dyestuffs, which can be crimson, red or orange. Around 155,000 insects are used to make a kilogram of cochineal (70,000 to the pound). Today, this natural dye has been largely replaced by modern synthetic ones and the cochineal industry is not nearly as thriving as it once was, surviving on a commercial scale only in the Canary Islands, Honduras and Mexico. However, cochineal is still used in the colouring of some cosmetics, food and drink and has a role in alternative medicine. In Mexico, cochineal insects have also been dried and used to make a kind of bread.

From the ancient Greeks to the present day, cicadas have been eaten, roasted or fried in many parts of the world from North America to Malaysia and Australia. The fully developed, emerging nymphs (Fig. 19), and adult females engorged with eggs are preferred to the adult males, whose air-filled abdomens do not provide much of a snack. The cicadas can be gathered when they emerge *en masse*, or dug out as nymphs from the ground; there have been reports of tribal peoples using hand-clapping or bird lime to attract the females.

A few other auchenorrhynchan bug species have been used as food. In Madagascar, certain species of fulgorid bug have been eaten. Treehoppers of the genus *Umbonia* congregate in large numbers on trees in South America at certain times of the year and, although armed with a sharp dorsal thoracic spine, they are apparently reasonable to eat if roasted. Despite the fact that many terrestrial heteroptern species are protected by their noxious metathoracic gland secretions, a variety of pentatomid bugs and others have been eaten by peoples in Africa, New Guinea, India and Mexico. In some places the bugs are first squeezed to empty the stink glands before cooking; however, some folk medicinal preparations use the fluids, which are thought to be good for the prevention of rheumatism and the curing of various stomach, liver and kidney complaints.

Giant water bugs (**Belostomatidae**) feature widely in the diets of people native to many parts of the Oriental region. Steamed, boiled or roasted, bugs in the genera *Belostoma* and *Lethocerus* are very popular and are caught with special nets or attracted to lights after dark. Although the eating of giant water bugs is no longer as widespread as it used to be, they are still considered a great delicacy by many humans and the bugs' scent gland secretions are sometimes used as seasoning or to make flavoured salt. Other species of water bug, particularly the **Corixidae**, can be eaten as adults; they also provide ample supplies of eggs, which can be used as a sort of flour. To harvest them, hundreds of bundles of a particular species of rush are prepared and lowered into the water. In a few weeks the rushes will become covered with corixid (and sometimes notonectid) eggs. The bundles are taken out, dried and beaten to release the eggs, which are then cleaned. In Mexico the resultant flour is used to make cakes called Hautlé. Corixid eggs have been used in a similar manner in parts of Egypt.

Several brightly coloured heteropteran species have featured in folk art, and the front wings of a few species find their way into jewellery. In areas of the world prone to drought, the hard, cyst-like, subterranean, resting nymphal stages of some species of *Margarodes* (**Margarodidae**), known as ground pearls, are threaded together and worn as necklaces. *Rhodnius prolixus*, a reduviid bug, will be familiar to anyone who has undertaken a degree course or further education in biology, where it is of great value as a laboratory insect. Pioneering physiological studies into the hormonal control of insect metamorphosis and development were carried out using this bug, and it continues to be much used in research and teaching today.

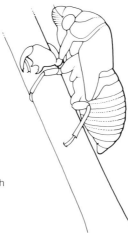

Fig. 19. A final instar cicada nymph crawls up a stem where it will moult into the adult form.

Further Reading

The following reading list is by no means exhaustive, but will enable the reader to study the subject of entomology in general and bugs in particular in greater depth; it also provides a good entry to the considerable literature available. Children interested in bugs are directed to McGavin (1988).

Allaby, M. (1985), *The Oxford Dictionary of Natural History*. Oxford University Press.

Arnett, R.H. Jnr (1985), *American Insects: A Handbook of the Insects of America North of Mexico*. Van Nostrand Reinhold, New York.

Arnett, R.H. Jnr and Jacques, R.L. Jnr (1981), *Guide to Insects*. Simon and Schuster, New York and London.

Borror, D.J., De Long, D.M. and Triplehorn, C.A. (1981), *Introduction to the Study of Insects* (5th edn). Saunders College Publishing, New York.

Borror, D.J. and White, R.E. (1970), *A Field Guide to the Insects of America North of Mexico*. Houghton Mifflin Co., Boston.

Chapman, R.F. (1982), *The Insects: Structure and Function* (3rd edn). English University Press, London.

Chinery, M. (1986), *Collins Guide to Insects of Britain and Western Europe*. Collins, London.

CSIRO, ed. (1991), *The Insects of Australia. A Textbook for Students and Research Workers*, 2 vols. Melbourne University Press, Carlton.

Daly, H.V., Doyen, J.T. and Ehrlich, P.R. (1978), *Introduction to Insect Biology and Diversity*. McGraw-Hill, New York and Maidenhead.

Dixon, A.F.G. (1973), *Biology of Aphids*. The Institute of Biology's Studies in Biology no. 44, Edward Arnold, London.

Dolling, W.R. (1991), *The Hemiptera*. Natural History Museum Publications, Oxford University Press.

Henry, T.J. and Froeschner, R.C., eds. (1988), *Catalog of the Heteroptera or True Bugs of Canada and the Continental United States*. E.J. Brill, Leiden, New York, Copenhagen and Cologne.

Linsenmaier, W. (1972), *Insects of the World* (trans. L.E. Chadwick). McGraw-Hill, New York and Maidenhead.

McGavin, G.C. (1988), *Discovering Bugs*. Wayland, Hove, England.

McGavin, G.C. (1992), *The Pocket Guide to the Insects of the Northern Hemisphere*. Dragon's World, Limpsfield.

McGavin, G.C. (1992), *Insects of the Northern Hemisphere*. Dragon's World, Limpsfield.

O'Toole, C., ed. (1986), *The Encyclopedia of Insects*. Allen and Unwin, London/Facts on File, New York.

O'Toole, C. (1985), *Insects in Camera: A Photographic Essay on Behaviour*. Oxford University Press.

Richards, O.W. and Davies, R.G. (1988), *Imm's General Textbook of Entomology* (10th edn, 2 vols). Chapman and Hall, London.

Index

Numbers in *italic* refer to line drawings. Numbers in **bold** refer to colour plates.

abdomen 29–31
Abedus 42, 175, *176*
Acalypta 48
Acanaloniidae 77
Acanophora 170
Acanthocephala **142**
Acanthocephala femorata 163
Acanthosoma 63
Acanthosomatidae 63, **64**, 68
Achilidae 76, 98, 117
Achilixius 77
Aclerdidae 95
Adelges 89
Adelgidae 89, 137
Adelgoidea 83, 89
aedeagus 31
Aetalion reticulatum **132**
Aetalionidae 82, **132**, 170
Aethus 64
air stores 31, 44, 46
Alcaeorrhynchus 68
Aleurocanthus 86
Aleyrodes 86
Aleyrodidae 70, 85, **85**, 118–20, 132, 138
Aleyrodoidea 83, 85
allelochemicals 151–2
Alydidae 61, **61, 128**, 133, 154, 161, **166**
Amblypelta 62
Ambrysus 41
ambush bugs *see* Phymatidae
Amphibicorisae 34
Amulius 156
Anaptus 52
Anasa 62
Anasa varicornis **184**
Androctenes 53
Aneurus 55
Anisops 44
Anoecia 88
Anoeciidae 86–7, 134
Anthocoridae 27, *49*, 51–2, 109, 112, 166–7
Anthocoris 51, 167
Aonidiella 93
Aphelocheiridae 32, 41, 127
Aphelocheirus 41
Aphididae 27, 70, 86, **88**, 88, **116**, **181**
Aphidoidea 83, 86
aphids *see* Aphididae
Aphis 88
Aphrania 52
Aphrophora 78
Aphylidae 69
Apiomeris 54, **154**
Apiomorphidae 95
Arachnocoris 156

Aradidae 47, *49*, 55, **56**, 98, 170, 174
Aradoidea 55
Aradus 55
Arhaphe cicindeloides **126**
Arilus **53**
armoured scales *see* Diaspididae
Arytaina 84
ash-grey leaf bugs *see* Piesmatidae
Asian Rice Brown Planthopper (*Nilaparvata lugens*) 72, 115
assassin bugs *see* Reduviidae
Asterolecaniidae 91
Asterolecanium 91
Auchenorrhyncha 10, 14, 69, *70*

Bacillus thuringiensis 98
backswimmers *see* Notonectidae
bark bugs *see* Aradidae
bat bugs *see* Polyctenidae
Bed Bug *see Cimex lectularius*
Beesonidae 95
beet bugs *see* Piesmatidae
Belostoma 42, 175, **187**
Belostomatidae 32, *37*, 42, 124, 127, 144, 153, 174–5, *176*, **187**
Bemisia tabaci 86
Berytidae *49*, 57, **57**, 132
Berytinus 58
biological control 48, 50–1, 91, 104, 112, 119, 131, 185
Biturritiidae 82
blackfly *see* Aphididae
Blissus 58
bodyguards 133–5
Brachycaudus cardui **116**
Brantosoma notata **125**
Brevicoryne 88
broad-headed bugs *see* Alydidae
Bromocoris foetida **17**
Brown Soft Scale (*Coccus hesperidum*) 92
Bucimex 52
Buenoa 44, 45
burrowing bugs *see* Cydnidae

Cacodmus 52
Callaphididae 86, **110**
Callococcus 91
Calocoris stysi **13**
Calophyidae 85
cannibalism 39
Canopidae 69
Carcinocoris 54
Carsidaridae 85
Centrotus 82
Ceratocombidae 38
Cercopidae 70, 77, **77**, 104, **108**, 111, 114–15, 133, 140, 149, 162
Cercopis 78
Cercopis vulnerata **103**
Cercopoidea 77
Cerococcidae 95
Cerococcus 91
Ceroplastes 92, **186**
Chagas' disease 54, 179–80
Chaitophoridae 86
chemical defences 122–32
Chiloxanthus 36

Chrysomphalus 93
Cicada Killer (*Exeirus lateritius & Sphecius speciosus*) 108
cicadas *see* Cicadidae
Cicadella 80
Cicadellidae 14, *70*, 78, **79**, 80, 100–11, 115, 120, 123, 133, 140, 149, 162, 177, 184
Cicadelloidea 80, 83
Cicadidae 27, *70*, 78, 99, 100, 140, **143**, 149, **160**, 161, 177, *187*
Cicadoidea 78
Cicadomorpha 69, 77
Cicadulina 80
Cimex 52, 97
Cimex hemipterus 179
Cimex lectularius 10, 11, 51–2, 178, *178*
Cimex rotundatus 52
Cimicidae *49*, 51, 52, 130, 144, 146–7, 153, 166–7, 177
Cimicoidea 51
Cimicomorpha 46
Cinch Bug (*Blissus leucopterus*) 58
Cixiidae *70*, **71**, 71, 11, 115, 133
Clastoptera 78
Coccidae *70*, 90, 92, **93**, 107, 137, **182, 183, 186**
Coccoidea 83, 90, 95
Coccus 92
Coccus viridis 92
cochineal (carminic acid) 92, 185–6
cochineal scale insects *see* Dactylopiidae
Coconut Scale (*Aspidiotus destructor*) 106
Cocoteris **171**
Coleorrhyncha 10, 14, 69, *70*
Colobathristidae 58
Colorado Potato Beetle (*Leptinotarsa decemlineata*) 68
Conchaspididae 95
cone-nosed bugs (Triatominae) *see* Reduviidae, *Triatoma*
Coptosoma 68
Coreidae **20**, 29, **30**, *49*, 62, **63**, 112, 114, **121**, **127**, **129**, 133, **139**, **142**, 146, 154, **164**, 170, 174, **184**
Coreoidea 61
Coriaria 76
Corimelaena 64
Coriplatus depressus **124**
Corixa 46
Corixidae 28, 31, *37*, 46, 98, 102, 110, 130, 161, 187
Corixoidea 46
Corn Hopper (*Peregrinus maidis*) 72
Corythuca 48, 172
Cotton Aphid (*Aphis gossypii*) 88
Cotton Boll Worm (*Heleothis zea*) 52
cotton stainers *see* Pyrrhocoridae
Cottony Cushion Scale (*Icerya purchasi*) 95, 106, 111, 159
crawlers 91, **183**
creeping water bugs *see* Naucoridae
Cryptochetum iceryae 111

Cryptognatha nodiceps 106
cuckoo spit **77**
cuckoo spit insects *see* Cercopidae
   78
Cyclotorna monocentra 107
Cydnidae *49*, 64, 114, 140, 170
Cydnus 64
Cymatia 46
Cyphostethus 63
Cyphostethus tristriatus **64**
Cyrpoptus 76
Cyrtopeltis 29

Dactylopiidae 92, 185
Dactylopius coccus 92, 185
Dactylopius opuntiae 92
damsel bugs *see* Nabidae
Delphacidae 14, 50, *70*, 71, 100,
   111, 114–15, 120, 162, 184
Deraeocoris 51
Deraeocoris ruber **153**
Derbidae 73, 98
Dialeurodes 86
Diaspididae *70*, 90, 92, 99–100,
   106–7, 137, 182
Dicranocephalus 63
Dictyonota 48
Dictyopharidae *70*, **72**, 73, 114
Dicyphinae 29
Dicyphus 29, 51
Dinidoridae 69
Dipsocoridae 38, 124
Dipsocoroidea 36
Dipsocoromorpha 36
Distantiella theobroma 50
dorsal pumping organ 33
Drepanosiphum 88
Drymus 58
Dysdercus 60, **113**
Dysdercus flavidus **61**
Dysodius lunatus **56**

Ectinoderus 156
Edessa **25**
egg dumping 173
Egg-plant Lace Bug (*Gargaphia
   solani*) 173, **175**
Elasmolomus 58
Elasmostethus 63
Elasmucha 63
electric light bugs *see*
   Belostomatidae
Embiophila 156
Emesa 156
Emesaya 54
Empicoris 54, 156
Empoasca 80
Encarsia formosa 119
Enicocephalidae 34, 144
Enicocephaloidea 34
Enicocephalomorpha 34
Enithares 44
ensign coccids *see* Ortheziidae
Eriococcidae 95, 107
Eriosoma 136
Eugubinus 156
Eurinopsyche 76
European Lanternfly (*Epiptera
   europea*) **72**

Eurybrachyidae 76
Eurygaster 68
Eurymelidae **81**, 81
expansion skating 41

faunal regions *20*
felted scales *see* Eriococcidae
Ferrisia 95
Fiji disease 72
filter chamber *147*, 149
fire bugs *see* Pyrrhocoridae
flat bugs *see* Aradidae
Flatidae **8**, 73, **74**, 114, **137**
flower bugs *see* Anthocoridae
fossa spongiosa 156
Frenchia 91
froghopper blight 78
froghoppers *see* Cercopidae
Fulgoridae 73, **75**, **94**, 114–15, 133
Fulgoroidea 71
Fulgoromorpha 69, 71
fungal diseases of bugs 98–100

galls 48, 87, 89, 91, 95
Gargaphia 48, 172
Gargara 82
Gelastocoridae *37*, 43, **43**, 124, 127
Gelastocoris 44
Gelastocoris peruensis **43**
Gelastocoroidea 43, 44
Gelastogonia erythropus **134**
Gengidae 77
Geocoris 58
Geocorisae 34
Geotomus 64
Gerridae *37*, 39, **40**, 110, 120, 124,
   152, 153, 174
Gerris lacustris **40**, **152**
Gerroidea 39
Gerromorpha 38
giant scales *see* Margarodidae
giant shield bugs *see*
   Tessaratomidae
giant water bugs *see*
   Belostomatidae
grapevines (*Vitis vinifera*) 90
Green Vegetable Bug (*Nezara
   viridula*) 66
greenfly *see* Aphididae
Greenhouse Whitefly (*Trialeurodes
   vaporariorum*) **85**, 86, 119
Greenideidae 86
ground bug *see* Lygaeidae
ground pearls *see* Margarodidae
Guayaquila 170
gula 22

Haematosiphon 52
haemoglobin 45
Halimococcidae 95
Halobates 40
Harlequin Bug **23**, **32**, **66**, 68
Harpocera thoracica 23
Hebridae *37*, 38, 153
Hebroidea 38
Hebrus 38
Helopeltis 50
Helotrephidae 45
Hermatobatidae 41

Hesperocimex 52
Hesperocorixa 46
Hesperoctenes 53
Heterogaster 58
Heteronotus reticulatus **26**
Heteroptera 10, 34, *49*
hoarding 42
homosexual rape 167
Homotomidae 85
honeydew 82, 84, 86, 87, 91, 111,
   119, 133–5, 185
Hormaphididae 86, 136
Hormaphis 88
Hyalymenus 61, **61**, **128**, **166**
Hydrocorisae 34
Hydrometra stagnorum **144**
Hydrometridae *37*, 39, **144**, 144,
   153
Hydrometroidea 39
Hyocephalidae 62
Hypochthonellidae 77
Hypsipterygidae 38

Idiostolidae 57
Idiostoloidea 57
Ilyocoris 41
insecticidal knockdown 17
intertidal dwarf bugs *see*
   Omaniidae
Ischnodemus 58
Issidae 76

Javesella 72
Joppeicidae 47
Joppeicoidea 47
Joppeicus paradoxus 47
jumping plantlice *see* Psyllidae

Kermesidae 95
Kerriidae 95, 185
Kinnaridae 77
kissing bugs *see* Triatoma

lac insects *see* Kerriidae
Lac Insect (*Kerria lacca*) 138, 185
lace bugs *see* Tingidae
Lachnidae 86
Lachnus 88
Lantana camara 48
lantern bug *see* Fulgoridae
lanternfly *see* Fulgoridae
Lanternia 76
Largidae 61, **126**
leaf-footed bugs *see* Coreidae
leafhoppers *see* Cicadellidae
Lecanodiaspididae 95
legs 28–9
Leotichiidae 36
Lepidosaphes 93
Leptocentrus 170
Leptocoris 62
Leptocorisa 62
Leptocorisa acuta 62
Leptoglossus 62
Leptopodidae 36
Leptopodoidea 36
Leptopodomorpha 36
lesser backswimmers *see* Pleidae
lesser water boatmen *see* Corixidae
Lestoniidae 69

Lethocerus 42, 187
Libyaspis coccinelloides **65**
Limnogeton 42
Liorhyssus 62
Lissocarta vespiformis **123**
Liviidae 85
Lophopidae 76
Loxaspis 52
Lyctocoris campestris 51
Lyctocoris flavipes 51
Lygaeidae 27, 47, *49*, 57–8, **59**, 100, 109, 112, 114, *125*, 126, 130, 140, 146, 153–4, 161, 163
Lygaeoidea 57, 58
Lygus 51
Lyramorpha **67**

Macrocephalus 54
Macrosiphum 88
Macrosiphum cholodkovskyi **88**
Macrosiphum rosae **181**
Macrosteles 80
Macroveliidae 39
Malcidae 58
malpighian tubules 148–9
Margarodes 187
Margarodidae 95, 106, 111, 138, 187
marsh treaders *see* Hydrometridae
Martarega 44
maternal care 48, 63, 68, 170–4, **171**, **172**
Meadow Spittle Bug (*Philaenus spumarius*) 78
mealy bugs *see* Pseudococcidae
Medocostidae 52–3, 166
Meenoplidae 77
Megamelus 72
Megarididae 69
Membracidae 25, 26, *70*, 81, **82**, 83, 99, 114–15, 120, **122**, 133, **134**, 162, 170, **172**, 177
Membracis 82, 170
Membracoidea 81
Merragata 38
Mesovelia 38
Mesoveliidae *37*, 38
Mesovelioidea 38
Metacanthus 58
Micronecta 46
Microvelia 40
Milkweed Bug (*Oncopeltus fasciatus*) 131
Mindaridae 86
minute pirate bugs *see* Anthocoridae
Miridae **13**, 14, *22*, 23, 27, 46, 48, *49*, **50**, 109, 112, 117, 122, 124, 130, 132–3, 140, **153**, 153, 155, 168, *170*
Miris striatus **50**
Miroidea 48
Monalonion 50
mounting techniques *18*
mummification 98–9, **116**, 118
Murgantia 68
Musgraveia sulciventris 68
mycetomes (mycetocytes) 87, 146–7

Myrmus 62
Myzus 88

Nabicula 52
Nabidae 14, *49*, 52, 53, 100, 109, **110**, 112, 133, 144, 153, 155, 161, 166
Nabis 52
Nabis rugosus **110**
Naucoridae 31, *37*, 41, 144, 153
Naucoris 41
Naucoroidea 41
negro bugs *see* Cydnidae
Neides 58
Nematopus indus **164**
Nepa 43
Nephotettix 80
Nepidae 30, *37*, 42, 98, 110, 127, 144, 153
Nepoidea 42
Nepomorpha 41
Nezara 68
Nicomiidae 82
Nipaecoccus 95
nitrogen 133, 149
Nogodinidae 76
Notocyrtus **97**
Notonecta 44
Notonecta glauca **45**
Notonectidae 31, *37*, 44, **45**, 98, 110, 124, 127, 144, 153, 161
Notonectoidea 44, 45
nuptial gifts **113**, 163
Nysius 58

ocean striders *see* Gerridae
Ochteridae 44, 110
Odontoscelis 68
Oechalia 68
Oeciacus 52
Omaniidae 36
Oncopeltus 58
Oncopeltus famelicus **59**
Oplomus dichrous **155**
Orius 51, 167
ornate pit scales *see* Cerococcidae
Ornithocoris 52
Ortheziidae 95
Orthotylus 51
Oxycarenus 58, 60

Pachycoris **171**
Pachycoris torridus **35**
Pachylis pharaonis **127**, **139**
Pachynomidae 54
Pachypsylla 84
palm bugs *see* Thaumastocoridae
Panstrongylus 54, 97, 179
Paracimex 52
Parajalysus nigrescens **57**
Paraphrynoveliidae 39
parasites and parasitoids
    Nematodes 111
    Diptera 111–14
    Lepidoptera 114
    Strepsiptera 114–15
    Hymenoptera 115–20
Parent Bug (*Elasmucha grisea*) 63
Parlatoria 93
Paropisoseys **94**
Parthenolecanium 92

paternal care **174**, *174*–6
peanut bugs *see* Fulgoridae **75**
Peloridiidae 69, *70*, 140
Pemphigidae 86, 87, 135–6, 146
Pemphigus 88
Pemphigus spirothecae 136
Pentatoma 68
Pentatoma rufipes 122
Pentatomidae **17**, **25**, *49*, 63–4, 100, 109, 112, 114, 122, **124**, 146, **148**, **150**, 153, **155**, 161, **169**, 170, **171**
Pentatomoidea 63
Pentatomorpha 55
Perkinsiella saccharicida 50, 72
Petalops thoracicus **63**
Phenacoccus 95
Phenacoleachiidae 95
Phenax 76
pheromones 121, 124, 130–1, 160, 163
Philaenus 78
Phloeidae 69
Phloeomyzidae 86
Phoenicococcidae 95
Phromnia rosea **137**
Phyllomorpha laciniata **121**
Phylloxera 90
phylloxerans *see* Phylloxeridae
Phylloxeridae 89, 109
Phymata 54
Phymata erosa **162**
Phymatidae 54
Phythia pulchella **21**
Phytocoris 51
Picromerus 68
Piesmatidae *49*, 56
Piesmatoidea 56
Pineus 89
pit scales *see* Asterolecaniidae
Plagiognathus 51
Planococcus 95
plant bugs *see* Miridae
planthoppers *see* Delphacidae
plantlice *see* Aphididae
plastron 32, 41, 168
plataspid shield bugs *see* Plataspidae
Plataspidae *49*, **65**, 68, 133
Platycentrus 170
Platycotis 170
Platymeris 177
Pleidae 45, 130
Ploiaria 156
Plokiophilidae 53, 155–6, 166, 167
Podius 68
Polyctenidae 53, 153, 166–7
Polyglypta 170
pond skaters *see* Gerridae
pondweed bugs *see* Mesoveliidae
pooter 15, *16*
predators
    birds 101
    spiders 102
    Diptera 103–4
    Neuroptera 104–5
    Coleoptera 105–7
    Lepidoptera 107
    Hymenoptera 107–9
    Hemiptera 109–10

Primicimex 52
Probergrothius sexpunctatus **151**
Propicimex 52
Prostemma 52, 167
Psallus 51
Pseudococcidae *70*, 90, 93, 107,
 118, 135, 137
Pseudococcus 95
Psitticimex 52
Psylla 84
Psylla alni **84**
Psyllidae 14, *70*, 83, **84**, 84, 120,
 146
Psylloidea 83, 84
Psyllopsis 84
pulsatile organs 33
Pulvinaria 92
Pulvinaria regalis **182**
pygmy backswimmers *see* Pleidae
Pyrrhocoridae 60–1, **61**, 100, 112,
 113, 130, 140, 146, **151**
Pyrrhocoroidea 60

Ranatra 43
Ranzovius 156
Recilia 80
red bugs *see* Pyrrhocoridae
Red Date Palm Scale
 (*Phoenicococcus marlatti*) 95
Reduviidae **19**, 28, *49*, 52, **53**,
 54–5, **97**, 100, 109, **112**, 123,
 125, 144, **145**, 146, 153, **154**,
 155, **157**, **158**, 158, 161, **162**,
 170, **173**, 174, 177
Reduvius 54
Reduvoidea 54
reproductive systems 163–5, *165*
Rhagovelia 40
Rhaphirrhinus phosphoreus **79**
Rhinocoris 174
Rhinocoris tristis **174**
Rhodnius 54, 97, 179
Rhodnius prolixus 179, 187
Rhopalidae 62, 112, 131
Rhopalosiphum 88
Rhopalus 62
Rhynchota 14
Ribaga's organ (organ of Berlese)
 167
Ribautodelphax 72
Ricaniidae 76, 114
Ricolla quadrispinosa **55**
rostrum *24*, 140–6, *141*

Sahlbergella singularis 50
Salda 36
Saldidae 36, *37*
Saldula 36
saliva 144–5
Salyavata variegata **158**, 158
San José Scale (*Quadraspidiotus
 perniciosus*) 93
saucer bugs *see* Naucoridae
scentless plant bugs *see* Rhopalidae
Schizopteridae 36
Scutelleridae **23**, **32**, 35, *49*, **66**, 68,
 114, 170, **171**

scutellum 25, **35**, **65**, 66, 68
secretion-grooming 130
seed bug *see* Lygaeidae
Sehirus 64
Sextus 170
shellac 185
shield bugs *see* Pentatomidae,
 Pentatomoidea
shore bugs *see* Saldidae
Sigara 46
siphons 42, 43
small water striders *see* Veliidae
soft scales *see* Coccidae
Sogatodes 72
soldiers 135–6
songs 161–3
sooty moulds (*Botrytis* spp.) 86,
 135
spermatheca 163, 164, *165*, 166–8,
 176
Sphaerodema 42
Sphagiastes ramantaceus **19**
sphagnum bugs *see* Hebridae
Sphongophorus 82
Sphonogophorus guerini **122**
spiny-legged bugs *see*
 Leptopodidae
spiracles 25, 30, 31, **32**
Spondyliaspididae 85
squash bugs *see* Coreidae
Stemmocryptidae 38
Stenocephalidae 62
Stenocephalus 63
Stenocoris 62
Stenolemus 156
Stephanitis 48
Sternorrhyncha 10, 14, *70*, 83
Stictocephala 82
Stictococcidae 95
stilt bugs *see* Berytidae
stink (scent) glands 25–6, **67**,
 122–31, **128**, **129**
Stiretrus 68
stridulation 45, 46
stylets *see* rostrum
Sugar-cane Planthopper *see*
 Perkinsiella saccharicida
Sugar-cane Woolly Aphid
 (*Ceratovacuna lanigera*) 135
swarming behaviour 35
Sycamore Aphid (*Drepanosiphum
 platanodis*) **110**

Tecaspis 93
Tectocoris 68
Tectocoris diophthalmus see
 Harlequin Bug
Teleonemia lantanae 48
Termitaphididae 56
Tessaratomidae **67**, 68
Tettigometridae 76
Thaumastocoridae 46
Thaumastocoroidea 46
Thelaxidae 86
thorax 24–5
Tingidae 47, **47**, 48, *49*, 131, 140,
 170, 172

Tingis 48
Tingis ampliata **47**
Tingoidea 47
toad bugs *see* Gelastocoridae
tracheae 31
traps 17, 34
traumatic insemination 51–3, 166
treehoppers *see* Membracidae
Triatoma 54, 97, 179
Triatoma dimidiata 179
Triatoma infestans *178*, 179, 180
trichomes 150
Triozidae 85
trophobioses 133
Tropiduchidae 76
Trypanosoma cruzi 54, 179, 180
Two-spotted Stink Bug (*Perillus
 bioculatus*) 68
tymbal organ 80, *161*, 161
tympanal organ *161*, 161
Typhlocyba 80
Tytthus mundulus 50

Umbonia 82, 170, 186
Umbonia spinosa **172**
Unaspis 93
unique-headed bugs *see*
 Enicocephalidae
Urostylidae 69

Vedalia Beetle (*Rodolia cardinalis*)
 106
Velia 40
Veliidae *37*, 40, 98, 153, 161
Velinus malayus **157**
Velocipedidae 53, 166
velvet shore bugs *see* Ochteridae
velvet water bugs *see* Hebridae
Venustria superba **160**
Vianaididae 48
vine aphid (*Viteus vitifolii*) 90
Viteus 90

water boatmen *see* Notonectidae
water measurers *see*
 Hydrometridae
water striders *see* Gerridae
water treaders *see* Mesoveliidae
watercrickets *see* Veliidae
waterscorpions *see* Nepidae
waxes and resins 136–8
wheel bugs *see* Arilus
whiteflies *see* Aleyrodidae
wing pads 27, *28*
wings 26, 27, *27*, *28*, **63**
woolly conifer aphids *see*
 Adelgidae
Woolly Apple Aphid (*Eriosoma
 lanigerum*) 136
world forests 20

Xylocoris 51
Xylocoris maculipennis 167

Zelus 174, *175*
Zicrona 68